MUMBY'S
Publishing
AND
Bookselling
IN THE
TWENTIETH CENTURY

Also by Ian Norrie

History/Travel

THE BOOK OF HAMPSTEAD (ed. with Mavis Norrie)
THE BOOK OF THE CITY (ed.)
THE HEATHSIDE BOOK OF HAMPSTEAD AND HIGHGATE (ed.)
THE BOOK OF WESTMINSTER (ed.)
HAMPSTEAD, HIGHGATE AND KENWOOD: A SHORT GUIDE
HAMPSTEAD: LONDON HILL TOWN (photographs by Dorothy Bohm)

Fiction

HACKLES RISE AND FALL
QUENTIN AND THE BOGOMILS
PLUM'S GRAND TOUR

MUMBY'S
Publishing
AND
Bookselling
IN THE
TWENTIETH CENTURY

Sixth Edition by
IAN NORRIE

BELL & HYMAN
London

Published in 1982 by
BELL & HYMAN LIMITED
Denmark House
37-39 Queen Elizabeth Street
London SE1 2QB

Sixth edition © Ian Norrie 1982
This edition by arrangement with Jonathan Cape Ltd.
Publishing and Bookselling by Frank Mumby
first published by Jonathan Cape Ltd. in 1930
Second edition 1949
Third edition 1954
Fourth edition 1956
Fifth edition by Frank Mumby and Ian Norrie revised and reset 1974

British Library Cataloguing in Publication Data
Mumby, Frank Arthur
Mumby's publishing & bookselling in the 20th century.—6th ed.
1. Publishers and publishing—Great Britain— History
2. Booksellers and bookselling—Great Britain— History
I. Title   II. Norrie, Ian
070.5'0941   Z326

ISBN: 0 7135 1341 1

Typeset by Computerset Ltd., Oxford.
Printed in Great Britain by
Thetford Press Ltd., Thetford, Norfolk
Bound by The Pitman Press Ltd., Bath

For my very good friend, Alan Steele,
printer, bookseller, publisher, bookman *par
excellence*, who has been of inestimable help
to me and to many others named in this book.

Contents

Introduction

Frank Mumby, man of letters and literary journalist, who was born in 1872, spent much of his life chronicling the history of the book trade in general and publishing houses in particular. In 1910 he published *The Romance of Bookselling* which was the forerunner of his greater work *Publishing and Bookselling: A History from the Earliest Times to the Present Day,* which, after its first appearance from Cape in 1930, quickly became a standard text. A second edition was issued in 1949 with a new preface which ended with Mumby's 'farewell salute to all those with whom it has been my present lot to be associated throughout my journalistic and literary career'. Notwithstanding, in 1954, the year of his death, a third edition was published but bibliographers may well conclude that this in fact was only a new impression. Two years later a revised and enlarged edition was edited by Max Kenyon who brought 'the story to Easter 1956, while keeping to the words, and to the structure of *Mumby* . . . . as far as possible'.

In 1967, Graham C. Greene, of Cape, invited me to bring the work further up to date. In the preface to the fifth edition (1974) I wrote, 'I re-read the work that I had long admired, and noted, as will some future reviser in his turn, that there were many omissions. After long heart-searchings I concluded that only major surgery would meet the case, because Mumby had recorded little of the history of bookselling, as distinct from publishing, in the twentieth century, and had also overlooked many specialist imprints . . . . . At first I thought it would be satisfactory to go back only as far as 1945 [to take up the narrative]; then 1919 seemed a more convenient date. Finally I opted for 1870 as my starting point'.

When my 'revision', which took six years, was ready it was apparent that there were two books of which the first part, with some corrections, was Mumby up to mid-Victorian times, and the second, mine. At that stage, it was my wish to see the work in two volumes but Graham, who had been most patient in awaiting the result of my labours, ruled otherwise, although he generously granted me copyright in my longer 'half'.

Published at the then high price of £12, in March 1974, the book sold out in just over two years, which was gratifying, but led to a demand for a new, corrected edition. As the result of discussions between Giles Gordon, my agent, Graham Greene and Robin Hyman, Cape's leased their rights in 'Mumby' to Bell & Hyman and this present volume is the result. It is based on my part of the 1974 'Mumby' but much of it has been re-written and there has been a rearrangement of chapters some of which have disappeared. Many names which were in the 1974 book will not be found here because I have tried to follow a rule of mentioning only those individual booksellers and publishers who illustrate a particular theme, trend or incident. In writing what is partly near-contemporary history one has to risk seeming invidious but no offence is intended to those who are not in the index.

For the 1974 book I consulted well over 200 people, all acknowledged, and some of whom supplied further information for this work. To determine which of them ought to be thanked for helping with this particular volume would require research amongst correspondence stretching over fifteen years, so I hope to be forgiven for offering sincere, blanket thanks to all who have assisted me with both books. Naming a very few names, however, I must record my gratitude to Gerry Davies and Colin Eccleshare for reading this latest typescript, commenting upon it from their deep knowledge of the trade and suggesting alterations many of which I was happy to accept; to James Coates, of Whitaker's, who provided most valuable statistical information; to Elizabeth Brooke-Smith of Bell & Hyman for her help in preparing the typescript for the printer; to my publisher, Robin Hyman, who, being an interested party in so many respects, added valuable comments in the margins as he received copy, chapter by chapter; and to Peter Cochrane, whom our mutual friend, the publisher, had the sagacity to engage as editor, and whose knowledge of the British book trade in the latter half of this century was of inestimable benefit.

Hadley Wood, 1982   *Ian Norrie*

Prologue

It would be appropriate to state that William Caxton was the father of the British book trade, because as printer, binder, translator, publisher and bookseller he was the complete bookman; but it would be untrue. Nor can the title be bestowed upon the Venerable Bede, the monk who wrote the first history of England and whose works were distributed rudimentarily to medieval seats of learning. Nor on Alcuin whose library in his native city of York became celebrated in many parts of Europe. There is no known individual we can honour with this title, but certainly the Roman book trade, itself modelled on the Greek, influenced the far-flung province of Britannia to which some of those manuscripts copied by slave labour in the seven-hilled city were surely sent.

The Roman publisher had advantages over his modern equivalent in not having to pay royalties to his authors and wages to his labour force or to face competition for foreign markets. He was untroubled by literary agents or the equivalent of a Society of Authors. There were no printers and the roles of publisher and bookseller were one, as they were to be for centuries to come.

There was scarcely even a veneer of civilisation after the Romans withdrew from Britain. In the centuries which followed, learning was kept alive in the monasteries, often under conditions of extreme privation for the scribes, illuminators and preparers of parchment who preserved all the literature which has survived from the Dark Ages. How much perished we do not know because, in the paper shortages of Norman Britain, manuscripts were re-cycled and over-written. In Ireland, which was largely ignored by the barbarian hordes, the art of the illuminated manuscript was perpetuated and, when circumstances permitted, copies were made for monasteries and courts in England and on the mainland of Europe, where there was an organised business in books, long before the practice of

11

printing. In university cities such as Oxford and Cambridge the authorised stationers (the term is synonymous with booksellers/publishers for a long while to come) were permitted to trade. In London, the scriveners and booksellers were similarly organised from 1404 into a guild which was the fore-runner of the present Stationers' Company.

Caxton, the first London printer, from 1476 until his death in 1491, and a mercer by calling, was not, apparently, objected to by the stationers, which is extraordinary when one considers the implications of Gutenberg's discovery. Possibly his decision to found his press near Westminster Abbey instead of in the City was relevant to this, though his Alsatian-born assistant and heir, Wynkyn de Worde, moved to Fleet Street after his master's death. In the next century however, the City, which had previously been tolerant of continental printers and booksellers, approved sanctions against them. The foreigners, heavily taxed, remained for a while trading around St Paul's Churchyard, which was to be the centre of the English book trade for more than four hundred years, but by the mid-sixteenth century they had withdrawn to their native countries where some of them engaged in printing the Bible in English and smuggling copies into the offshore island. Details of their names and operations may be found in the learned works of E. Gordon Duff (see Bibliography).

Long before this, Caxton had accepted the need to farm out work to printers in Paris and Rouen because he could not cope with the demand for grammars and service books. He also had 'competition' at home from presses set up in London, St Albans and Oxford. At the last city the first press was at work in 1478 but activity there, and at Cambridge, was intermittent until the late seventeenth century.

The publishers/booksellers of the early centuries of printing had to contend with an official censorship which could lead to ear-cropping or worse, and a rigorous monopoly exercised by the Stationers' Company whose standing was strengthened by the support of monarchs, Protestant and Catholic, who believed it would be simpler to control what was printed if all publications had to be registered with the Company. By a decree of 1637, the Star Chamber reduced the number of printers to twenty-three (an indication that printing was already in the main separated from bookselling/publishing) and ordered that all books should be licensed as well as registered. The import of English books printed abroad was prohibited, apprentices to the trade were to serve for seven years before becoming masters, and provision was made for one copy of every book to be delivered to Stationers' Hall for deposit in the library of Oxford University.

The 1637 Act was repealed by the Long Parliament four years later. The Stationers lost their monopoly in Bibles and some categories of books, so publishing activity in other directions was stimulated. When this caused official alarm the virtues of freedom were championed by John Milton in his

Areopagitica, published, unlicensed, in his own name in 1644.

> Who kills a man kills a reasonable creature, God's image: but he who destroys a good book, kills reason itself, kills the image of God, as it were, in the eye. Many a man lives a burden to the earth; but a good book is the precious life-blood of a master spirit.

The words have echoed down the centuries although, even today, the law has not clarified what is a 'good book' and what is to be termed seditious or obscene.

During the Commonwealth there was official freedom of the press, although levity was frowned upon; censorship returned with the monarchy but its imposition was hampered by the calamitous plague of 1665 and the Great Fire of London in the following year. Towards the end of the century the public taste for bawdiness was catered for by the printed and acted plays of the Restoration dramatists. Allowing for the social pressures exerted on printers and publishers by Victorian moral fervour, there has been little political danger in trading in books ever since, although a few practitioners have been humbled by authority, and even imprisoned.

By the end of the seventeenth century the licensing laws had lapsed, the two university presses were firmly established and richly endowed, and the third oldest publisher in the United Kingdom, the Society for Promoting Christian Knowledge (S.P.C.K.), was already a healthy two-year old planning books in Arabic and French and laying down the basis of a world-wide distribution service. Jacob Tonson and Bernard Lintot had established themselves as leading London booksellers, catering for the widest possible market, keeping Shakespeare and the classics in print, but also attracting the satire of Pope in his *Dunciad* (an early instance of author/publisher antipathy). There was also a marked move towards legislation to define the rights of writers and booksellers which exacerbated both sides because each believed they should have everlasting copyright in what they had penned or purchased.

The Copyright Act of 1709 was the first of many which limited the term of an author's rights in his own work but at least it recognised that he had some. The day of the professional author was dawning, and as the century progressed literacy increased. Booksellers were, naturally, eager to exploit the growing market and the publication of Samuel Johnson's dictionary of the English language is an apt example of both the new spirit of cooperation between publishers (it was sponsored by Robert Dodsley, the foremost bookseller of his time, and the first Thomas Longman, amongst others) and of the need for a basic work of reference. The cost of publication was shared, so were the profits, and Johnson's accolade was earned: 'The booksellers are generous liberal-minded men'. Few authors since have been so positive in their admiration of the trade.

Circulating libraries sprang up to meet the wider demand for literature. Lending, instead of selling, books for a fee, or against a subscription, they existed in Bath, Birmingham, Bristol, Cambridge and Norwich, by 1751, and one, founded in Hull in 1775, is still in business. Earlier, in London, a variant of the system had been introduced by which clients paid to read books in stock but on the premises with chairs provided.

More readers meant more books, more speculation, and, inevitably, more failures. The first to cash in on the remainder market was James Lackington who founded his Temple of the Muses in Finsbury Square, in the City of London. There he sold, at bargain prices, books the like of which publishers had previously burned because they couldn't find another way of disposing of them. He built himself a chariot adorned with the motto 'Small Profits do Great Things' and travelled the land, recording his journeys for posterity. On the trade of his day he made as much impact as Paul Hamlyn was to have on his in the 1950s. In Glasgow, Lackington would have called at John Smith's shop in Trongate, now the oldest bookselling business in the U.K. still trading under its original name; in Cambridge, at No. 1 Trinity Street, then bearing the name of Thurlbourne and Woodyer, he would have visited a shop in which books have been sold since the early 1600s. Today it is part of W.H. Smith, as Bowes & Bowes. Elsewhere in the provinces, and in Scotland and Wales, he would not have found shops bearing names familiar to us now but in London, just before his retirement, he should have become aware of John Hatchard who opened his doors to the public in Piccadilly in 1797, though possibly ignorant of the first Smith, ('H.W.' not 'W.H.') who was in a small way of business in Belgravia. Lackington retired in 1798. His cousin, who succeeded him, knew of the imprints of Constable and Nelson, of Murray and W.H. Allen, and others still embossed on the spines of books in 1980. In this introductory chapter reference to few of them will be made because it will be more useful to the reader to have their historical background sketched in when accounts of their twentieth-century achievements are recorded.

At the start of the nineteenth century many publishers/booksellers were still also printers and binders. By its end at least three of these occupations had been separated although there were major exceptions. Bookselling and publishing had long been moving apart. The coming of the railways, making for swifter communication and transport, led to independent printers establishing themselves in small country towns. Publishing remained based chiefly on London and Edinburgh, although towards the end of the century most of the Scottish firms who had formerly had agents in the southern capital, opened their own offices there, in some cases even transferring their headquarters. The two great university presses also established London bases without the Syndics of the one, or the Delegates of the other, losing academic control over them, but with the great bookselling chains the move was in the opposite direction. Smith's of London and Menzies' of Edinburgh both decentralised, opening branches in the wake of the ever-expanding railroads.

In 1800 there were no official organisations for booksellers, publishers or authors. About 600 titles were issued annually, poetry was for a while to be in the ascendant although novelists were soon to attract a larger public; books specifically for children, which had emerged in the previous century thanks to the industry of John Newbery, were still a novelty. Medical literature had existed for centuries and there was already some activity in technical books because the industrial revolution had begun. Another uprising, in France, had also broken down barriers and there was an air of greater licence amongst writers, especially poets.

By the end of the nineteenth century the publishers and booksellers each had their own associations, as had the authors; literary agents were professionally active for the first time; and a Net Book Agreement, by which publishers fixed the price at which most of their books should be sold to the public, had been introduced. Novelists, rather than poets, were now household names, some of them deservedly rich from their writings; there was a new trade in school textbooks following Forster's Act of 1870 making education compulsory for all; and overseas markets had become so important that most leading publishers had already established offices in New York and the then colonies. Steam power had been harnessed for printing. Large editions of books and pamphlets could be produced quickly; mass production was a reality.

In the new century there were even more drastic changes. The motor car, steam locomotive, telephone and electricity all existed in 1900 but there were no airplanes as yet. The cinema was in its infancy, radio and television were decades away, the atom had not been split, no man had landed on the moon, and although Charles Babbage's work on mechanical calculating machines had won him respect in academic circles the development of the computer and the microchip was as remote as heart transplants and sex changes. More real were social changes. Education was already a right, not a privilege. Trades unions were groping towards power and the end of cheap labour was in sight, and there was to be a revolution in public taste which removed all taboos about what were or were not proper subjects for literature. Women played little part in trade or public life in 1900; by 1980 the feminist movement was in full swing, having already made successful incursions into bookselling for half a century.

Before considering in detail what happened to the book trade after 1900 something needs to be said about how it organised itself in the previous century.

Booksellers/publishers had been represented in guild terms by the Stationers' Company since the fifteenth century but it was not until 1812, when publishing was fast severing itself from retailing, that some London booksellers attempted to found an association of their own to counteract underselling. This failed, as did another effort in 1828. Six years later a movement by Glasgow booksellers was temporarily effective but collapsed under threat of transportation for conspiracy. The fight returned to London where, in 1852, another four-year-old group disbanded in the face of popular approval of free trade: but the demand for the right to organise prevailed, with the emphasis always on the need to prevent price-cutting in the interests of maintaining an efficient and healthy trade. In the 1870s Eyre & Spottiswoode announced that they had closed accounts with booksellers who refused to sell at recommended prices; ten years later Lewis Carroll attempted his own remedy by insisting that his books be supplied at not more that twopence-in-the-shilling discount, thus leaving no margin for underselling. *The Bookseller,* which had taken over *Bent's Literary Advertiser* in 1858 and become the self-styled Organ of the Book Trade, campaigned resolutely for a union of retailers and, in 1890, printed a momentous letter from Frederick Orridge Macmillan, son and nephew of respectively Daniel and Alexander who had founded the family firm, and one of whom had tried to net an edition of Shakespeare as early as 1864. Frederick maintained that it was up to publishers who wished to see well-stocked bookshops to take the initiative, and here commences the story of the modern British book trade. He echoed his author, Lewis Carroll, in advocating a low discount to booksellers, and none to the public. *The Bookseller* polled its readers but received so few replies that Macmillan's proposal went unheard although he started to net some of his books, the first of them, significantly, being Alfred Marshall's *The Principles of Economics.* He closed the account of a City of London chain which refused to conform and did not listen to the pleas of the newly-formed London Booksellers' Society which asked for only high-class publications of limited circulation to be netted. In 1894, the Society changed tack and became, with colleagues in the country, dedicated to the introduction of the net system through the Associated Booksellers of Great Britain and Ireland. The formation of the latter led to an informal meeting of publishers which, inevitably, was the basis of the Publishers Association, inaugurated in 1896. For two years the A.B. and the P.A. negotiated, in consultation with the Society of Authors (1884), to come to terms about the conditions of supply of net books to retail booksellers. As the century neared its end, so did their deliberations and, on 1 January 1900, the Net Book Agreement came into being. John Murray, for the publishers, said they had not wanted it but had committed themselves to it for the booksellers, but he hoped publishers would honour it despite pressures from the lending libraries. Serious undercutting recurred only once in the next half-century, and to many, the prosperity of the book trade seemed assured.

16

1900-1939

Trade Affairs

If Frederick Orridge Macmillan typified those far-sighted publishers in late-Victorian times who saw the necessity for organising the book trade, then in the early twentieth century Stanley Unwin emerged as the embodiment of a concerted effort towards cooperation.

He made his contribution through the Publishers Association, of which he later became president, the Society of Bookmen, of which he was a founder member, the National Book Council and, behind the scenes, the British Council.

The detailed history of the P.A.'s first fifty years is admirably recorded by another ex-president, R.J.L. Kingsford, in *The Publishers Association 1896-1946*. Here we are concerned only with the main events and policies which attracted its Council's attention. We know the Association was formed as a direct result of the Associated Booksellers' demands for a net book system. Before 1896, publishers had only been stronger than booksellers as individuals, but from that date they were able to muster collective strength for joint action. By 1900 there were sixty-eight members; in 1910 eighty-nine. Collective action was sometimes effective, as in 1903 when booksellers were refused $33\frac{1}{3}$% discount on non-net books; sometimes less so as in the case of the 328 local boards created by the Education Act of 1902. The P.A. recommended that they should buy through booksellers but emphasised that it could not force its members to refrain from selling to local authorities. The Boards of course clamoured for full trade terms, the London School Board having established a precedent in 1875. The majority were refused, some, including the London County Council, were not. The daft system whereby booksellers give discounts on the books they buy at worst terms but none, except to libraries and school book associations, on those they buy at best terms, continues to this day, although there is now a tendency for booksellers to make their own rules and turn a blind eye on the regulations.

Publishers, secure in the knowledge that teachers wanting their textbooks must come to them, directly or through a middleman, were reluctant to allow booksellers sufficient margin to make school supply profitable. Yet they recognised the advantages of a well-organised retail trade. The argument was really about efficiency and it was obtuse of publishers not to realise that it could only be effected by awarding better terms. Slowly they conceded more, while the P.A. condoned the trend paternalistically, as it had the Net Book Agreement, the first challenge to which came in the famous 'Times Book War'.

The Times newspaper was struggling to survive. To boost circulation a book club and library was established in the West End of London, and five-year contracts were signed in 1905 with many publishers. Soon it became apparent that books were being sold at a discount after being loaned as seldom as twice or three times, so that members of the Times Book Club were able to purchase virtually new books for much less than the advertised published price. The trade associations protested and a new condition of sale was introduced into the N.B.A. with a clause forbidding the sale of a book as secondhand until six months after publication. Most booksellers signed this readily; the Times Book Club, supported by editorials in *The Times* which attacked the new agreement, did not. The 'Book War' was on.

The P.A. declared the Club 'black' and many publishers ceased supply. However, those who had signed contracts with *The Times* were bound to honour them. Messrs Constable had their own particular problem with Bernard Shaw who approved of underselling, and produced his own edition of one of his plays imprinted 'Issued by the author for the Times Book Club'. (Shaw, in fact, was his own publisher, employing Constable as his agent.)

The battle continued for some two years and involved thousands of people, vast numbers of whom signed a petition protesting against the N.B.A. on the ground that publishers sold books at half price to the colonies but objected to British citizens enjoying the same privilege at home. It was a rabble-rousing argument, but ignored the difficulties of publishers wishing to boost export.

The climax came in the autumn of 1907 when John Murray published *The Letters of Queen Victoria* in three volumes at three guineas. The Book Club was obliged to buy at full price and a *Times* reviewer complained about the high retail cost. He was backed up by a correspondent (actually a member of staff writing to the Editor under a pseudonym) who accused Murray of extortion, coupling his name with that of Judas Iscariot. Murray sued and won damages of £7,500. By then the Book Club was losing substantially each week, and the new proprietor of the newspaper, Lord Northcliffe, was negotiating peace with the P.A. In September 1908 the Times Book Club signed the N.B.A. and, one month later, *The Times* and

Murray's jointly published a cheap edition of the Queen's letters. Underselling had again been stamped out and the agreement (extended in 1905 to cover maps as well as books) was not seriously challenged again until the 1950s (but see p. 168).

P.A. Council members were also concerned in these early years with piracy of colonial editions by indigenous publishers and with newspapers quoting excessively from books under the guise of reviewing them. Some, of course, thought the Association should be more effective. John Lane, in 1907, suggested a central London showroom for new books, a weekly catalogue of new titles and an 'on approval' scheme for librarians and booksellers for all books over 5s. The Council did not even consider Lane's proposals, but partly resulting from this official snub, a ginger group, The Publishers' Circle, was formed a year later, at the suggestion of Arthur Spurgeon of Cassell. It was blessed by the Association and, at its luncheons, concerned itself with those problems which the P.A. chose to ignore.

The International Congress of Publishers, formed in 1896, continued to meet every two or three years up to the outbreak of World War I. International copyright was always on its agenda but progress towards a universal agreement was slow, and made slower by military conflict between the main literate nations, although German copyright was respected by the P.A. in 1914. In Britain a new Copyright Act, 1911, protected an author's work during his lifetime and for fifty years after death, and the National Library of Wales was added to the list of deposit libraries, although not all new publications were to be theirs free of charge, a privilege enjoyed by The British Museum; the Library of the Faculty of Advocates, Edinburgh (later the National Library of Scotland); the University Library in Cambridge; the Bodleian, in Oxford; and the Library of Trinity College, Dublin.

Trade union troubles were experienced in 1913 when there was a dispute with binders, heralding bitter struggles in other workshops in the following decade, though there had been an earlier rumbling in 1910 when thirty booksellers' assistants in Oxford petitioned humbly and politely for a half-day off each week. The local branch of the Associated Booksellers refused to discuss the proposition because some employers might not agree. Feudal inclinations were not confined to the Council of the P.A.

The price of novels caused dissatisfaction and there were vehement exchanges between publishers and booksellers and publishers and publishers. Cloth-bound fiction reprints at 7d upset the sale of 6s. editions. Booksellers officially deplored this; so did the publishers, but their Association, neither separately nor jointly, could alter it. Other familiar issues fomented discontent, providing the trade press with correspondence. Censorship was often news. The commercial libraries, stamping-grounds for Mrs Grundy, banned books by H.G. Wells, Compton Mackenzie, Hall Caine and others, and the Doncaster Free Library Committee ordered copies of *Tom Jones* to be burned. (Decades later another northern authority sought its ratepayers' protection from Boswell's *London Journal*, but no actual incineration was recorded; probably Boswell even returned to the shelves during the period known as the permissive society.)

William Heinemann attacked literary agents, some of whom prospered (A.P. Watt died in 1914 worth £60,000), while others failed disastrously, even dishonourably (Arthur Addison Bright committed suicide in 1906 having swindled his friend J.M. Barrie out of £16,000; A.M. Burghes and his son were convicted of fraud in 1912).

Publishers were suspected by authors of earning too much. Conan Doyle, at a Society of Authors dinner in 1905, commented that an eminent writer on astronomy had left £1,200, another on zoology a mere £300, but that Smith, of Smith, Elder & Co, had died worth £750,000 (although Smith made most of his fortune from mineral waters). Conan Doyle joined Shaw and Wells in promoting a company dedicated to sell books on behalf of authors; nothing came of the project.

New branches of the Associated Booksellers were started. H.W. Keay, the first president in 1903 (previously he had been chairman), sold his Eastbourne shop two years later. The rules of the Association were then altered to allow him to remain in office although he was no longer in business. Keay was president until 1923. He gave his Association's approval to a discount demanded by the Library Association for public libraries. The P.A. refused even to discuss it.

The number of books published increased from some 7,000 in 1900, to 10,914 in 1911. It rose again in 1913 to 12,379 but by 1918, predictably, it had fallen to 7,716.

The war brought a paper and a staff shortage. There was little damage to property but appalling losses in people. *The Bookseller,* which had become a weekly in 1909, reverted to monthly publication in 1915, in which year the Associated Booksellers called for all books to be netted. This was not acceptable to the P.A. so local agreements came into being in some areas to fix the discount on school books. In 1916 the East Midlands Branch of the A.B. reported that booksellers' profits had fallen from 8.46% net in 1914 to 1.7%. In 1917 the P.A. Education Sub-committee held its first meeting but a year later Mr W.M. Meredith, the P.A. president, was complaining of the lack of organisation in the trade.

His words were not unheeded. On 19 November 1929 there was a reception at Stationers' Hall to celebrate a decade of cooperation, not only between members of the P.A. but between booksellers, authors and publishers; the groundwork done since 1895 had borne fruit in an upsurge of activity prompted by the determination of various individuals to produce a better book trade in the aftermath of a war which created new economic conditions in Europe.

Trade with Germany was at a standstill because of inflation. Reparations demanded by the victorious Allies caused the German government to devalue the mark again and again until, by the end of 1923, it was worthless. Other central European and Scandinavian countries also had to devalue so drastically that foreign books became prohibitively expensive for them. Britain too, was in a financial crisis and could not afford to be represented at the Florence Book Fair in 1922 until free space and transport was offered to our publishers to whom the British government gave a grant for the 1925 fair. The crisis at home prevented a similar subsidy in 1928, by which time Germany was competing successfully with British books in other parts of the world, notably Japan.

Against a background of trading chaos in the export markets of the world the Council of the P.A. came under heavy criticism from its younger members who thought resolutions should be binding on all. But the Council could not impose its will on the whole membership; it could only hope, as it became more organised, to influence individual publishers for what it saw as the general good, which it did, although it was always up against the unfortunate truth that economics is not an exact science. Councils look to the opinions of experts, and experts are as fallible as popes, so it was correct for the younger publishers to become back-bencher irritants.

To the existing Publishers' Circle was added in 1921 the Society of Bookmen, which embraced the whole trade. It was founded by the novelist Hugh Walpole as the result of a meeting of another homogeneous group, The Whitefriars. Membership, restricted at first to seventy-five, later increased to one hundred, was open to men concerned with the creation, distribution and production of books. It held monthly dinners at which papers of interest to the trade were read and discussed freely, without being reported. From its *in camera* deliberations arose the National Book Council (afterwards the National Book League), the Book Tokens scheme and working parties formed to examine the structure of the book trade in other European countries. One of its earliest positive suggestions was for a system of cooperative advertising of books as books to be paid for jointly by publishers and booksellers. The project was never adopted by the trade but almost every year since at least one publisher or bookseller has recommended it.

The National Book Council, not at first officially supported by the P.A., came into existence on 14 May 1925 with the object of promoting the reading and the wider distribution of books, as the result of a joint meeting of the Publishers' Circle and the Society of Bookmen the previous year. Maurice Marston was secretary of both the Bookmen and the N.B.C. which had a grant from its sponsors of £750 for the first year. By 1928 there were 1575 members, and a reference library of books about books had been founded.

In 1926 the Bookmen sent a delegation to Holland and Germany to study the clearing-house system for the dispatch of orders, and on its return plans were made to form a committee to advise on how existing conditions in the British trade could be improved.

The P.A. told the Bookmen that the creation of a joint committee was none of a dining club's business. The Society responded by saying it was only concerned that note should be taken of the findings of the delegation and that it would be absurd for acrimony to arise because half of its members were also members of the P.A. So the committee was appointed jointly by the A.B. and the P.A. and its findings in three reports in 1928 and 1929 were eventually published with the Bookmen reports on trade matters in *British Book Trade Organisation,* edited by F.D. Sanders. This concise and lucid description of the day-to-day working arrangements of a complex industry, with practical recommendations for improvement, was the first comprehensive anatomy of the book trade in Britain. It is a monument to detailed research.

The twenties also saw the organisation of other groups within the trade. The reps – publishers' travelling salesmen – found collective identity in the Book Publishers' Representatives Association (B.P.R.A.) which sprang from a meeting in December 1923 called by Leslie Munro, of Heinemann, and William Grant, of Nisbet. The Association, formed the following year, fostered friendship among members and between them and their bookseller customers. A samaritan fund was instituted to help the needy.

Publishing employers looked with favour upon the B.P.R.A. but were less enthusiastic about the collective action of other workers who joined trade unions. When the packers at Macmillan's struck because their weekly wage was reduced from 70s. to 60s. on the grounds that the cost of living index had gone down, there was no attempt at conciliation. The strike there, as elsewhere, was broken and the packers crept back to their benches to work at the lower rate. John Baker, a young trainee who had sided with them, was ordered by the uncompromising management to work beside them amongst the corrugated paper and cardboard. Baker, naturally, resigned, and continued his career at Sampson Low's. (Macmillan's still had a distinctly feudal attitude: a boy from the warehouse who dared ascend the directors' staircase was instantly dismissed for his effrontery.) The strike was similarly broken, after three months, at Simpkin Marshall's, W.H. Smith's and at Wyman's, another chain, where many staff had enrolled in unions at the end of the war. The General Strike of 1926 soon followed, affecting books less than other trades because of the poor organisation of the workers. On the retail side bookshop managers and assistants might join a union if they wished, or dared, but membership did nothing to increase their income. Shop-workers remained underpaid and ill-organised, even in 1980, when the minimum wages laid down for them were still absurdly unrealistic.

In the late 1920s publishers came under pressure again from the Library

Association which demanded a 10% discount on purchases through booksellers. Commercial libraries, dealing directly with publishers, received the same discount as booksellers (in most cases they *were* booksellers as well) and loaned their books for a fee. The public libraries who loaned theirs free, and were a charge on the rates, were quick to appreciate this but booksellers, who realised it would be their 10%, and not the publishers', objected strongly. Nevertheless, in 1929 the Library Agreement was concluded, granting the 10% for which the librarians had asked. The P.A. gave in because there were so many evasions of the net ruling by bookseller suppliers that it was thought better to regularise the situation by agreeing a fixed discount. Booksellers, who were given better terms on single copies sold to libraries, resented this but those of them who were large enough to run public library supply departments still found methods of giving extra services at competitive rates, so the arguments against the concession must be seen as frail.

It was simpler for publishers to resist demands for higher wages than it was for them to beat down printers. By 1920 printing charges stood at 200% above the pre-war level. Printers faced with a 5s. a week increase for their workers slapped 5% on their prices but, two years later, when printing workers' wages fell by 7s.6d a week, prices were reduced by only 3%. The cost of paper, which had soared during the war, fluctuated wildly in the twenties but the average novel settled to retail at between 7s. and 7s.6d in 1918, and remained at that price for twenty years. It should also be noted that as early as 1916 printers and binders had begun to charge publishers for storing sheets and bound stock which formerly they had held gratis.

In international copyright the Indian states in 1923 gave protection to books produced in the British Empire but in 1924 Egyptian publishers grandly announced that they would not pay for any translation they made into Arabic from English. One step forward, one, even one-and-a-half, backwards.

The invention of broadcasting brought a new opportunity for selling subsidiary rights in books. There was never any quarrel between the British Broadcasting Corporation and the P.A. about payment for material used on radio, the BBC accepting the principle that it should pay for what it used, although there was continuing argument about how much. Some alarm was created by the Corporation's own publishing activities, especially in connection with talks reproduced in the BBC journal, *The Listener*. Publishers questioned whether the BBC's Charter gave it any right to publish; the law ruled that it did. Qualms were gradually allayed as it was realised that even broadcasts to schools would not end the demand for textbooks, and the fears were not revived until television arose as a further apparent threat to the printed word.

The P.A., noting the usefulness to the German book trade of its official paper, the *Borsenblatt,* was bothered by the absence of a similar journal in Britain. There were two trade papers, each privately owned, each willing to be wooed. In 1928 the Whitaker family agreed to transfer their journal into the care of the P.A. and A.B. as *The Publisher and Bookseller,* reserving the right to keep 20% commission from sales for themselves. G.S. Williams was appointed editor and the experiment lasted five years after which Whitaker's terminated the agreement. The journal reverted to being *The Bookseller* and in 1933 Edmond Segrave, from Heinemann's, became editor. *The Publisher's Circular,* owned by the Marstons, then became the joint trade paper until 1938 when, after two profitless years, the arrangement was suspended, finally lapsing with the outbreak of World War II.

The A.B. celebrated its silver jubilee in 1920 by appointing a paid secretary, W.J. Magenis. He was installed in a room in Paternoster Square, donated by Simpkin Marshall and designated the Association's headquarters. In 1923 at a three-day conference in Nottingham F.W. Denny succeeded the long-serving H.W. Keay as president, and, thereafter, presidents were in office for not more than two years. As with the P.A. the A.B. spawned committees which considered the problems besetting the trade. In 1925 membership stood at 877 and a year later the financial report showed a deficit of £127. Subscriptions were increased and by 1935, thanks mainly to the success of Book Tokens, the membership had grown to over 1200. Miss Hilda Light succeeded Magenis as secretary in 1930 and the Association moved to larger offices in Warwick Lane, from which Miss Light organised the now annual Conference which became more social as publishers were invited to participate. The publishers, it should be noted, resisted all suggestions that they should hold their own conference, or sponsor one jointly with booksellers.

Hilda Light regarded it as her duty to harry the enemy, which is how she saw publishers, according to her opposite number at the P.A., Frank Sanders, who found her 'charming but formidable'. She captained England at hockey and brought the tough qualities demanded on the sports field into the secretariat and conference room.

The 1930s began with the depression and ended with the outbreak of another world war. In this difficult and dark decade the book trade pursued its policy of cooperation and organisation against a background of unemployment and mounting international tension. There were two important innovations within the trade – Book Tokens and book clubs – and one, equally valuable but hard to quantify, in the political world – The British Council.

The idea of selling vouchers exchangeable for books in all bookshops was first suggested by Harold Raymond of Chatto & Windus at a meeting of the Society of Bookmen in 1926. It took six years of committology and private lobbying to get the scheme off the ground and, when it was introduced, there was bitterness from some publishers, particularly Stanley Unwin, because the National Book Council, which agreed to operate it, did so on the understanding that Book Tokens were the property of the A.B. The latter, for once, had shown more initiative than the P.A. in being willing to back it, and it never did a wiser thing.

The tokens scheme simply consisted of printing stamps of various denominations from 3s.6d up, which the issuing bookseller was required to affix to a card designed by Book Tokens; $12\frac{1}{2}$% of the token value was retained by the bookseller selling it, and the whole cost of the card, at first 3d, was passed on to the customer by the bookseller, who then handed it over to Book Tokens to cover their administrative and production costs. The bookseller exchanging the token for a book received $87\frac{1}{2}$% of the stamp value from Book Tokens, so that on the one hand the issuing bookseller received $12\frac{1}{2}$% commission without risk, and on the other the exchanging bookseller $87\frac{1}{2}$% of the price of the book held in stock or ordered in at the usual discount. The scheme at first attracted only 30% of the A.B. membership but, as it became popular with the public, more joined. Eventually the right to sell and exchange Book Tokens led scores of tobacconists, stationers and sub-postmistresses to apply for membership, but they were not accepted unless they already sold books. This later proved a mixed blessing to those who wished to organise the actual sellers of books rather than those who applied their commercial expertise to the adhesion of stamps to card. Profits accrued from Tokens which were never redeemed, the A.B. gained an unexpected hold over its members and the National Book Council lost its only chance of financial independence.

In the thirties there were other vouchers which endeared themselves less to booksellers – cigarette coupons which were exchangeable for 'free' books from fifteen publishers' lists. Books also became bait when newspaper proprietors attempted to attract more readers during the circulation war. Sets of Dickens and other classics, encyclopaedias, atlases, cookery books, were offered for so many coupons cut out of a newspaper, plus a small cash sum. The *Daily Mail* advertised a complete Shakespeare for 5s.9d plus six coupons. Basil Blackwell instantly counter-attacked by offering his Shakespeare Head Edition of the plays for 6s. and no coupons. Naturally Bernard Shaw stepped into the ring, once again to Constable's annoyance, and through the *Daily Herald* his collected plays to date were any reader's for six coupons, plus 3s.9d. It is a pity that Shaw's natural polemic and flair for self-advertisement were never channelled into the benefit of the book trade, which, nevertheless, he enriched. With their joint pertinacity and debating skill, he and Stanley Unwin might have cleaned up for a generation or more of authors, publishers and booksellers. Instead of which they died rich men in their own right, the one having done great service to his fellow bookmen and all authors, the other contributing to the gaiety of millions.

The practice of dangling books as carrots before newspaper readers died a natural death when it became too costly for the press barons who agreed a truce, and an unsuccessful experiment by a new publisher with coupon advertising perhaps proved that booksellers had little to fear from such competition. The difficulty of accepting this calmly was shown by their outcry against book clubs which they saw as an innovation designed to bring about their immediate ruin. It was all right for Messrs Foyle because they joined in and started their own clubs; most booksellers had neither the capital nor the initiative to take similar action and waited to see their businesses dwindle as the public learned to buy books on the cheap.

In fact the first book club did not undersell. The Book Society, founded by Alan Bott in 1929, offered its wares at full published price by post. A panel of authors – J.B. Priestley and Hugh Walpole were amongst the first judges – made a monthly choice and, as membership grew, the publisher of the selected book was able to reduce its price because he could order a large run. Later still, he was obliged to reduce it further because the Society would not otherwise choose the book. Many Book Society members were expatriates, or lived in remote parts of the country, far from bookshops. There was no evidence that the Society harmed the retail bookseller who, nevertheless, remained wary of a potentially dangerous competitor.

The creation of Reader's Union by John Baker in 1937 seemed even more of a threat, especially as it enrolled 17,000 members in a year. Baker had been involved in selling new books on the instalment plan (sometimes for as little as 1d per day) through the Phoenix Book Company since 1928. Even this was too expensive for those on small incomes so, through Reader's Union, he offered them the same books, in tastefully designed editions, at 2s.6d each, a reduction in the case of the first choice of 13s.6d; but members had to wait for a period after original publication before getting this bargain. Foyle's formed another general book club, later branching out into numerous specialist subjects; the Student Christian Movement Press inaugurated a Religious Book Club in 1937 and Victor Gollancz's Left Book Club, which started in 1936, soon had 60,000 members.

Booksellers learned to cooperate with the clubs by accepting subscriptions on behalf of their customers but it became apparent that the clubs had found a new market and were not poaching on the booksellers' traditional preserves. The size of the cake, it transpired, was not fixed but it took years of suspicion before the majority of retailers, apprehensive during a period of difficult trading conditions, accepted the evidence.

The British Council was set up by the government in 1934 to project to the world at large Britain and the British way of life. Stanley Unwin, who had for years maintained that trade follows the book, was appointed to the executive committee of the Council which established libraries in foreign countries and organised exhibitions of books with increasing cooperation from publishers. English was already a world language. The good sense of such a promotion seemed obvious to publishers.

To return to the A.B. and its members' chronic fears of competition, the growth of 'other traders' amongst Twopenny Library owners alarmed booksellers at the 1932 Chester Conference. At the end of that year sixteen firms, including a chain of tobacconists, had been recognised for trade terms in this field of activity, and the number increased by 42 in 1933, by 73 in 1934, and by 91 in 1935 with Foyle's offering the attendant benefit to newsagents and stationers in Greater London and the home counties. During a depression the slightest innovation is bound to concern those who see their livelihood threatened.

The cinema and radio had already arrived; soon there was also to be television, its effects only delayed by the outbreak of war. Rents were rising, overheads going up, and booksellers in northern towns particularly were being forced out of business as unemployment grew. If for no other reason than raising morale like a good general, it was necessary for Basil Blackwell, when president of the A.B., to make rallying noises. He invited Stanley Unwin, then president of the P.A. (and no two presidents have ever been better matched or equally distinguished), to be joint host with him at an unofficial weekend conference of booksellers and publishers. Blackwell and Unwin had already inaugurated fortnightly meetings, at which each paid for his own lunch, to keep each other informed about the feelings of their respective members; the Ripon Hall Conference, Blackwell's idea, was an outcome of these, one supposes, spartan culinary occasions. At Ripon Hall those present were under no constraint. They were not guests, they had paid 50s. each to be there, so they spoke and argued together freely about the important issues of the time, thus enhancing the work of the joint committee whose deliberations had done much to bring them together. Such opportunities were less frequent then than in later decades when most publishers were invited to booksellers' Conferences and the habit of party giving had grown extensively.

Lasting friendships were made at Ripon Hall in 1934, and sealed when the experiment was repeated in 1936. The cooperation resulting from these two inter-war decades was to serve the trade nobly in the harrowing and nearly disastrous early years of World War II.

Fathers and Sons

Many of the publishing dynasties of the nineteenth century prospered through much of the twentieth; a few, a precious few, were still by 1980 ruled by descendants of their founders but all had become limited or public companies.

In 1900 the family links were stronger, although the second oldest private publisher, Longman, had bought the oldest, Rivington, ten years previously. *The Bookseller* described this as the most important amalgamation since Longmans had taken over John W. Parker, Son & Bourne in 1863. The latter's name means little, if anything, to us now, but that of Rivington is familiar because Septimus, the seventh son of Francis Hansard Rivington, who sold to Longman, had started his own list, using his own name, in 1889, and it was to remain a family partnership for seventy-five years. Fifth generation Longmans entered what was also still a partnership in the 1870s, Thomas Norton Longman (V) succeeding his father in 1879 as head of the firm and living on until 1930 by which time much of the management was exercised by men who were not of the family. The first was an elementary schoolteacher, J.W. Allen, who joined in 1884 and altered the balance of the business by building up the school book side and developing markets in India and elsewhere. The second was an accountant, Kenneth Potter, who brought much-needed finance through his family, who were in shipping. He joined in 1921 and became a director when Longmans, Green & Co Ltd was formed in 1926. (The name of Green, denoting another father and son concerned mainly with sales, had been included in most of the many imprints the house had published under since 1823.) Potter gave to Longmans the same drive and ability that members of the family had devoted to it for just on two centuries, and understood the traditions of the business and of the trade in which he played an influential part. Not all accountants who entered publishing had the same inherent sympathy with book-making as distinct from book-keeping.

Mention of Allen and Potter should not lead the reader to suppose that there were not Longmans a-plenty still intimately involved in the management of the firm throughout, and before, this period. Most became octogenarians. More may be learned of their contributions to the list in Philip Wallis's *At the Sign of the Ship, 1724-1974.* Wallis joined Longmans in 1929 and by 1938 was Head of the Publishing Department.

The Longman family attracted an eminent dynasty of authors in the Trevelyans. Sir George Otto (nephew of Lord Macaulay) was on the list in 1900 and his son, George Macaulay Trevelyan, became the most distinguished Longman historian of this period. In the 1930s four other Trevelyans, including R.C., graced the imprint.

The thirties brought novelists Stella Gibbons, Mary Renault and Thornton Wilder and, in the ever-important educational department (still small enough at the time not to be called a division) C.E. Eckersley (English) and W.F.H. Whitmarsh (French), whose textbooks were to serve several generations. From 1931, E.W. Parker, who had spent years visiting schools and colleges as a representative, managed this side of the list, editing many titles himself.

There were fewer Murrays than Longmans but the various Johns never allowed the family fortunes to rest upon the laurels of the Byron industry. The thirteen-volume edition of that poet's letters and poems appeared in 1895 too late for publication to be celebrated by Murray III. He had issued Darwin's *Origin of Species* and Samuel Smiles' *Self-Help* on the same day in 1859, which is as nice a double as I have encountered. He too inaugurated the famous series of guide books, four of which he wrote himself, creating a market which is still insatiable. Murray IV was a scholar and author like his father. During his reign Reginald Smith, of Smith, Elder, died (1917) and his list, with the exception of *The Dictionary of National Biography* which went to O.U.P., was acquired. This brought the Conan Doyle stories and novels to Murray and the *Cornhill Magazine,* a valuable source of new authors. Sir John Murray IV died in 1928 and was succeeded by his son, who, having no issue of his own, brought in his nephew, John Grey. Grey later changed his name by deed poll to preserve the identity of the house which during the thirties added John Betjeman, Osbert Lancaster and Freya Stark to the general side of a list also sporting P.C. Wren and that enduring bestseller, Axel Munthe's *The Story of San Michele.*

The first Murray was a Scot who always published from London although his successors had important links with Edinburgh. The first William Collins founded his business in Glasgow in 1819, in partnership with a celebrated divine of his time, Dr. Chalmers, who in a temper twenty-seven years later walked out and joined Oliver & Boyd. The list had been only partially built on religious writings, Collins himself having developed a market in school books earlier than most English publishers, and also diversified into printing. When he died his son, 'Water Willie' (a teetotaller) combined his business duties with being Lord Provost of Glasgow. When he was appointed Queen's Printer for Scotland in 1862 he was already well known for his editions of the scriptures, having published the Bible in seventeen different types and sizes, in 300 styles of binding, achieving an annual sale of nearly 300,000 copies. With his sons William and Alexander he expanded at dynamic pace, widening Collins' markets at home and abroad. Ahead of his time in many respects, William II made his firm into a limited company as early as 1879. He died in 1895, handing over to William III, an eccentric who dressed in the first garment which came to hand, took his own meat and game into restaurants so that he might be certain of the quality of his meals, and paid his wife £5 every time (which was often) he failed to attend divine service on a Sunday. He modernised the printing presses at Glasgow, established a stationery manufacturing department in Sydney, N.S.W., and proudly inaugurated Collins' Illustrated Pocket Classics in 1903, three years before the first volume of Dent's Everyman's Library. Unlike his father, he was no puritan and conducted his working life and the pursuit of wealth with some gaiety. He died, as he had lived, in too great a hurry, unlocking the lift gates of his London flat and stepping impatiently into a void.

William IV, nephew not son of the previous chairman, had a happy working relationship with his younger brother Godfrey, who took on the book side of the company and produced 7d reprints of novels in competition with Nelson's. After the war Godfrey, by now a politician and *Sir* Godfrey, and later to be a Minister, shared the responsibility for joining in direct competition with London publishers with his nephew William V – 'Billy' Collins, who was to become one of the most enthusiastically dedicated of publishers of any age. Increasingly taking over from his uncle, 'Billy' scoured the literary agencies (as well, some claimed, as his fellow publishers' lists) for saleable fiction. The Crime Club was started in 1930 by which time Agatha Christie, attracted from John Lane four years earlier, was already a Collins author.

The Collinses, numerous and energetic though they were, also called on outside help. Sir Godfrey brought in F.T. Smith as chief editor, R.J. Politzer as publicity manager, and Sydney J. Goldsack to run sales. Goldsack, who opened the New York office in 1923, then made two world trips, was a Collins in spirit, and spent his life selling their list. Politzer, working in a field where it is difficult to judge to what extent success or failure is due to the actions and inspirations of the individual concerned, was revered. Certainly, until the Hamlyn marketing adventures of the 1950s and 1960s, no books were promoted with more zest and belief in the product than when Politzer and Goldsack ran their respective departments.

Much of the nineteenth-century prosperity of A. & C. Black (founded in Edinburgh in 1801) was based on the *Encyclopaedia Britannica,* bought at auction after Constable's failure for £6,150. By the end of the century, however, following piracy on a huge scale of the ninth edition in America, James Tait Black, the elder surviving son of Adam Black, the founder, sanctioned a deal with Horace Everett Hooper, an American, on behalf of James Clarke of New York, one of the pirates. Hooper then negotiated successfully with *The Times* to promote a new sale of the same edition; aware of the financial difficulties of the newspaper, he averred that it needed him even more than he and his associates needed it. He was correct. *The Times* agreed to offer the encyclopaedia to its readers provided Blacks guaranteed delivery of stock. Its readers gratefully seized the opportunity of buying the *Britannica* at less than half price, and in 1900 Hooper and another bought out Clarke and became sole proprietors of the *Encyclopaedia* on payment of £5,000 to A. & C. Black, who had already received £46,500 from Clarke. Thus a work of British scholarship, founded in Edinburgh in 1768-71, was sold to America on the eve of the new century, a deed very much heralding the pattern of things to come. (It is perhaps worth recording that at Frankfurt in 1968 I met a German employee of Encyclopaedia Britannica Inc who assured me that I was quite wrong in supposing the *Encyclopaedia* to be of British origin.)

Adam Black, who became politician as well as publisher, representing his native Edinburgh at Westminster, did not live to see his sons establish a London office in 1889. The partnership, which became a private limited company in 1914, began the century at a low ebb but recovered with the development of *Who's Who*, acquired for £30 when Adam Black III tossed with George Whitaker for it, and won. Black and his cousin Adam Rimmer Black extended the market for this work of reference by broadening the text to include the eminent in all fields, and not just the rich and noble. To *Who's Who* was added, in 1906, *The Writers' and Artists' Yearbook* and *Black's Medical Dictionary*. But it was W.W. Callender, who joined as a boy in 1876, who realised the potential of three-colour printing and inaugurated a highly successful series of topographical and natural history books which ran to some eighty titles produced over fourteen years. Callender became joint managing director, retiring in 1928.

Blackie, two years younger than Black, and based on Glasgow where their headquarters remained even after a London office was opened in 1837, built up a fine list of religious, technical and historical works in the nineteenth century, and also opened a printing works. When John II, eldest son of the founder John Blackie, predeceased his father by one year in 1873, his brother, Dr. W.G. (Walter), took command and pursued plans for entering the school book market, widened the juvenile list and turned the partnership into a limited company in 1890. The Blackies expanded in a quieter way than, and along different lines from, the Collinses and Blacks. They were associated with subscription publishing (direct sale to the public) and in 1898 formed a subsidiary, The Gresham Publishing Co Ltd, for this purpose, and produced sumptuous volumes for children and adults in an age accustomed to elegance. John Alexander, who took the chair on his father's death, lost his only son in World War I and died himself in 1918. (A Nelson, two Dents, a Blackie, a nephew of Heinemann, and so many others who might have graced the publishing scene of the twentieth century died in that senseless war.) Blackie's, like others, rallied from the blow and the Bisacres, related by marriage, carried on the imprint, Frederick Bisacre's experience as an engineer lending practical value to the expansion of the technical list.

Black, Blackie, Blackwood, might almost be a conjugation. The house of Blackwood, which had published much of George Eliot's work in the nineteenth century, entered the twentieth under George William Blackwood, great-grandson of the founder. It was in his time that the firm published the early work of Ivy Compton-Burnett and E.M. Forster.

Older than any of their Scottish competitors were Thomas Nelson, established in Edinburgh in 1798. They opened a grand new building in Paternoster Row in 1870. In the Edwardian decade their classics were successful although the range did not grow to be as wide as Collins', with whom they were also in competition in the 7d reprint market. In 1906 John Buchan, a prolific writer who yet found time to edit others, joined them in Parkside, Edinburgh, after which district a series of their classics was named. He remained with them until long after World War I, the history of which he wrote for them, recording among many other deaths that of Captain T.A. Nelson whose younger brother Ian succeeded to the business. In 1938 H.P. Morrison joined Nelson's as managing director and his bent for philosophy soon showed itself in the list. John Hampden, also a writer, followed Henry Scheurmier as London editor for many years and was succeeded by Mervyn Horder, whom he first engaged 'to do the advertising': who is to say it was any less effectively done than nowadays when a whole department can be employed upon it?

Another Edinburgh firm, William and Robert Chambers, was founded in 1832 and their *Encyclopaedia,* which first appeared in 520 weekly parts from 1859-1868, continued to compete for sales with the *Britannica.* In the same fair city Oliver & Boyd could trace its origin back to 1778 when Thomas Oliver became a printer, using the hearth in his mother's house as an imposing stone. By 1896 the firm was jointly owned by the booksellers Thin and Grant but had temporarily ceased to be publishers of the *Edinburgh Medical Journal.* The leading medical publishers in the city were E. & S. Livingstone who had opened on South Bridge in 1863. A year earlier, the first Medical Officer of Health had been appointed, with far-reaching results reflected in the new list which was to become strong in nursing titles following sweeping changes in techniques initiated at the Edinburgh Royal Infirmary.

It was customary then for shops to open on Christmas Day in Scotland, but the benevolent Edward Livingstone announced one year in the nineties that they would shut early on the 25th, adding that there would, therefore, be no need to light the fires. At three o'clock he returned from lunch to his pinched and frozen employees, who had failed to make a single sale, and exclaimed cheerfully, 'Well, well, we must not work any longer on such a day as this'. (Normal working hours were from 8.30 a.m. to 8 p.m.)

To return to the larger dynasties in London, the Macmillans produced sufficient offspring, though not always in direct line, to carry on the tradition. Sir Frederick Macmillan became chairman on the death of his uncle Alexander in 1896; the imposing new offices were opened soon after in St. Martin's Street. The Bentley list was purchased for £8000 in 1898, the Bombay branch opened in 1901. Novels by Hardy and Shaw had been rejected but a volume of essays by Henry James accepted although the reader considered them 'mediocre'. In the years ahead they were to make large profits from Hardy but considerably less from James. Correspondence to them from authors, ranging over nearly a century, was selected by Simon Nowell-Smith for a fascinating publication, *Letters to Macmillan*. It reveals much about author-publisher relations.

Sir Frederick remained at the helm for most of this period and made frequent visits to America where the New York agency, opened as early as 1869, had become incorporated as a separate entity under George Platt Brett in 1896. Thereafter Macmillan, New York and Macmillan London acted with virtual autonomy, although closely linked in that they frequently sold rights to each other. The older company opened overseas branches in Melbourne (1904) and Toronto (1905), and its list strengthened and grew, becoming broader-based as the ultra-conservative editors Mowbray Morris and John Morley who had rejected Yeats, among others, were followed by younger men. On to the list came Hugh Walpole, Charles Morgan, A.G. Macdonnell, James Hilton and two of the Sitwells, Edith and Osbert. Rudyard Kipling, in editions for every occasion, was a moneyspinner long after his publishers feared they might have brought out the same collection of stories once too often. Lewis Carroll was another. H.G. Wells had a turn with them as he did with so many other publishers, but *Kipps* sold only 180 copies during the year to July 1907, so the author requested that it should be offered to Nelson's for their 7d library, in which during a few months of 1908 it sold 43,000.

All this while the Macmillans expanded their educational list, particularly in classical texts, often in their original bindings, still favoured by some schools in the 1970s. The leaning towards economics became more marked in the twenties when J.M. Keynes, Joan Robinson and A.C. Pigou appeared in the catalogue. The historians Lewis Namier and E.H. Carr published with them as did the great anthropologist Sir James Frazer, whose *The Golden Bough* at last found a wider public when it was put out in an abridged edition in 1922. For a company which produced a Conservative prime minister Macmillan's had a good record of progressive literature. That particular Macmillan, Harold, and his brother Daniel, assumed control in 1936 when their father, Maurice, their second cousin, George, and their uncle, Sir Frederick, all died within three months. Yet such was the sound basis on which the company was run that the boat scarcely rocked at all when these losses occurred.

The first Batsford was Bradley Thomas, an orphan boy from Hertford who served an apprenticeship with his cousin Bickers, a discount bookseller in Leicester Square. He set up his own shop at 30 High Holborn in 1843, began publishing in the next decade and by the end of the century, with three generations working in the firm, the retail side was of lesser importance. The founder, whose practice it was until late in life to walk most of the five miles from Kilburn to his daily work in Holborn, continued to work regularly until 1903, and died the following year at the age of eighty-three. His eldest son, Bradley II, outlived him by only two years, leaving the direction of the firm in the hands of his youngest brother Herbert and nephew Harry, who in 1917 became the sole surviving male Batsford in the business, although Aunt Florence had travelled the list during World War I, and may well have been the first woman book representative.

Under Harry Batsford the firm not only endured but actually thrived through the hard times of the twenties and thirties. Charles Fry joined in 1924; working hours, he was told, were 9 a.m. to 6.30 p.m. On the first day, on the dot of nine, he rang the bell in High Holborn, and after a long time an 'elderly crone' opened the door and invited him in, saying, 'Mr 'Arry's not 'ere yet; 'e's out with some bird, I suppose'. It transpired that Mr 'Arry and others were wont to appear nearer to ten than nine which must have made Bradley Thomas I turn over in his grave. But the founder could scarcely have failed to admire the industry of his grandson and Charles Fry who were joined in 1928 by Brian Cook, son of Harry's sister. Cook, who subsequently changed his name to Batsford, entered the family business as an enthusiastic artist with a predilection for gaily coloured jackets which became the image of the imprint within a short while.

On the very eve of the great slump Batsford's moved west to North Audley Street, Mayfair, taking their bookshop with them. That they survived the depression was due to their adaptability. In Holborn they had specialised in fine editions, sumptuously illustrated. Fry and Cook saw that they must produce cheaper books. Harry Batsford not only listened to them but entered zestfully into the planning of the British Heritage Series which aimed to provide a text of 40,000 words with upwards of 130 illustrations per volume. To achieve this at a popular price of 7s.6d it was necessary to print first editions of 10,000 copies. Most of them had to be reprinted and a similar series, the Face of Britain, was then launched.

Batsford, Fry and Cook not only published these books; they also wrote and illustrated many of them, travelling the country in an old car to do their research. Sam Carr, who had spent time in a bookshop, as all prospective publishers should, took up editorial duties in time to savour these frolics vicariously before World War II put an end to them.

It is improbable that such frivolity would have been countenanced within the mausoleum-like portals of York House, Portugal Street, where the descendants of George Bell, who started in the same decade as Bradley Batsford, continued to prosper steadily, not least from the sale of school texts. Edward, son of the founder, was an early president of the P.A.; Colonel A.W. Bell, a grandson who joined the board in 1927, became chairman in 1936. Outside the family were Guy H. Bickers, managing director for many years, and A.W. Ready, who came from Cambridge University Press in 1921 and was for long a leading figure in educational publishing. Bell's books went by the million into many schools and colleges but the firm also nurtured a trade list with a leaning towards crafts and chess.

Frederick Warne dissolved his partnership with his brother-in-law George Routledge in 1865, inheriting Nuttall's *Dictionary* from the split. With this and his Chandos Classics – 154 titles at 1s.6d paper and 2s. cloth which sold over five million copies – he got off to a good start. He lived in elegant Bedford Square, at No. 8, where he had the eccentric habit of calling all his male servants John and all his maids Mary. He opened a New York branch in 1881 and retired in 1894, by which time his three sons, Harold, Fruing and Norman were in the firm. It was to the last named that Beatrix Potter became engaged. Warne's published *The Tale of Peter Rabbit* in 1902 and were to sell millions of her twenty-three little books, in many languages, in the decades ahead because she remained loyal to them after her fiancé had died in 1905. Two years earlier Frederick Warne Stephens, grandson of the founder, joined the business and was followed by his son, Arthur L., and grandson, Cyril, so the family connection was firmly sealed. In 1938 the Observer series of genuinely pocket-sized guides to everything from Astronomy to Zoo Animals was launched, providing a back list for fifty years.

Ward and Lock, another imprint associated with popular children's books, began in 1854 and had a stroke of luck twelve years later when Samuel Orchart Beeton, widower and publisher of the famous cook, became their 'licensee in bankruptcy' through the failure of a discount house. George Lock and Ebenezer Ward gave Beeton £400 p.a. and one-sixth of the profits in exchange for all his copyrights. Subsequently they became acquisitive, buying the Edward Moxon list in 1870, and opening, as was the fashion, in New York. The famous Wonder books for children, with their comic endpapers, did not, however, start to appear until 1905. Various Locks remained in the business throughout the period when the firm had popular successes with such novelists as Dornford Yates, E. Philips Oppenheim ('prince of storytellers') and Edgar Wallace. Colonel E.A. Shipton, descended from the co-founder through his mother, joined the business in 1914 when there was only one female on the staff, she being described in the official history as 'a critic'. Shipton soon went to the war; by the time he returned there were more than sixty women on the payroll.

Sampson Low & Marston, proprietors of *The Publishers' Circular,* continued the book side of their enterprise under Fred Rymer who received authors with his own brand of informality, presiding over affairs in shirt-sleeves, waistcoat and bowler hat. The Whitaker family, owners of the competing trade journal, *The Bookseller,* had also been producing the *Almanack* bearing their name since 1868.

Sir Isaac Pitman whose list dated back to 1849 died in 1897 leaving two sons of very different stamp. One preferred to work on idealistic lines, the other said he would as soon brew and sell beer if that made more money. The former's son James (later Sir James) inherited his father's outlook and subsequently became head of the firm. Pitman's was always in the forefront of educational publishing, as befitted the pioneer of shorthand and typewriting books, which Sir James believed did as much to emancipate women as giving them the vote. Pitman's took over the technical house of Whittaker (not to be confused with the proprietors of *The Bookseller*) in about 1920, the same period when they moved into offices in Parker Street, sold in 1981. In the twenties much of their business was in direct selling, not only to schools and institutions but to industry and the professions. Sydney Hyde who worked in their publicity section in the late twenties has recorded that because of this his department was 'not in a position of subservience to the editorial and production departments'.

Hodder & Stoughton (pronounced *Stoaton*) was formed in 1868 when Matthew Henry Hodder, of Jackson, Walford & Hodder, was joined by Thomas Wilberforce Stoughton, who had worked at Nisbet's. Both men were interested in evangelical and low church theology, so it is not surprising that they acted for a while as official publishers to the Congregational Union and embarked on a monthly journal for serious Christians, *The Expositor,* in 1875. Nine years later when the editor's views became distasteful to the publishers and a large section of their readers he became an early recipient of the golden handshake and was replaced by the Rev. William Robertson Nicoll who became chief editor and literary adviser, introducing J.M. Barrie and others to the list. He also edited many books, including forty-eight volumes of *The Expositor's Bible.* In the illuminating chronological list of Hodder & Stoughton's principal publications, an appendix to John Attenborough's *A Living Memory,* the development of the firm may be traced. From heavy emphasis on theological and allied subjects there is a broadening out into fiction (Baroness Orczy, A.E.W. Mason and Sapper), general history and books for children. In 1910 shares were bought in the University of London Press Ltd and in Leicester a Midlands sales office was set up which was eventually to become the Brockhampton Press. The grandson of Matthew Hodder, J.E., later Sir Ernest, Hodder-Williams, played an increasingly dominant part in the development of the business but at first under the eye of the founders who took up their position each morning on the first floor of St Paul's House, Warwick Square, behind two roll-top desks. Mr Hodder with his 'flowing white beard, piercing blue eyes and (a) benign presence' lived until 1911; Mr Stoughton, who then became senior partner, until 1917.

The change of name to Hodder-Williams is explained by the fact that Matthew's only child was a daughter who became Mrs John Williams. All of Matthew's male grandchildren were given a third Christian name of Hodder which, in 1919, they officially hyphenated with Williams to create the present surname. When Ernest died in 1927, only fifty years old, his brothers Percy and Ralph took over, soon to be joined by their nephews Paul Hodder-Williams and John Attenborough, both great-grandsons of Matthew. The last two named began their careers in 1931 and were destined to see changes which might well have startled the two Congregationalists who began it all. On the eve of World War II, Leonard Cutts (who was not of the family) presided over the publication of the first, now ubiquitous, Teach Yourself books, known initially as Steeplejacks.

George Hutchinson, who had travelled for Hodder & Stoughton, founded his imprint in 1880 and issued paperbacks, 'the Sixpenny Blacks', some fifty-five years before Allen Lane's similarly priced Penguins appeared. There were twenty-five titles in the first year and their success enabled him to move out of his basement office into 34 Paternoster Square. He also pioneered part-works at a half-penny per issue, a branch of publishing which was to be revived, in some cases successfully, in the 1960s.

Walter Hutchinson succeeded his father in 1925 as head of a company which, between the wars, absorbed so many imprints that no complete record of them exists. Certainly they included Rider (established c. 1700), Hurst & Blackett (1812), Skeffington (1840), Stanley Paul (1908) and Jarrold's (1916). The young Robert Lusty joined in 1928 and when he had the audacity to ask for a list of his own, he was told 'You can have Selwyn & Blount – but only as a hobby. It must not interfere with your Hutchinson work'. Selwyn & Blount had been started by Roger Ingpen, who became an antiquarian bookseller after selling to Hutchinson. In his autobiography Lusty refers to Hutchinson's 'benevolent malevolence' but reports that he 'was kind to animals'. His treatment of human beings was often savage as countless numbers of ex-employees have recorded. Many, like Robert Lusty, survived to have distinguished careers in publishing. Some – Robert Hale and William Kimber for instance – founded their own imprints. Kimber was involved in the purchase of *Mein Kampf* which Hurst & Blackett brought out in the 1930s and which Lusty, when he returned to Hutchinson as managing director over twenty years later, felt reluctantly compelled to reissue. Of the hundreds of authors whom Walter Hutchinson published successfully Ethel Mannin and Dennis Wheatley stand out as two who stayed the course. The former's first novel, *Martha,* appeared in 1923 and fifty years later she celebrated her golden jubilee with the firm, paying particular tribute to thirty years of understanding with her editor, Cherry Kearton. Wheatley wrote sixty-two books for them and achieved world sales of over forty million copies.

Joseph Malaby Dent, an apprentice book-binder from Darlington, arrived in London in 1867 to look for work with 1s.6d in his pocket. Seven years later he opened his own bindery which he ran successfully for fifteen years until it was burned down. In the same year his wife died. Rallying from these twin blows he carried on business in new premises and took up publishing as well. His associations with Toynbee Hall in London's East End suggested to him the need for a cheap pocket Shakespeare, which was the origin of the Temple edition completed in 1896 in forty volumes. Meanwhile he had started The Temple Library, earning the praise of Bernard Quaritch for 'the best piece of book-making for years'. The public, said Quaritch, would soon want to know more of the man who had made them. The man, according to Frank Swinnerton, was less than medium height, lame, stingy and had a violent temper. 'He never praised; he paid very poorly; he frightened everybody who worked for him', including Swinnerton whom Dent liked, for some years trusting only him to bring in his meagre lunch of a penny roll, cheese, apple and ginger beer.

Dent remarried in 1890 and travelled to Italy which inspired the Medieval Towns series of guidebooks; he was soon to be 'overwhelmingly, even passionately' engaged in his publishing, as he recalls in his memoirs. He took over Macmillan's old offices in Bedford Street because of their literary associations, and from there, in the next decade, began to issue Everyman's Library, perhaps his greatest contribution to publishing. When he brought out the first title – Boswell's *Johnson* in two volumes, 1905 – he had the clear idea that he wished to publish a cheap library of the greatest works ever written. Not just the greatest novels, but the most important classical works, biographies, religious and philosophical treatises, political and social theses, plays, poems and chonicles of travel and adventure. The knowledge to be derived from the series would benefit not only men like himself with little formal education but anyone, of whatever standard of education, who was willing to continue learning.

Dent had the simplicity and imagination to see that what he was doing was both of cultural benefit to his fellows as well as immensely profitable. In the note that Ernest Rhys, first and foremost editor of Everyman, added to many of the volumes, he quoted Victor Hugo as saying that a library is 'an act of faith'. Everyman's Library was precisely that, with its decorative end-papers embellishing the words

Everyman, I will go with thee
and be thy Guide
In thy most need
To go by thy side.

Everyman's Library at 1s. a volume paid off at every level. Dent started it when he was fifty-seven. Seven years later he published the first encyclopaedia issued exclusively through the book trade. This work has been often revised and forms part of a library of reference works under the general Everyman symbol which exists to this day.

Dent lost two sons in World War I but the family retained control through a surviving child, Hugh, who purchased the freehold of Aldine House in Bedford Street. Hugh Dent died in 1938, twelve years after his father, and was succeeded by W.G. Taylor, who was president of the P.A. from 1935-7. His colleague, A.J. Hoppé, was by then also on the board and was one of those who combined responsibility for sales with being an able editor. He too played his part in trade affairs, becoming chairman of Book Tokens, then a committee of the National Book Council, and also of the Publishers' Circle. He was also a founder member of the Publishers' Publicity Circle and both he and Taylor were members of the Society of Bookmen for many years. Their 'other' activities, between them, typify what was expected of busy and successful publishers, in the way of voluntary work.

Other Pre-Twentieth Century Publishers

Older than any of those mentioned in the previous chapter were the Oxford and Cambridge University Presses whose publishing evolved differently but whose interests remained linked through their common official rights in the Bible.

The nineteenth century witnessed a transformation at Oxford, aided by the large profits of the Bible Press. The sale and distribution of Bibles was organised from London, where Henry Frowde was first employed as warehouse manager in 1874; the productions of the Learned Press also began to be published in London, though by Alexander Macmillan between 1863 and 1881. Frowde started publishing secular books for the general reader rather than for scholars, and by the time he was succeeded as London publisher by Humphrey Milford in 1913, O.U.P. was a major publisher in its own right. The Delegates remained a committee responsible to the University for all printing and publishing and had direct control over Clarendon Press (learned publishing), but the publisher for the university had editorial responsibility for O.U.P. output and organised sales and distribution for both.

Milford widened the range of O.U.P.'s publishing, expanding the World's Classics (bought by Frowde from the bankrupt Grant Richards), launching new series and himself editing volumes of verse; it was he who instigated the *Oxford Dictionary of Quotations*. Clarendon saw the completion (1928) of the great *Oxford English Dictionary* which in turn spawned the *Shorter,* the *Concise,* the *Pocket* (that of a voluminous overcoat) and the *Little,* all of which were sold at home and also through the overseas branches opened in Toronto (1904), Melbourne (1908), Bombay (1912) and Cape Town (1915). In the twenties the New York branch started to publish autonomously although continuing to distribute books originating in London and Oxford, and O.U.P. began to cater specifically for schools abroad by instituting the overseas education department, heralding the time when books would be published locally in some three dozen African and Asian languages and dialects, as well as in English. The London office moved to Amen House, Warwick Square, in 1924, and six years later a warehouse was built at Neasden, north-west London.

The breadth and depth of Oxford publishing knew no bounds. A children's book department started in 1907, an International Series of Monographs in Physics in 1931. There were medical and musical offshoots, Medieval and Early English texts, and the Oxford Standard Authors, definitive editions of the works of major and minor poets.

The Clarendon Press developed under Charles Cannan, R.W. Chapman (a scholar in the disparate fields of Johnson and Jane Austen) and Kenneth Sisam. The great dictionary was its prime consideration but the *Dictionary of National Biography* also came under its wing in 1917 (see page 29). To the public, even to the book trade, the O.U.P. and Clarendon imprints were one, and equally distinguished. There were no shareholders; the profits from its commercial ventures provided, until 1921, a subvention to the University and financed the publication of learned works with small sales.

As the Delegates ruled at Oxford, so did the Syndics at Cambridge, with a manager in London who was solely concerned with sales and promotion. The Syndics allowed their press to expand more slowly than Oxford's, and concerned themselves much with the quality of their printing and production, to which Walter Lewis and Stanley Morison particularly lent distinction. Their story belongs to the history of printing and may be read in *Two Men,* issued in 1968 by Brooke Crutchley when he was Printer to the University.

The administration of C.U.P. underwent radical changes at the beginning of the century when official recognition was given separately to the Printer and the Publishing Manager, the positions, previously doubled, going to the sons of C.J. Clay. A.R. Waller became Secretary to the Syndics in 1911, succeeding R.T. Wright who had contracted with Hooper to publish the eleventh edition of the *Encyclopaedia Britannica*. On publication eyebrows were raised at high table — the new edition lacked the desired academic excellence. The twelfth edition did not appear under the Cambridge imprint. Publishing took a new lease of life in the twenties and thirties with some remarkable bestsellers by Sir James Jeans, A.S. Eddington and others. The Cambridge Modern History, born earlier in the century, grew as planned. The London office, under R.J.L. Kingsford, moved in 1937 from Fetter Lane to a new building in Euston Road named Bentley House.

Other university presses in existence by 1900 were those at Glasgow, founded in the seventeenth century, Aberdeen (1840), and Liverpool (c. 1898). The University of Manchester published occasionally through the booksellers Sherratt and Hughes until 1912 when they founded their own press, using Longmans for distribution until 1931 when they took it over themselves; the University of Wales Press, Cardiff, started in 1922.

A joint interest in the Bible linked Oxford and Cambridge with the firm of Eyre & Spottiswoode, which had rights in the Bible by virtue of owning the patent of King's Printer. This patent was objected to by many members of Parliament but the Select Committee considering it always renewed it, for the last time in 1901, not for a fixed term but 'during Her Majesty's will and pleasure'.

Also connected with Oxford University Press were Bailey Brothers which began as a Bible bookshop in Seven Sisters Road, Holloway, in 1825. Its proprietor, Frank Evans Bailey, left his brother to mind the shop and opened a bindery which worked for O.U.P. Epworth Press, founded in 1739 as the Book Room in John Wesley's chapel on Finsbury Square, published that preacher's writings, and other works of Methodist interest.

At the other end of the religious scale were Burns, Oates & Washbourne, Catholic publishers and booksellers since the 1830s, started by James Burns, a convert from high Anglicanism. From publishing the work of the Oxford Movement, he turned to Rome, which nearly ruined his business until he was saved by a more famous convert, John Newman, whose writings set him on his feet again. Finally, in Edinburgh, were T. & T. Clark, uncle and nephew, and both named Thomas, of whom the elder had been the chief law bookseller in the City and publisher to the university. Their publishing list, however, was largely theological and ran to many series from Great Texts of the Bible in twenty volumes down to forty-four Bible Class Primers which, in 1940, were still priced at 1s. paper, 1s.3d cloth.

The great legal house of Butterworth all but qualifies for inclusion in the previous chapter on dynastic publishers. It was founded by Henry Butterworth who had been apprenticed at the age of fifteen in 1801 to his uncle Joseph, a law publisher and bookseller whose fortune was said to be 'the largest ever known in bookselling'. Henry set up on his own in 1818 in Fleet Street where the new business prospered (his uncle's old firm was 'disposed of to Strangers') and Butterworth became Law Booksellers and Publishers to the Queen. At his death in 1860 his second son Joshua became sole proprietor, remaining so until 1895 when his executors sold to Shaw and Sons for £5300. Shaw's, another family firm dating from 1750, was by now owned by the Bonds, great-grandsons of the founder. Richard Bond carried on the printing and law stationery business of Shaw's, while Charles and his son Stanley ran Butterworths (in Bell Yard from 1889) to which the Shaw law books were transferred.

Stanley Shaw Bond, despite suffering a sickly childhood, lived to become a forceful proprietor of the company. His innovations included legal encyclopaedias such as *Halsbury's Laws of England* which were quickly established as authoritative and essential reference works for lawyers. Bond opened branches in Australia, New Zealand, Canada, South Africa and India. The Indian company, the only failure, added medical publishing to its legal list and then attempted to enter the general market, which contributed to the losses. It was closed in 1946. Bond was patriarchal in his attitude to Butterworths and it is said in the official history that 'he owned people rather than employed them'. Like Joseph Butterworth he became immensely rich and in 1939 still presided over a private limited company.

Major competitors to Butterworth were Sweet & Maxwell, and Stevens & Sons. In the early nineteenth century Stephen Sweet and Alexander Maxwell (then trading separately) joined with Stevens and three others to form Associated Law Booksellers, a consortium which agreed to share equally the costs and rewards of publishing. They also undertook not to sell copyrights without unanimous consent. From this consortium emerged Sweet & Maxwell in 1889, and there have been Maxwells in the company until recently. The Sweets were represented by sons-in-law for a long while until John James, great-great-grandson of Stephen, joined in 1935. They expanded more slowly than Butterworths and did not open any overseas branches during this period. Nor did Stevens & Sons, also based in Chancery Lane, a company with which they retained contact through joint ownership of Woodfall's *Landlord and Tenant.*

Jean-Baptiste Baillière of Paris opened in London in 1826 and went on to establish offices in New York and Madrid. The English branch, managed by his younger brother Hippolyte, began by importing French medical books but later started to issue original native works. When Baillière died in 1867 his widow continued the firm for two years before selling to A.A. Tindall and William Cox under whose aegis the Students' Aids Series was born, to be followed several generations later by the Nurses' Aids. The veterinary interest came in 1875 with the purchase of a journal which naturally gave rise to a whole new section of the list. The other leading medical publishers were J. & A. Churchill, the family connection in which had worn somewhat thin by 1934 when it became a public company, E. & S. Livingstone, already mentioned, and Henry Kimpton, founded 1854 and still unlimited in 1939.

What was to become the largest specialist publisher of all, Her Majesty's Stationery Office, first became an imprint to be reckoned with — and paid for — by the public in 1883, when it took over the issuing of Parliamentary Papers. H.M.S.O. was established in 1786 but its actual publishing activities did not commence until well into the nineteenth century, when certain departmental publications began to be offered for sale. Prior to this it was primarily concerned with printing though it did not become responsible for producing *Hansard,* the record of parliamentary debates, until 1909.

Amongst the oldest of the general publishers who saw in the twentieth century was W.H. Allen which claimed an origin in the eighteenth. In a

Bookseller of 1858 they advertised themselves as 'publishers to the India Office' and offered various new titles on the sub-continent from an address in Waterloo Place, just off the Strand. By 1939 they were, however, virtually moribund and they are not listed in Whitaker's *Reference Catalogue of Current Literature* for the following year, by which time the list, such as it was, had been bought by a provincial journalist, Mark Goulden, whose exploits will be recorded in a later chapter.

Chapman & Hall, established in 1830, were Dickens's first publishers with *Pickwick Papers;* after a period with other firms he returned to them in 1859 and remained on their list until his death. Trollope, too, moved from Smith, Elder & Co to Chapman & Hall.

In practice it became Chapman & Chapman in 1847 when William Hall died. Edward Chapman's cousin Frederick took his place and became head of the house in 1864 by which time George Meredith had become its literary adviser. He remained so for over thirty years at a salary of £250 p.a. He turned down Mrs Henry Wood's *East Lynne* (which sold over one million copies elsewhere), Samuel Butler's *Erewhon,* and also novels by Shaw and Ouida, but he accepted G.A. Henty's offerings and Olive Schreiner's *Story of an African Farm*. In the 1890s when he requested a rise of £50 p.a. he was turned down. So both he and his future work moved to Constable's where his son, W.M. Meredith, was a partner. There is evidence that Chapman & Hall did not fit into the climate of the *fin-de-siècle* and it is said that the now aged chairman could not be made to understand that though the company had made a profit of so many thousand pounds that sum was not necessarily in its bank account.

In the next decade it was to recover under Arthur Waugh as managing director from 1902. He was advised that if it wasn't for Dickens (whose copyrights were running out) 'we might as well put up the shutters tomorrow' and that Mr. Chapman had averred that there was no money to be made out of miscellaneous publishing. He ignored both warnings, noted the increasing success of the John Wiley technical list for which his company held the agency, and fathered two highly successful novelists. Before their emergence as writers, however, he had an Arnold Bennett success with *The Old Wives' Tale,* not that that author stayed with him or any other publisher for long. Nor did the elder Waugh son, Alec, commence his career with Chapman & Hall, *The Loom of Youth* written in his eighteenth year coming out in 1917 from Grant Richards. Most of his later work went to Cassell. He joined his father beside whom he worked throughout the twenties, at the end of which Arthur semi-retired and Alec became a full-time novelist. By then the second son, Evelyn, had matured and soon established himself as the foremost satirical novelist of his age. No author shed such lustre on the Chapman & Hall list for forty years. In 1938, Philip Inman, into whose hands the company had fallen, sold it to Methuen.

Algernon Methuen Marshall Stedman, born 1856, was a classical scholar who opened a school in Surrey where, according to a former pupil, he gave the boys 'something to get on with' whilst he sat on the dais writing textbooks. These were published by George Bell until the author, by then a publisher himself, bought them back. In 1889 he rented a back room in Bloomsbury in the premises of W.W. Gibbins, a remainder merchant. His first book, a long-forgotten novel by Edna Lyall, sold 25,000 copies in its first year. Gibbins was appointed trade manager, another room was rented, twenty titles were published in the second year and then, in 1892, Kipling's *Barrack-Room Ballads* was an overnight success. Stedman gave up his school, changed his name to Methuen in 1899, moved to Essex Street and set about broadening his list, which from quite early days was a splendid amalgam of fiction, non-fiction and academic works catering for all brows. Marie Corelli's *The Life Everlasting,* in 1911, had a subscription of over 100,000 copies. Poor Henry James never earned the advances of between £150 and £300 on six novels. D.H. Lawrence brought only trouble when *The Rainbow* was successfully prosecuted for obscene libel.

Methuen suffered a curious publishing failure in 1904-5 when his Standard Library of Classics was met by praise from the reviewers but indifference from the public, which shortly after took Dent's Everyman Library to its heart. The Sixpenny Library — reprints of classical and contemporary authors — fared better, so did the Arden edition of Shakespeare and the Little Guides to the Counties of England. In 1908 he brought out Kenneth Grahame's *The Wind in the Willows* which at first went unnoticed but began to sell about two years later — inexplicably to its publisher — perhaps through word of mouth, the best and cheapest form of advertising.

Methuen also secured the first prose book of T.S. Eliot, *The Sacred Wood*. When he had become a director of Faber & Faber, who published most of his later work, Eliot sought to buy the rights back for his own firm. Methuen, recalling his own deal with George Bell, might well have acceded but he was dead by then and his successors have never parted with the book. Methuen left £250,000, an impressive sum which would have been much larger had he lived to see the publication of A.A. Milne's four enormously popular children's books which have between them gone into hundreds of printings in nearly sixty years. Methuen left an eccentric will by which the sales manager, C.W. Chamberlain, inherited the managing directorship and E.V. Lucas, an editor, the chairmanship. A year earlier E.V. Rieu had been made editor of academic books. In 1928 the company went public and fell into the hands of a biscuit manufacturer, Sir George Roberts, who did not take a seat on the board but interfered from a distance. In the interests of property speculation he jeopardised the company which was taken over by Lloyd's Bank who appointed Philip Inman, of Chapman & Hall, as chairman.

In a decade when finance was short, only a company as broadly based as Methuen could have rallied from such disasters. Eventually it did, under the financial backing of Nutcombe Hume (of the Charterhouse Trust), James Pitman and Stanley Unwin. One who stayed the course with them was a future managing director, J. Alan White, who joined the firm in 1924 at a time when the staff worked on high stools at sloping desks and speaking tubes had only just been declared obsolete.

Older than Methuen and having a more tumultuous history was Cassell which began when a teetotal tea and coffee merchant felt the urge to bring enlightenment to all at low prices. In the 1840s John Cassell launched the first of many journals, periodicals and part-works which ranged from *The Working Man's Friend and Family Instructor* at a penny a week to *Cassell's Popular Educator* and the *Illustrated Family Bible*. In 1855 his printers, Petter & Galpin, called in a large loan and bought him out, although retaining his services. He was taken into partnership in 1858, the premises in La Belle Sauvage Yard, Ludgate Hill were rebuilt and Cassell, Petter & Galpin, as it had become, expanded apace, a New York branch opening in 1860. By 1865, in which year Cassell died, the staff numbered 500; by 1888 it was 1200 but the period of prosperity was over.

No publisher had worked harder through propaganda and its own publications to help create the climate of opinion which led to the passing of Forster's Education Act in 1870, but the company failed to keep abreast of its competitors in the nineties, by which time a whole generation had benefited from compulsory education. Ironically the secretary of the company was then H.O. Arnold-Forster, adopted son of the sponsor of the Act. He and his colleagues were more interested in politics than in publishing and the new century dawned not at all bright over La Belle Sauvage Yard. Recovery was delayed until 1905 when Arthur Spurgeon became general manager. He made drastic cuts in staff and concentrated on boosting the circulation of the various magazines, which, in 1908, resulted in the shareholders receiving their first dividend for many years. Then Spurgeon turned to books, forming the Waverley Book Company (1909) to sell expensive illustrated volumes on the instalment plan directly to the public. Three years later Newman Flower, editor of the *Penny Magazine,* was deputed to revive the hopelessly languishing trade book department — only two titles having been announced for the spring list. Flower used the successful magazines to attract authors, promising them that he would not bother them again if he failed to sell their books. G.K. Chesterton obliged with the Father Brown stories, H.G. Wells with *Mr. Britling Sees it Through.* Arnold Bennett came to him in 1916, thus ending his wanderings amongst publishers, and remained loyal to Flower until his sudden demise in 1931. Ernest Raymond went to Cassell with his first best-selling novel *Tell England* in 1922 and stayed for fifty years, outstripping even Warwick

Deeping's length of service which began in the doldrum year of 1907. Sheila Kaye-Smith was another novelist with a long connection based on genuine friendship and respect between editor and author.

At the beginning of the 1920s the Berry brothers (later the newspaper barons Camrose and Kemsley) bought all the shares in Cassell. In 1923 the company went public and a few years later the Berrys decided to close down the printing works because of continued industrial disputes. This was followed by the sale of the magazine interests to the Amalgamated Press and of the book side to Newman Flower.

The years until the start of World War II were to be ones of solid achievement, with Louis Bromfield and Robert Graves joining the list, and when Alfred Knopf of New York closed his London office Cassell acquired British rights in Dashiell Hammett, and in English translations of Guy de Maupassant and André Gide.

Another imprint which had enduring relationships with many of its authors was Chatto & Windus whose beginnings lay with one of the most colourful figures in nineteenth-century publishing, John Camden Hotten, who began in 1855 in a Piccadilly bookshop. From various addresses in that thoroughfare he published numerous American authors and was none too scrupulous in taking advantage of the absence of international copyright. His widow sold out to his partner Andrew Chatto for £25,000. W.E. Windus, a minor poet, joined Chatto but never played a very active role, unlike Percy Spalding who became a partner in 1876. According to Frank Swinnerton, their reader for many years, Spalding 'did not pretend to any literary taste but put his hands in his pockets, jangled his keys and coppers, whistled *Meet Me Tonight in Dreamland* and said to all authors, whatever their pretensions, "Nice, give us a rattling good story".'

Chatto & Windus seem to have been adept at attracting eccentrics. From 1905-10 there was Philip Lee-Warner whose practice it was to lie flat on his back on the floor whilst dictating letters. He set a high standard for production and inaugurated a series of costly art books before going on to the Medici Society. Chatto's son (also Andrew) was a not over-interested partner until 1919, and *his* son Tom defected to the antiquarian trade. Meanwhile Frank Swinnerton and Geoffrey Whitworth had joined as editors, so with Charles Prentice, Harold Raymond and Spalding, the firm had a good blend of age and youth to see them through the first post-war years of boom and depression. When Spalding died Prentice became chief partner and he and Ian Parsons, who joined on coming down from Cambridge in 1928, carried on the tradition of good design. Parsons shared the partnership with Harold Raymond and J.W. McDougall, after Prentice's retirement. He was a notable critic of poetry in the thirties, an attribute very strongly reflected in the list.

Between the wars the new authors included Lytton Strachey, Wilfred

Owen (posthumously), Aldous Huxley and Marcel Proust, and Daisy Ashford, whose *The Young Visiters,* a highly sensational novel written when she was nine, is still strong backlist, as is Helen C. Bannister's *Little Black Sambo,* despite being denounced as racist. The Constance Garnett translations of Chekhov also went to Chatto after Heinemann had turned them down. The lit. crit. list was enlarged with controversial and original works from the tempestuous F.R. Leavis and the scintillating William Empson while art was the province of the erudite Clive Bell. Chatto & Windus, housed in shabby premises near Charing Cross, had a list which was nicely balanced between what would sell and what deserved to.

An equally well proportioned list was Allen & Unwin's, although not as exciting in literary quality as Chatto's. It began in 1871 when John Ruskin decided to sell his own books direct to the public, a line which other authors have tried to follow and failed. George Allen, whom Ruskin met when he was teaching at the Working Men's College in Great Ormond Street, and with whom he had been on a geological study tour in the Swiss mountains, became his assistant. The first publication was *Fors Clavigera* at 7d a copy. Ruskin told his readers that it cost him £10 to print one thousand copies, £5 more for a picture, and 1d off his 7d to send them the book. When he had sold the whole edition he and Allen would have made £5 each; 'we won't work for less, either of us'. 'And,' he went on, 'I mean to sell all my large books, henceforth, in the same way, well printed, well bound and at a fixed price. . . I, the first producer, answer to the best of my power for the quality of the bookpaper, bindings, eloquence and all; the retail dealer charges what he ought to charge openly; and if the public do not choose to give it they can't get the book. That is what I call legitimate business.' Which was a fine gauntlet to fling down at the trade and the public.

Allen's press at Orpington eventually took over all Ruskin's works and made a handsome profit, despite the opposition of booksellers with whom, in 1882, Ruskin came to terms because he saw that his high prices made his works prohibitive to the very public he wished to reach. He made £4,000 per year from his publishing and writing over the next fifteen years, partly through lowering his prices and dealing with retailers. George Allen was allowed to take on other authors and to open a London office in Bell Yard, in 1882. The two men remained friends and partners until Ruskin's death in 1900, by which time Allen had moved to Charing Cross Road and published Maeterlinck and the first of Gilbert Murray's translations from the Greek. In 1911 he amalgamated with Swan Sonnenschein (of whom more below) but became bankrupt two years later. His name is perpetuated in George Allen & Unwin Ltd.

Unwin, born 1884, was regarded as so sickly an infant that an over-frank friend of his father's remarked, 'if you can't do better than that you'd better stop'. The sickly child, who died in harness aged eighty-four, was descended from printers on both sides but began his working life as a shipping and insurance broker's clerk. Always careful about money, he contrived to save sufficient to enable him to travel, which pursuit later framed his life's work. On the day he gave notice to the broker he visited his childless uncle, T. Fisher Unwin, whose imprint dated from 1882, and who was looking for a partner and successor. Stanley agreed to join him after spending a year in Germany and France.

In Leipzig in 1903-4 Stanley Unwin worked six days a week for a bookseller and theological publisher. He was only absolved from working also on Sundays by protesting that his parents would not approve. Wishing to widen his experience he suggested to his uncle that he should visit Berlin with Fisher's list. He was granted three pounds for the trip and sold £120 worth of books, which, he noted in his autobiography, would have paid him better had he been operating on the usual traveller's 10%. (He did not recall, in the same volume, that his London rep in the 1950s, working on 10s. per week fares allowance, put in for a 2s.6d per week subsistence rise but was granted only 2s.)

At Fisher's request Stanley returned to England ahead of schedule only to find his services were not required immediately, so used the time fruitfully at his father's printing works learning about typesetting and the cost of standing type.

In his autobiography Unwin describes Fisher as 'tall, handsome, bearded ... physically as straight as a dart, a keen mountaineer ... wonderfully good company out of office hours'. Stanley started in that office as an invoice clerk, but later went on the road to travel the list. When T. Werner Laurie, Fisher Unwin's manager, left to start his own imprint, he returned to the office, first to inaugurate an export drive, then to take over gradually the day-to-day management of the business. His uncle sent him to America, and came to lean on him increasingly while preserving the appearance of being in command. It was too much for an ambitious young man who had introduced saleable books and watched the profits grow from around £600 a year to more than £6,000. Twice he offered his notice, twice his salary was doubled. On the third occasion, seeing that he would never gain control of the business, he resigned. At once he planned a world tour with his future brother-in-law, Severn Storr. They visited countries to which no British publisher had been before. Stanley made copious notes which served him well in later life when he was alleged to arrive at a print number by calculating that three copies would be sold in this capital, ten in that, five in such-and-such a university city in the Far East, fifty in another, and so on. The story is no doubt apocryphal, as are so many relating to this remarkable man, but it holds a grain of truth.

Back in England in 1913 Stanley Unwin looked for a bankrupt list to buy. On 1 January 1914 a receiver was appointed to George Allen. Unwin, unemployed for eighteen months, accepted the receiver's onerous terms which restricted his powers because although he held more shares than any other director, *all* of them had to agree about each book submitted for publication and any one of them could exercise a veto. It was on the fateful date of 4 August 1914 that he entered into his obligations. In the same year he married and, true to his essential business acumen, commissioned a book from the officiating cleric in the vestry after the service.

Unwin craftily chose for himself a tiny ground floor office from where he could see all approaching visitors, while his co-directors were accommodated in more splendid rooms on the upper storeys. This did not impede one of them, however, from preventing publication of Marie Stopes' *Married Love,* apparently in retaliation for Unwin's vetoing a novel which he judged would be thought obscene. *Married Love* eventually sold over one million copies under the Fifield imprint; the novel, published by C.W. Daniel, was successfully prosecuted.

Two of the three directors were called up in the war; Unwin was classified B3 and published Bertrand Russell, who was imprisoned for his pacifist views, Ramsay MacDonald, a Hampstead neighbour who also objected to the war, and a reissue of *Praeterita,* (there was a warehouse full of unsaleable copies) under the new title *Autobiography of Ruskin,* which was a sell-out.

Frank Mumby maintained that Allen & Unwin made a bigger contribution in proportion to its size to the common stock of knowledge than any other publishing house in the country. Stanley Unwin, who built his list scientifically, no doubt regarded this as obvious to all right-thinking persons. He was not accustomed to being wrong. There was little humour in his make-up (he even boasted of this during his eightieth birthday celebrations) and his autobiography is riddled with earnest Pooter-style anecdotes of How to Succeed. 'I have always maintained,' he wrote, 'that if it is by a recognised authority, and was the best on the subject, my firm would publish any book regardless of whether it was particularly in our line or not.' He refers to his younger son, when a boy, reading *The Hobbit* by J.R.R. Tolkien 'eight or nine times, so absorbing did he find it. Many years were to elapse before the publication of its sequel — not addressed to children though they will enjoy it — *The Lord of the Rings,* in three large volumes'. That is the voice of Pooter and also the authentic voice of a publisher with absolute belief in himself. He was a professional who knew his business from the packing-floor upwards. It was said of him that when he was not on a foreign tour, or on the holidays which he rightly considered essential to maintaining his extremely good (B3) health, he always opened the morning mail himself, and vetted every outgoing letter before it left the office. In the twenties Unwin acquired debentures and more shares in Allen & Unwin, bought the Swarthmore Press and Maunsel & Co, and attracted the attention of the law for publishing Freud's *A Young Girl's Diary.* Typically, he wore down the public prosecutor and won his case. He travelled extensively and wrote *The Truth about Publishing* which Jonathan Cape dubbed 'the publisher's bible', and this it has long remained. In the thirties he was rid of the last of his co-managing directors together with the Williams & Norgate imprint which he had bought in 1928. It was appropriate timing because he was soon to become the president of both the P.A. and the International Congress of Publishers.

Through buying Williams & Norgate, Allen & Unwin laid claim to the future work of Lancelot Hogben whose *Science for the Citizen* and *Mathematics for the Million* sold in huge numbers. When the latter was offered to them in 1936, C.A. Furth, a respected senior editor who became a director, 'pronounced it as quite outstanding and all of us who looked at it agreed with him'. Furth had the fortitude to endure the rigours of travelling abroad with his Chief, or 'Uncle Stan' as the trade called him, although never to his face. One to whom he was truly uncle was Philip Unwin who had also begun his career with Fisher. That Unwin was forced to sell his company in 1926. Ernest Benn bought it in return for an annuity for Fisher Unwin and his wife. Philip went to 40 Museum Street, A. & U.'s home since its beginning, for the rest of his publishing life and wrote a memoir, *The Publishing Unwins,* in which there are fascinating portraits of his uncles.

The Swan Sonnenschein whose list became part of Allen & Unwin had opened his doors in 1878 in Paternoster Square, at the age of twenty-three. The son of an immigrant Moravian, he was a man with considerable flair, who after publishing Bernard Shaw's first novel and J.M. Barrie's *Better Dead,* advised G.B.S. that he thought the author would do better to write plays. (Someone must have given the same advice to Barrie.) He became a member of the first Ethical Society in England, publishing Hegel, Bergson, Bradley, Beatrice Webb and others, and founded the Muirhead Library of Philosophy. In 1887, four years after Marx's death, he published the first English translation of *Das Kapital,* edited by Engels. This appeared under the imprint of Swan Sonnenschein, Lowrey & Co, as the firm was known until 1888, when Francis Lowrey emigrated to be replaced in 1891 by Colonel Philip Hugh Dalbiac. Sonnenschein's intellectual vigour and business acumen did not allow him to rest on his laurels. In 1902 he abandoned his own business to Dalbiac (who thus became one of the directors whom Stanley Unwin was obliged to accept with the George Allen list) and went off to resuscitate George Routledge & Co which had fallen upon bad times since the death of the founder in 1888.

George Routledge was an experienced bookseller and publisher when he opened a modest shop, dealing in secondhand books and remainders, off Leicester Square in 1836. Understanding the opportunities which lay in improved methods of communication, he began the Railway Library for which W.H. Smith & Son's gave a standing order of 1,040 copies for each volume. The Library grew to nearly 1300 titles by 1898. Routledge's sons had long been in command by then and seen the growth of Morley's Universal Library, issued in sixty-three volumes at one shilling which, like Cassell's National Library (also edited by Morley) was a precursor of Dent's Everymans. Neither lasted which must have been partly due to one Routledge son's becoming a literary agent and another's untimely death in 1899. The firm limped on until 1902 when a banker, Arthur E. Franklin, bought it with William Swan Sonnenschein. Sonnenschein's action in abandoning his own brain child to breathe life into a moribund list can only be explained by his lust for work, already evident in his compilation of *The Best Books,* a bibliography recording the literature of all subjects. This would have been a full-time occupation for many people; to Sonnenschein it was a hobby, after the long working day at Routledge, for whom he bought up in 1903 the then valuable copyrights of J.C. Nimmo, and in 1911 the company of Kegan Paul, Trench & Trubner, of early nineteenth-century origin.

Sonnenschein (who took his mother's maiden name of Stallybrass in 1917) brought in C.K. Ogden to create an incomparable series of books, The International Library of Psychology, Philosophy and Scientific Method. Ogden, a pacifist who had run the Cambridge Bookshop during the war, was both businessman and scholar, arranging for a small royalty to be paid to himself on every work he introduced. (His authors included Jung, Adler and Wittgenstein.) In personal industriousness he rivalled Stallybrass, using his spare time to compile a system of Basic English reducing the language to 850 words.

Into the antiquated house in Carter Lane, off Ludgate Hill, of Routledge & Kegan Paul, Fredric J. Warburg was introduced as an apprentice publisher in 1922. Warburg, an Oxford graduate, had served in the artillery in France and entered publishing by accident. Not attracted to banking, he entered Routledge as substitute for his brother-in-law. Stallybrass set him to work at a desk in the office he shared with Cecil Franklin, son of Arthur Franklin. The new apprentice admired his master as 'the greatest scholar-publisher of his day' and as 'modest, shy, a trifle puritanical, learned, energetic, with broad interests, humorous and honest. . .' For all the adulation later expressed in his memoirs, Warburg nevertheless shocked his master by suggesting translations of bawdy Greek and Italian classics; some were sanctioned, but others permitted publication only in the original — a compromise making alleged pornography available solely to the learned. They succeeded and were, wrote Warburg, 'lively, unconventional and scholarly. They were *mine,* my first creative effort in publishing, and in some ways my best'. But Stallybrass panicked when the *Casanova Memoirs* were bought. An old-school publisher did not lightly risk prosecution for obscene libel in those days, so the edition was remaindered to Grant's of Edinburgh who cleaned up handsomely on the deal and were never brought to court.

When Stallybrass died in 1931 aged seventy-five, Warburg, now a director, felt an urge to introduce fiction. This was not appreciated by the Franklins so the inevitable rift occurred, and is humorously related by Fred Warburg in *An Occupation for Gentlemen.* Routledge survived his departure, and, in 1939, took to publishing the novels of Georges Simenon.

William Heinemann was born in Surbiton in 1863 of German-Jewish stock. His father, naturalised in 1856, came from Hanover, his mother from Manchester. He was tough, cosmopolitan, cultured, successful in business, single-minded and immensely energetic. After finishing his education in Dresden, he learned his publishing with Nicholas Trubner, whose death in 1884 left him running the business which was much concerned with orientalia. Trubner was sold to Kegan Paul, and in 1889 Heinemann bought Hall Caine's novel, *The Bondman,* turned down by Cassell, and issued it on 1 February 1890, establishing an author and an imprint with one blow. From offices in Bedford Street he then began to publish in translation the works of great European writers of the nineteenth century. It was his peculiar contribution to his trade, puncturing the chauvinism of so many of his colleagues. (Henry Vizetelly, to be strictly accurate, had first introduced Dostoevsky, Tolstoy and Lermontov to the English public in the eighties; but he received no thanks for it and, when he turned to French literature, translations of Zola only brought prosecution.)

However the way was paved for Heinemann who, in addition to the great Russians, published Bjornson and Ibsen (although the famous William Archer translations of the latter came from Walter Scott), Gerhart Hauptmann, George Brandes, Guy de Maupassant and Gabriele d'Annunzio. He offered the British the opportunity of appreciating contemporary European literature and also competed for a time with Tauchnitz of Leipzig by operating on the Continent with English language editions. Sir Edmund Gosse edited his International Library and also his Literature of the World.

Heinemann published the plays of Arthur Wing Pinero but turned down Shaw's because, he said, the public would not buy plays. He produced a ledger showing Pinero's accounts to make his point. (His own plays were published by John Lane.) Swinnerton describes him as above middle height, with a pale round face and a rather resentful mouth. In addition to his translations he published many British authors but failed to keep Kipling, Robert Hichens and H.G. Wells — but then nobody kept Wells for long. In the twentieth century, however, John Galsworthy, Somerset Maugham and John Masefield, amongst others, came and stayed. Heinemann had, apparently, a habit of over-editing which infuriated some authors, but he did not notice when they reinstated their own words at proof stage and in any case he spent less time editing as he became involved in publishing as an international activity.

A notable series was started when he readily took to James Loeb's idea of a classical library with original texts on one page and a sound translation on the opposite. Loeb's wishes were deferred to unless they did not conform with those of the practical publisher, but they had good relations although Heinemann advised that there was no need to advertise so excellent a venture because the library would find its own level. It did despite Loeb's illness and Heinmann's threatened blindness.

On a less academic level was the publication, arranged simultaneously in nine European languages, of the explorer Shackleton's *Heart of the Antarctic* (1910). This feat of organisation pre-dated the work of Walter Neurath and George Rainbird by nearly fifty years. It was one of Heinemann's last achievements. The war was for one of Anglo-German origins a particularly unhappy period, and there was the added frustration of seeing his work for international copyright and the International Congress of Publishers come to a standstill. He died, without the consolation of wife or family, soon after the Armistice of 1918. During thirty years of publishing he issued new books by over five hundred writers, half of whom were novelists.

In 1920, Doubleday, Page & Co of New York bought Heinemann's but the English company was continued with Theodore Byard as chairman and Charles S. Evans as managing director. It was at the latter's suggestion that nine novels by Galsworthy were turned, with interpolated bridging passages, into *The Forsyte Saga, A Modern Comedy* and *The End of the Chapter.* Evans also advised the young Graham Greene, when he accepted his first novel, to find a literary agent, a suggestion upon which Heinemann would have frowned. By the end of the twenties Heinemann's was again British owned, with its offices at 99 Great Russell Street, a William and Mary house in which some of the incidents recorded in Boswell's *London Journal* took place. William Heinemann Medical Books was formed in this era, as was Heinemann & Zsolnay, the latter as a practical form of help to Paul Zsolnay, a refugee from Hitler's occupation of Austria in 1938.

Shortly after William Heinemann started publishing, the house of Constable was revived by the grandson of the Edinburgh publisher whose crash in 1826 involved Sir Walter Scott and revealed him as the author of the Waverley Novels. The third Archibald Constable retired after only three years handing over in 1893 to his nephew H. Arthur Doubleday who planned the ambitious Victoria History of the Counties of England, and also *The Complete Peerage*.

Constable's most noted author during the first half of the twentieth century was George Bernard Shaw though his footing was different from that of other writers because, like Ruskin, he was his own publisher. Constable's had only a commission for handling his work, but he was a valuable property. Under Michael Sadleir, who followed W.M. Meredith, the firm acquired other distinguished authors — Harold Nicolson, Damon Runyon, Patrick Hamilton among them — and also an apprentice, Ralph Arnold. In his memoirs Arnold, who became a director, described the bleak-looking office building in Orange Street which belied the homely atmosphere within. He wrote of Sadleir and other colleagues, among them Martha Smith, one of the first women to achieve executive status in British publishing. After seventeen years as publicity manager and associate editor she was appointed to the board in 1937.

The nineties brought many new publishing names. Edward Arnold (not to be confused with E.J. Arnold of Leeds, the West Country printer who had laid the foundation of his huge educational supply business in 1863) was the grandson of Arnold of Rugby, and his list became noted for standard school texts, although in his early years fiction featured on it as well. Through one author, E.M. Forster, he was to retain a foothold in the general market, although when *A Passage to India* was published in 1924 Arnold, who took over the earlier titles published by Blackwood, could not know that Forster would not publish another novel during his long life. His short stories went to Sidgwick & Jackson, perhaps because by then the main interest in Arnold's Maddox Street offices lay in academic works catering for a broad market from secondary school upwards. Forster turned in an occasional biography or critical work and was an undemanding author, enjoying happy relations with Arnold, who retired in 1930, and with Brian Fagan, his successor.

John Lane, who began his working life as a railway clerk, was the most dazzling of the new *fin-de-siècle* publishers. He persuaded Elkin Matthews, who had a bookshop in Exeter, to open in Vigo Street, Mayfair in 1887 at the sign of The Bodley Head, and joined him full time four years later. By then their first book had been issued, *The Romantic Nineties*. Its author Richard Le Gallienne related how Aubrey Beardsley tried Lane's patience by slipping into his drawings for *The Yellow Book* minute indecencies which often could only be discovered with the aid of a magnifying glass. *The Yellow Book* above all his other publications established Lane as a fashionable publisher although as J.E. Morpurgo records in *King Penguin,* the biography of Lane's nephew, 'very few titles in the Bodley list had an initial run of more than 1000 copies'. The Lane-Matthews partnership lasted only a few years, at the end of which each invited their authors to choose between them. Most plumped for Lane, who crossed Vigo Street to new premises and enjoyed a brief heyday publishing some of the more exotic figures of the time, not least of whom was Oscar Wilde. In the new century he introduced Anatole France and André Maurois from across the Channel and Stephen

Leacock from Canada. He married a rich American widow who had much influence on the authors selected but by the end of World War I their star was waning. Like Fisher Unwin, having no son of his own to continue the firm, he looked to a nephew, the Bristol-born Allen Lane who was soon appointed a director. The young man kept the list afloat after John Lane's death in 1925; ten years later he issued his first ten Penguins bearing The Bodley Head imprint, but in 1937 his uncle's old company passed into the joint control of Allen & Unwin, Jonathan Cape and J.M. Dent.

Another exotic figure of the nineties was Grant Richards whose early books included A.E. Housman's *A Shropshire Lad*. He had a curious contractual arrangement with the poet by which he did not have to pay any royalty as long as he kept the book in print at 6d. For a while he published Bernard Shaw, as well as bringing out his own novels, founding the World's Classics Library at 1s. per volume, and introducing Dumpy Books, one of which was the original edition of *Little Black Sambo*. Bernard Shaw said of him that it was his tragedy to be a publisher who had allowed himself to fall in love with literature. His fortune vacillated, with two bankruptcies which entailed the forced sale of his best publishing ventures. His business failure was due not so much to lack of acumen about what to publish, as to his inability to scale down his style of living to match what he could afford to take out of his firm. In the twenties he became a victim of the economic climate. By then, many distinguished writers had made their first appearance under his imprint, including Ronald Firbank whom he considered overrated and G.K. Chesterton. After his second crash he became for a time chairman of the Richards Press but resigned when he realised that the appointment carried little real authority. He was much travelled, twice married and an incorrigible optimist who wrote an entertaining memoir, *Author Hunting*. (Corvo portrays him amusingly, but with undoubted malice, in *Nicholas Crabbe*.)

Several other houses started in the nineties, among them The Studio, which remained family-owned for many decades; Gale & Polden (1892), publishers of militaria from an address in Aldershot; The Temple Press (1892); John Tiranti (1898) and Gerald Duckworth, in the same year. The last survived throughout the period without making a sensation, building in an orderly and quiet fashion a splendid backlist. Duckworth learned his publishing with J.M. Dent in whose offices he worked with A.R. Waller who became his first partner. He engaged Edward Garnett as his reader and, later, Jonathan Cape as his London traveller. He was the stepson of Sir Leslie Stephen and, therefore, the obvious publisher for Virginia Woolf's early works. He lost the later ones, and also the services of Cape whom he would not make a partner because he didn't consider him a gentleman. Strange sentiments from one who made sexual overtures to his half-sister.

In the twenties Duckworth published much of what the Sitwells wrote, and in the next decade started his Great Lives series, potted biographies which eventually extended to over one hundred volumes. He died in 1937 and a year later Mervyn Horder, who was to preside over the company for more than thirty years, joined the board.

There were other new publishers (as at all periods of book trade history); the names of a few will occur in later chapters, but mention must be made here of William Morris. Originally published by Reeves & Turner, he was inspired by Ruskin's do-it-yourself example to found the Kelmscott Press in 1893. From that date, with few exceptions, the books he produced to standards as near to his ideal as possible bore the legend 'Published by William Morris at the Kelmscott Press', an imprint which was to make them of impressive value in the antiquarian market.

The New Publishers

In 1900 there were more British publishers with offices in New York than American ones with London branches. Harper's were already here, with the young Jonathan Cape as their traveller until he left for Duckworth, and remained until 1931 when Hamish Hamilton, their last London manager, started his own list. Samuel French, New York publisher of playscripts, had bought out his English opposite number, Thomas Hailes Lacy; but the oldest resident American company was Putnam, George G. Putnam having come to London in 1841. His son George Haven took over in 1873 and continued his father's work for international copyright. In 1930 control passed to Constant Huntington, a compatriot and relative, who was responsible for introducing many European authors, such as Sholokov, Italo Svevo and Erich Maria Remarque whose *All Quiet on the Western Front* was a huge success on publication in 1929. James MacGibbon who joined the firm from school in that year recalls that the office was so chaotically run that some review copies had not been sent out but that the novel sold by word of mouth. MacGibbon maintains that, although a pillar of New England rectitude, Constant Huntington had a deep urge to shock the public, which was why he approved publication of Charles Sale's *The Specialist,* an incomparable comic masterpiece about an American backwoodsman building himself a privy, and why he took over Marie Stopes' evangelising tracts on birth control, which Stanley Unwin had been prevented from publishing.

George G. Harrap who started in 1901 was the first important new native publisher of the century. He was active in the educational field and also promoted numerous series of cheap children's books. His son Walter joined him in 1912 and, after war service, believing that publishers worked too much in isolation, formed the Advertising Circle, later known as the Publishers' Publicity Circle. Apart from the Harraps, there were George

Oliver Anderson and his son, Reginald Olaf, and also John Edmund Mansion at directorial level. The last named was a scholar too, creating the *Standard French and English Dictionary,* which was a landmark in dictionary publishing.

The years to 1914 did not produce any new publishers on the scale of Heinemann, Methuen and Dent, although Martin Secker could have proved the exception, He entered the trade with Eveleigh Nash (formed 1902) for whom he read and strongly recommended Compton Mackenzie's *The Passionate Elopement.* Nash took a second, less favourable opinion, and turned it down which led Secker to start his own imprint. He had an instant success in 1910 with Mackenzie's novel and went on to publish Kafka, Lawrence, Mann and Norman Douglas, becoming for a while the most fashionable house in London for works of originality and high literary quality. However, whether as a result of the financial climate of the twenties and thirties, or because Secker pursued what interested him without sufficient regard for making a profit, or both, in 1935 he failed. The Lawrence titles were sold to Heinemann to clear pressing debts, and, a few years later, the list was revived under Fredric Warburg as Martin Secker & Warburg Ltd. Secker remained for only a short while, leaving to follow his own bent with the Richards Press, which grew out of Grant Richards' last crash.

The Medici Society, to which Philip Lee-Warner turned his talents after breaking with Chatto & Windus, set up as specialist art publishers in 1908. The Architectural Press (1902) served another specialist cause as did the Shakespeare Head Press, started by A.H. Bullen (1904). On the technical front Concrete Publications and Macdonald & Evans began in 1906 and 1907 respectively whilst newcomers in the religious sphere were the Kingsgate Press (Baptist , 1903) and the Faith Press (Anglo-Catholic, 1905).

Most notable of the new non-specialists who have survived is Sidgwick & Jackson (1908) formed when Frank Sidgwick left Lawrence & Bullen, a nineteenth-century imprint which has not lasted. Sidgwick was primarily a publisher of poetry (Rupert Brooke, John Drinkwater, etc) and brought out *Poems of Today,* compiled by the English Association, in six figure editions. He also issued the plays of Harley Granville-Barker during the first great era of the Royal Court Theatre in Sloane Square. In his latter years (he died in 1939) he depended much on the Brooke copyrights. The company's archives, in the Bodleian Library, include eighty-five volumes of letters – 62,000 in all – written during the years 1908-40, to authors, booksellers, printers and literary agents.

Mills & Boon began in 1909, both of the original directors, Gerald Mills and Charles Boon, having worked previously for Methuen as educational and sales manager, respectively. In their first year they turned over £16,650. Before 1914 Hugh Walpole, P.G. Wodehouse and other famous names had graced their list but in the twenties they failed to prosper with their 1s. cloth editions of which there were stocks of quarter of a million. Mills died in 1928 and fresh capital became necessary. Boon exploited the rising market of the commercial libraries with his romances, thus enabling the company to recover.

Herbert Jenkins gained his early trade experience with John Lane. He began publishing for himself in 1913, his own Bindle tales bringing him almost as much fortune as the works of P.G. Wodehouse, who had joined him by the end of the war. Unfortunately his health broke and he died in 1923 having willed his business, and his own copyrights, to the Royal Society for the Prevention of Cruelty to Animals. The R.S.P.C.A. sold them to J. Derek Grimsdick who continued the Jenkins imprint.

Bertram Christian, described in a 1940 reference book as 'sole partner', started the educational house of Christopher's in 1906, in the same year that Robert Evans began Evans Brothers (where he was 'sole brother' until Edward joined him in 1908) in one room in Newgate Street. Five years later the journal *Teachers' World* was acquired; it complemented a steadily expanding schoolbook list. In due course Robert Evans was knighted for his services to education. Christian, to his chagrin, never received the accolade. He served as president of the P.A. and had an interest in James Nisbet. A colleague in that company was John Mackenzie Wood who, with his wife, created the world-famous Janet and John readers. James Brodie, a firm dedicated to helping teachers and pupils achieve better examination results, started in 1907; its notes on chosen English texts are still in demand on the Pan list.

Country Life magazine first appeared in 1897 but the book list of the same name did not emerge until 1903. For the remainder of this period, and for long after, high quality illustrated volumes about antiques, furniture, architecture, gardens, were issued. From the start George Newnes was associated with *Country Life* (although it was Edward Hudson's idea), and his family firm was part-owner until 1905 when Sir Edwin Lutyens designed a grand new building on the edge of Covent Garden from which the magazine was thereafter edited. In the late twenties the Collingridge list of gardening and horticultural books was purchased, and by 1940 the chief directors were Sir Frank Newnes and Sir Neville Pearson, pioneers of popular literature in their youth, and both of whom published from the same address in Southampton Street, Strand, adjoining the Lutyens building.

Nothing could illustrate more forcefully the notion of fact being stranger than fiction than the history of the Hogarth Press. One of the most seminal poems of the twentieth century, T.S. Eliot's *The Waste Land,* was set by hand by Virginia and Leonard Woolf, in the dining room of their home in Richmond, Surrey. Was ever a work of creative imagination so cradled by another literary genius in the twentieth or any other century? How it came about deserves a chapter to itself; here a paragraph must suffice but the story, in greater detail, may be found in Leonard Woolf's *Beginning Again*, and later volumes of his autobiography. Woolf returned to England in 1912 after seven years as a colonial administrator and married Sir Leslie Stephen's daughter Virginia who was on the threshold of her writing career, and already prone to the fits of nervous depression which temporarily unbalanced her for the rest of her life. It was her custom to work on the current novel in the mornings, and on criticism for the *Times Literary Supplement* in the afternoons. Leonard, perceiving that she would benefit from a change of activity, bought a small handpress and installed it in their home, Hogarth House. Together they learned to print, and soon issued a small edition (150 copies) of a booklet containing stories by each of them. 134 copies were sold. Encouraged, they produced a longer story by Katherine Mansfield and, in 1919, four books including some poems by Eliot, whose *Prufrock* had already been published by *The Egoist*. Harriet Weaver, editor of that journal, offered the Woolfs the first part of James Joyce's *Ulysses* but they felt it was beyond their technical skill. In 1922 Virginia's *Jacob's Room* was ready. Gerald Duckworth waived his option on it and thereafter all of her books came from Hogarth, although the printing of them was farmed out. The press grew modestly. In 1923 there were thirteen new books including *The Waste Land*. The next year the publications of the International Psycho-Analytical Library were signed up, bringing ultimately the entire works of Freud to the list and in the following decade Christopher Isherwood and C. Day Lewis were published. Eliot left them when he became a director of Faber but many other writers depended on the Woolfs so that, even though tempted to do so because of their own work, they could not give up the press. A succession of young men, including John Lehmann, helped them to manage it, but they always remained in control, moving from Richmond to a house in Mecklenburgh Square, Bloomsbury. There the Woolfs continued to take part in the invoicing and despatching of books, the therapy of packing being especially helpful to Virginia. Leonard also wrote and was active politically. He did not build an ivory tower to shield himself or Virginia from reality but it is certain that without his love and care she would not have produced the work she did. His last three volumes of memoirs are essential reading for students of the book trade, and his comments on the optimum size of a publishing house, and the supposed necessity for chasing turnover, should be remembered when we come to consider the events of the sixties and seventies. The press began on a capital of £136.2s.3d and never had to find further finance. Woolf prided himself on his business acumen and financed each year's publishing programme on the profits of the previous years. He deliberately restricted his list to not more than twenty books a year and refused to listen to what he described as his one-time partner, John Lehmann's 'siren song about expansion'.

In the twenty years between the wars a number of other gifted men established imprints, using their own names. Those who began in the twenties fared better in the long run than those who started in the following decade.In 1980, Faber, Gollancz and Benn were still independent, and Cape was part of a private merger involving among other imprints the Hogarth Press, although the founders of all four were dead; but Hamish Hamilton, Michael Joseph, Secker & Warburg, and even Penguin Books, had joined bigger brothers.

Jonathan Cape's first list appeared in 1921, he having spent the two years since demobilisation helping Philip Lee-Warner at the Medici Society where he met his future partner, G. Wren Howard. They became as perfect a combination as any in between-the-wars publishing. Cape was tall, slim, handsome, with a gentle charm for his authors and friends, and a cool hard stare for booksellers. 'Bob' Howard, the younger and shorter one, was as smart in mind and appearance as he was shy. Jonathan got the books; Howard produced them, as Michael S. Howard (Wren's son) notes in the best of all histories of an individual house, *Jonathan Cape, Publisher,* a work which does not idealise either of the founding fathers.

From the start Cape went regularly to the U.S.A., by preference in slow ships, in search of books and authors. His list was strong in American writing. Native writers were not neglected and one with whom Cape persevered was Mary Webb, whose *Precious Bane* was published in 1924 but did not become a bestseller until four years later when the prime minister, Stanley Baldwin, praised it at a Royal Literary Fund Dinner. Her reputation was made, although too late for her own enjoyment; she died in 1927. Robert Graves, a year later, was permitted the satisfaction of commercial success in his own lifetime with *Goodbye to All That,* of which Cape sold 30,000 copies in a week. The list was broad-based, with a strong bias towards history and fiction, and featured two cheap series, the Traveller's Library, pocket editions in neat format running to over 200 titles by 1940, and the Florin Library of 2s. cased reprints of contemporary and nineteenth-century writers.

Wren Howard maintained that the foundations of the firm were built upon T.E. Lawrence who wrote an introduction to Doughty's *Arabia Deserta,* which was published jointly with the Medici Society. Later came *Revolt in the Desert,* condensed from a privately printed version of *Seven Pillars of Wisdom,* the complete edition of which was not published until after Lawrence's death in 1935. *Seven Pillars* was an immediate and continuing success; *The Mint,* Lawrence's frank diary of R.A.F. life at Uxbridge, was kept in cold storage too long and, when finally published in 1955, was something of a damp squib.

In his first year Cape bought the A.C. Fifield list which brought him the books of Samuel Butler and Bernard Shaw's praise; three years later he purchased Harriet Weaver's Egoist Press, thus acquiring several James Joyce titles but not *Ulysses,* which was still a hot property, 499 of the 500 numbered copies in the edition published by Miss Weaver having been seized by the Customs at Folkestone in 1923. (It was re-issued by Sylvia Beach in Paris in 1924, but Cape, wisely, left it alone.)

In 1924 a lease was taken of 30 Bedford Square, an elegant terrace house in the most perfectly preserved square in London, which provided as fine a setting for good publishing as it had previously for good living. Into it came the young Rupert Hart-Davis with instructions from Jonathan that as he was to be a director, he must direct. Hart-Davis complied with resultant skirmishes but he survived until his call-up in World War II. When Edward Garnett died, William Plomer succeeded him as reader and Daniel George arrived on the list but not, until later, the staff.

Neither Cape nor Howard took much part in the social life of the trade, but the latter worked for the P.A., sitting on its Council for thirty-five years, and being president (1937-9). Cape himself did little for the P.A., and even less for booksellers. When *Seven Pillars* came out one hundred copies had to be ordered to qualify for $33\frac{1}{3}$% discount. Jonathan sought to publish at the cheapest possible prices. Yet, as he did not seek to sell his books direct to the public, or through other channels, he was relying on the bookseller whilst wilfully refusing to understand the economics of the retail trade. From 1924 until 1969 his company contracted with Arthur Child, a dapper little cockney, to operate a personal delivery service. Child did more, and took it upon himself to become salesman when circumstances warranted it. His catch phrase, uttered with immense aplomb as he thumped parcels on to booksellers' floors and counters – 'Ree-marrk-ab-le weather for the time o' the yee-ar' – deserves inclusion in any compilation of London street cries. Standardisation of distribution has denuded the trade of men like Arthur Child whose irrepressible good humour lightened the days of many a harrassed bookseller and his assistants.

Geoffrey Faber's first partner was Lady Gwyer who inherited the Scientific Press from her father. Thus, Faber and Gwyer, the former coming into the picture via O.U.P., the army, a family brewery and All Souls College, where he was Estates Bursar. That was in 1924. Five years later he bought out Lady Gwyer and with his wife Enid formed Faber & Faber. He gathered distinguished colleagues around him, amongst them T.S. Eliot (as already noted) and Frank Morley, an Anglophile American who remained here for most of his life. The scientific origins of the company were not over-looked – there was a director from the original press – but other branches of literature, usually indicating a particular director's special interests, were reflected in a rapidly growing list. Young poets of the thirties were obviously drawn to it but it was not only Eliot's presence which attracted the likes of Spender, Auden and Pound. Faber himself was a poet and shared with

Frank Sidgwick and Ian Parsons an abiding interest in publishing verse. Richard de la Mare was allowed to indulge his passion for art and gardening; Morley Kennerley, his for sport; W.J. Crawley, sales manager from 1934, his for children's books. Sales and editorial have too often in publishing been thought of as watertight compartments but in Faber's the sales personnel always had an editorial say. Faber published sixty books in 1930, in which year he employed only thirteen people. They included Ethel Swan whose voice uttering the single word '*Fay*-ber' was to become familiar to telephone enquirers down the decades. In 1940, he published 177 titles.

A very different style of publishing was evolved by Victor Gollancz who took over the Henrietta Street offices of Williams & Norgate. Gollancz, henceforth 'V.G.', had spent some years, after giving up school teaching, with Ernest Benn, of whom more shortly, before committing himself to his own imprint. At 14 Henrietta Street he remained all his publishing life in offices which made no concession to modernity for as long as he thumped the bare floorboards or clattered down the uncovered stairs to his trade department in Maiden Lane where booksellers' collectors were likely to have the counter bashed into their backsides by his sudden descent. The stark austerity of the offices utterly belied the image of the new firm as it was projected in the press. Publishers' advertising took on a new note with V.G. who made it vulgar and eye-catching like his yellow-jacketed books. It was also arrogant and did not play down to any supposed lower level of literacy. The authors he named were not explained. The reader was supposed to know about them, as about him. Often he did not bother to append the word GOLLANCZ to his advertisements – their style and layout were unmistakable. He spent lavishly on advertising where other publishers invested in three- and four-colour jackets. His bindings were usually black, his paper often greyish-white, his jackets uniformly daffodil, but his typography was acceptable and he drove printers and binders berserk by increasing his print orders in derisory quantities. 'You mean, of course, seven fifty, Mr Gollancz?' 'No, seventy-five.'

V.G. got his authors by paying large advances, guaranteeing them publicity and sales, and by commanding their personal loyalty. He believed in big sales as he believed in himself as a salesman, possessor of a *mana* which he defined, via the *Encyclopaedia Britannica*, as a 'wonder-working power'. At sales conferences he confused his colleagues by stopping to listen to Moses, the voice which told him what to do. He was a latter-day St Joan with all the conviction and single-mindedness of Shaw's saint. The fact of being sometimes wrong never deterred him, probably because he was too busy to notice it. He didn't work scientifically, like Stanley Unwin, but emotionally, explosively even, always one-hundred per cent committed to what involved him. He did not know the meaning of half-heartedness. He was a large man, in every way, and often a tiresome one, but his socialism was based on humanitarianism. He adored music and bridge and lunched regularly at the Savoy Grill, but with a modesty which must have disturbed the staff. His own employees were more upset by his refusal to commit himself to holidays. He was an impossible and lovable man for those who could live at his pace, though some fell by the wayside.

His first publishing success came with a play, R.C. Sherriff's *Journey's End* which plunged both playwright and publisher into the limelight. V.G. soon cashed in on it, building up a list of saleable authors as well as using his publishing house as a platform for his political and anti-Fascist views. He started the Left Book Club, to warn the world about Hitler. It was successful in publishing terms but it did not stop the drift to war. For V.G. publishing was always a crusade as well as a business but he applied himself diligently to both. One of his monuments is Dorothy L. Sayers, whose detective novels earned vast sums for him as well as for their author. She was also a scholar and devout Christian who translated Dante and wrote plays about Jesus. Nothing perhaps highlighted more the lifework of V.G. than this combination of religion, popular appeal and scholarship in the work of one of his most successful authors.

Ernest Benn was further to the right politically than Gollancz was to the left, but tolerated V.G. for many years of the twenties. Benn Brothers was primarily concerned with trade journals; V.G.'s task was to develop the technical book department. Soon he was dabbling with the notion of art books, so in 1923 Benn formed a separate book publishing company for him. The list ranged from scholarly and expensive items of orientalia to a Sixpenny Library covering many worthy subjects. It was broadly based when V.G. left in 1927, the year after Benn arranged to buy the Fisher Unwin list. The Blue Guides were taken over from Macmillan in the thirties, and there were twenty-two of them in print in 1940, by which time Benn was also noted for the Mermaid series of dramatists and the E. Nesbit children's series. At that date too they had 115 titles available of the Augustan Books of Poetry, all at 6d. Never before or since have there been so many libraries which publishers could afford to keep in print, against probably small but steady demand. Labour was still comparatively cheap, so were standing type charges and warehousing.

The first prominent newcomer in the dark decade of the thirties was Hamish Hamilton, half Scot, half American, who had served a two-year, mostly unpaid, apprenticeship with Jonathan Cape and also studied for the bar before managing Harper's London office. His aim was to publish books which would contribute to greater Anglo-American understanding in the face of the growing menace of renewed German aggression. Hence John Gunther's *Inside Europe,* the first of a series of popular reference books concerned with contemporary events. The list always tended towards biography, fiction and general literature however and the solid foundations laid in these difficult years bore fruit in plenty after the war.

Michael Joseph, once a literary agent, published his first list in 1935 with the backing of Victor Gollancz who also provided him with office space. The association did not last long, and within three years Joseph had found both fresh offices and capital, and also a bestselling author in Richard Llewelyn to whom he paid an advance for an unwritten novel, much to V.G.'s fury. Robert Lusty moved from Hutchinson to join him and the youthful Charles Pick, whose feats of salesmanship were recorded in the Gollancz company minutes, also changed houses. He provided another bestseller when he met Monica, a great-granddaughter of Charles Dickens, at a dance and persuaded her to write down her experiences as a maidservant. By the outbreak of war Joseph already had a notable list of authors. His cousin, Herbert Joseph, ran a separate, profitable line in cookery books compiled by the Countess Morphy.

Secker & Warburg was a year younger than Michael Joseph Ltd, and somewhat less healthy. Fredric Warburg noted in his memoirs a loss of £3,197 in 1938 on a turnover of £11,358. (V.G. advised Joseph that he should aim at a turnover of £40,000 in his first year.) It was, he insisted, a distinguished loss and he was proud of his twenty-six general books and nine novels which had been responsible for it. Warburg started with £1,000 borrowed from an aunt and with rather more put into the firm by his partner Roger Senhouse. More, but not enough, so Warburg went back to his aunt who provided a further £5,000 although she regretted that he published 'so many of those horrid Socialist books'. So Secker & Warburg approached the unexpectedly boom years of wartime with fresh heart and a backlist which already included Thomas Mann and Gabriel Chevallier. They also had H.G. Wells, who had by then run through thirty-three publishers, and whose *The Fate of Homo Sapiens* came out in August 1939 and sold 13,000 copies which helped to reduce the annual loss by half.

The Phaidon Press, still a prestigious name in art book publishing, started in Vienna in 1923 and moved to London after Hitler's annexation of Austria fifteen years later. Its founders were Bela Horovitz and Ludwig Goldscheider but by the time they arrived in London as refugees they had sold their stocks and assets to Allen & Unwin so that The Phaidon Press officially had no Jewish connection when the Nazis marched in. Another publisher of art books, born on the continent, was Anton Zwemmer who bought Jaschke's bookshop in Charing Cross Road in 1924, commenced publishing in the following year and acquired the agency for Albert Skira of Geneva in 1936, thus introducing a fine series for which the British public was not then ready. His shop became a haunt of painters and art historians, one of them, Herbert Read, writing a monograph on another, Henry Moore. The home trade subscription was thirty-six copies; Zwemmer sold most of the edition in Japan.

The twenties was a time of boom for what were called the private presses, small imprints mostly operated on a shoe-string from the owner's house. They specialised in sumptuously produced editions which were sold mainly to Americans. The bottom fell out of the market with the Wall Street slump but many of the names are remembered today by collectors. Outstanding amongst them were the Golden Cockerel Press and the Scholartis Press, the latter owned by the lexicographer and etymologist Eric Partridge, an Australian who arrived in Europe with the 'digger' troops during World War I and returned to remain for the rest of a long life as scholar and publisher. The Cresset Press, formed by Dennis Cohen in 1927, was also concerned with first editions and the high standards of production of the private press movement, but when the slump came it quickly adapted to the general market and survived, as did many others, despite hard times. Geoffrey Bles tempered a learned list which included such authors as Berdyaev and Stanislavsky with bread-and-butter thrillers; Peter Davies and his brother Nicholas (who were reared, with other orphaned brothers, by J.M. Barrie) allied their company to William Heinemann; Frederick Muller, Robert Hale (a refugee from Walter Hutchinson), Lindsay Drummond, Andrew Dakers and Ivor Nicholson & Watson (who paid the then enormous sum of £15,000 advance for Lloyd George's memoirs) ploughed middle courses and got through to the end of the second war. Lovat Dickson, despite some spectacular successes, as related in one of his volumes of autobiography, *The House of Words,* did not remain independent for long, and moved to Macmillan where he became an editorial director.

The Blandford Press, a magazine publishing company, issued its first books in 1927 as the result of a demand for back numbers of journals on catering and display. They also inaugurated in 1932 a lasting horticultural list with *Cactus Growing for Beginners*; it has remained in print ever since. Blandford's kept a low profile within the book trade, as did Wills & Hepworth which, although it does not appear in Whitaker's *Reference Catalogue of Current Literature* for 1940, was registered as a company in 1924. Its origins go back to World War I when William Simpson Hepworth, a printer with little in his order book, decided to launch a series of children's books with the name Ladybird. Between the wars publication was spasmodic because Hepworth was again concentrating on quality printing but the renewal of hostilities brought Ladybirds back and their enormous success, together with that of a Leicestershire neighbour, The Brockhampton Press, will come later.

I have saved until last the most famous of all the new imprints of the thirties, one which quickly became a household name – Penguin Books.

Allen Lane spent his twenties finding out how difficult it was to sell case-bound books, as he travelled the country with the Bodley Head list, and directed its affairs after the death of his uncle John. What is surprising in retrospect is that it wasn't until 1935 that he founded Penguin because he was a man who loved action. That he played along with his fellow directors at the Bodley Head for ten years is remarkable. In New York he bought a book of cartoons upon which his colleagues frowned, so he improvised an imprint and sold 8,000 copies. He also conducted a personal experiment with a 2s.6d juvenile of Walt Disney's *Three Little Pigs,* later selling it through Woolworths. Then he went to Paris and posted himself in London a copy of *Ulysses* in a package clearly bearing the message THIS CONTAINS A COPY OF ULYSSES BY JAMES JOYCE. It reached its destination unopened and the Bodley Head published the book in a 63s. limited edition in 1936, a trade edition following later.

Neither of these anecdotes is included in J.E. Morpurgo's biography of Lane. The first came from an interview given by Lane to *The Times* in 1969 and it is possible it is apocryphal because he was given to spreading different tales, retrospectively, about his various ventures; the second was in an official handout from Penguin Books during his lifetime, but the same comment will serve. Allen Lane was not a liar but he enjoyed helping to perpetuate his own myth.

What is undisputed fact is that, whether or not the idea came to him whilst he was waiting for a train on Exeter railway station, or during one of the morning bathroom sessions in Talbot Square, London, with his brothers, or somewhere else, on 3 July 1935 the first ten Penguin titles went on sale at 6d a copy, bearing the Bodley Head imprint.

Lane had observed the careers of Jonathan Cape and Victor Gollancz and could no longer be contained. By 1935 he was ready to risk everything and gamble on 6d reprints of popular books in paperback, and he had won over his brothers, especially Richard, with whom he had a closer relationship than with John. The three shared a flat in which, at the morning bathing and shaving ritual, they discussed their business ideas as well as their social achievements.

There had been cheap paperback series before but Penguins were to be different. The Lanes were not relying on Bodley Head titles but they planned to issue ten books every three months for an indefinite period. Allen went first to Cape who was the publisher of the moment and offered £25 down payment for each title against a $\frac{1}{4}$d royalty but settled for £40 against $\frac{3}{8}$d. Cape later confessed that he thought the venture doomed, disliked paperbacks anyway, but wasn't averse to making something out of it, and them.

The actual name of Penguin was suggested by Allen's secretary, Joan Coles. Edward Young, on the Bodley Head staff, was sent off to Regent's Park Zoo to make drawings of the birds for the colophon, and the series was launched on £100 capital. The trade did not respond kindly so Clifford Prescott, chief buyer for Woolworth, was wooed. He gave a first order of 34,000 copies, encouraged by his wife Blanche, who called at his office whilst Allen Lane was pressing for an order. She was asked to react as 'ordinary member of the public' and came down heavily on Penguin's side.

The Lanes took offices, so-called, in the crypt of Holy Trinity Church in Euston Road. The petty cash was kept in one empty tomb, the invoice book in another. The packers pinned up nudes above their stone benches and the management arranged for blinds which could be quickly lowered when the vicar called. The new venture had an air of improvisation and fun which it always, to some extent, retained whilst Allen Lane lived. In the early years he transported the entire staff to Paris for the weekend when the mood took him, encouraging the young to make men of themselves. Nothing quite like it had happened in British publishing before. Joseph Malaby Dent, not to mention Mr Hodder and Mr Stoughton, must have revolved in other hallowed sites, as the Penguins came and went from the Euston Road crypt.

Penguins were an almost instant success, so Lane looked around for possibilities of expansion. He was already publishing non-fiction titles when one day, at King's Cross bookstall, he heard a woman enquiring for 'one of those Pelican books'. Not wanting a rival with so similar a name, he instantly arranged for works by Shaw, Wells, Julian Huxley etc, to appear, not in orange covers like his firstborn, but as Pelicans, in blue. (There are other versions of the story and they are all true in spirit.) What, again, is a matter of fact, is that the young Indian, Krishna Menon, later to become India's representative to U.N., and High Commissioner for India, was appointed first editor.

Soon another series, the Penguin Specials, was established, born of much the same desire which motivated Gollancz and Hamish Hamilton – to alert public opinion to the dangers of a totalitarian Europe. The pace of Penguin publishing was dazzling from the start. It was as though the pent-up frustrations of fifteen years at the Bodley Head had exploded. By 1939 there were already eighteen volumes of the Penguin Shakespeare, six guides to English counties, ten English classics, and the first two King Penguins, volumes with short texts and numerous colour plates, in stiff jacketed boards. The last are now collectors' items. The enterprise soon outgrew the crypt, and subsequently moved to a modern factory at Harmondsworth near the present London Airport.

Penguin Books reflected the concern of contemporary publishers with presentation and production. For all their cheapness they were impeccably printed and designed and this played a part in their instant success. They sold to those who wanted the best they could afford, and when Pelicans came along, they appealed at once to those who – like Allen Lane himself – had not received higher education, but were interested in learning. In later years Lane told an interviewer that Pelicans were introduced to compensate for his own lack of university training, but by then he had become so accustomed to being told that he had sparked off a social revolution singlehanded, that he may well have invented the reason on the spot, with a wicked twinkle in his eyes.

Bookselling in London

The retail book trade's battle against underselling during the Edwardian decade, provoked by the Times Book Club, has already been noted. W.H. Smith & Sons faced as big a crisis in 1905 when their contracts for railway bookstalls were cancelled in bulk. These had been opened in the mid-nineteenth century as track spread across the country. To replace them 200 shops were opened in ten weeks, all situated, for obvious reasons, as near as possible to railway and London Underground stations. This amazing feat occurred during the reign of W.H. Smith III, who was the second Viscount Hambleden, and his partner Charles Harry St. John Hornby. (Smith II, during whose time circulating libraries were developed, entered Parliament in 1868, and was awarded a viscountcy for his services.) In addition to catering for the newspaper and periodical trade the new shops developed on the bookselling side, of which David Roy emerged as head in 1920. He was highly regarded by publishers. The face of Stanley Unwin has been seen to take on a mellow, wistful look as he recalled the great Roy of Smith's who must have bought in most satisfactory quantities. And sold similarly, because his reign at Strand House outlasted the thirties, and he survived the transition of W.H. Smith into a limited company after the second Hambleden's death in 1928. Five years earlier the small Truslove & Hanson chain was purchased. The three shops, in fashionable streets in south-west and west-one London, were precursors of the later Bowes & Bowes Group, of which the surviving one is part.

As Smith's lost bookstall contracts, Wyman & Sons gained them, the first in 1906, and then 349 more over the years. Both companies opened wholesale houses in provincial towns and cities to cope with their trade, and Wyman's followed the older firm into retail bookselling in 1930 when they opened the first of many branches at Acton, in west London.

Most wholesalers remained centred on London, including Simpkin,

Marshall (an amalgam of three nineteenth-century wholesaling firms) who formed a special company to take over the Stoneham group of shops which went bankrupt in 1907. (E.J. Stoneham, who was often in dispute with publishers about price-cutting, began in 1874, opened seven more shops in five years, all in the City, and died aged fifty in 1888, earning the epitaph 'the well-known underselling bookseller of Cheapside and elsewhere'.) Simpkin's was a cornerstone of the distribution structure, booksellers having far fewer direct accounts with publishers than were forced upon them when wholesaling broke down after World War II. They operated on small margins and paid poor wages but many later successful booksellers gained their knowledge of the trade working for Simpkin's, which handled all publishers' books and dealt with most retail outlets in the United Kingdom. Its managing director from 1894 was Joseph Shaylor who wrote much about bookselling and books, historical and contemporary, for the *Publishers' Circular* and other journals. Later in this period Arthur Minshull, who joined in 1908, became the dominant figure.

Simpkin's also found their way into wholesale exporting to overseas booksellers, a branch of the trade which did not always operate on the same narrow margins as at home. The customer was charged the invoice price of the book plus a commission of 5% or 10%, but there were dodges to make transactions more profitable. The wily Frederick Joiner, who started William Jackson (Books) Ltd in 1918, bought at colonial rates from publishers by pretending that he was exporting to South Africa or New Zealand, but sold at home rates to the U.S.A., where the market was usually closed anyway. (Thus he would buy a 7s.6d novel at 3s.9d but invoice it out at 5s. plus 10% commission. He also charged his customers insurance of 3d in the £ and gambled on there being few, if any, claims.) Joiner was a character of Dickensian proportions, uneducated, foul-mouthed and gross but with redeeming qualities.

Some large Commonwealth booksellers had their own London offices, notably Whitcombe & Tombs, of Wellington, New Zealand, and the Australian Book Company which was bought by Angus & Robertson in 1938.

Of the firms established in the eighteenth century Bumpus's and Hatchard's entered the twentieth century as London's two main 'pedigree' shops. The former moved from Holborn Bars to Oxford Street in 1903 but did not acquire the services of John G. Wilson, perhaps the most distinguished of London booksellers, until 1923. 'J.G.', a Scot, trained with John Smith of Glasgow, came south as a publisher with Constable and then, finding bookselling the stronger attraction, joined Jones & Evans, in Queen Victoria Street. Frederick Evans of the latter was described by Shaw as his 'ideal bookseller' and, according to Grant Richards, he dictated to the City what it should read. Wilson came to perform much the same function in the

West End where he was much beloved by customers and representatives. These were the days before sale-or-return, when booksellers operated on small overheads, paid starvation wages and took on apprentices. In the 1920s J.G. found himself training John Knox, the son of the man who trained him. Then there was still a carriage trade and Ian Parsons, a trainee at the time, remembers that when Harold Nicolson's *Some People* was first published, J.G. stood at the door of his shop, handing copies enthusiastically to customers, saying, 'I'll charge it to your account'. One admires the drive but a cautionary rider must be added: when Bumpus's passed into new ownership in the 1950s the incoming manager discovered credit accounts not settled since the thirties. Fortunately, Bumpus's did not rely solely on the carriage trade. In *The Book World Today,* Wilson emphasised the importance to London booksellers of the tourist and visitor. Even so, although seasonal changes were less marked in central London than elsewhere, between 20 and 25% of his annual trade was done in December.

J.G. urged publishers to adopt 'sale or return', pointing out that many excellent books were not on booksellers' shelves but in warehouses, but he was not apparently affected by Jonathan Cape's harsh terms for *Seven Pillars*. Instead of grumbling he noted with enthusiasm that a bestseller stimulated trade all round. He believed very strongly in the personal relationship between bookseller and customer and thought young people were reading hard, and with a purpose — to change a world with which they were not over-pleased.

At Hatchard's A.L. Humphreys, a Bristolian who had been taken on by Edwin Shepherd, the new owner of the business, in 1881, remained until 1924. After his departure Shepherd's two sons managed the business but it deteriorated. In 1938, Sir Thomas Moore MP bought it with one Clarence Hatry, against whose conviction for fraud he had campaigned. They cleaned up the shop, which was half-empty of books, and opened a meeting-room in which political and literary celebrities met and spoke with the public. This was in the John Hatchard tradition, and proved popular.

Other survivors from the nineteenth century were A.R. Mowbray's and Alfred Wilson's. Mowbray, still concentrating on theological books, moved to Margaret Street, north of Oxford Circus, in 1908. Wilson, who had bought Gilbert & Field of Gracechurch Street in 1885, continued to operate successfully in seventeenth-century premises until his death in 1928. His son Hubert, who moved into nearby Ship Tavern Passage two years later when the ancient edifice was condemned, also opened a branch in Victoria Street, and took over another shop of long lineage in Hampstead High Street. Frank Denny had succeeded his father, Alfred, in the shop in the Strand opened in 1886. Here he received travellers in a confessional style cubicle. One of them remembers subscribing a book in which the word 'knickers' occurred. In shocked tones the sometime president of the Associated

Booksellers read him a lecture on where he was likely to end up if he continued to circulate such filth, and ordered him from the shop. That was in the late twenties.

The S.P.C.K. was operating from various addresses in the City and Westminster; Hachette of Paris had opened a London branch in 1859; Edward Stanford specialised in maps and allied products from the premises he had taken in Long Acre at the turn of the century, and in Cecil Court, a paved way between Charing Cross Road and St Martin's Lane, booksellers had begun colonising the small shops in the nineties.

The founder of the most famous of circulating libraries, Charles Edward Mudie, died in 1890, leaving a thriving business whose management, at least until the end of the century, could dictate terms to publishers because of their buying power and their position in fashionable society. Mudie's, once almost a national institution, collapsed in the very decade when popular circulating libraries were flourishing all over the country. F.T. Bell, who worked for them in 1929 for £2 a week, believed that failure was due to their moving from New Oxford Street into Kingsway where there was not sufficient room for the stock. Subscribers, exasperated at being kept waiting whilst books were fetched from a store across the river, moved to the Times or Harrods.

The Times Book Club was reorganised after the famous 'war' and in 1911 the library was thrown open to the general public at a subscription rate of £2.12s. for three volumes (Mudie's and Smith's charged £1.17s.). Three years later, ever the innovator, the club invited the public to browse amongst the actual books, hitherto an unheard-of privilege. As a result the accumulated loss was turned to profit by 1918. Four years later new premises were taken in Wigmore Street.

Harrods were already selling books in 1900 and other stores soon followed them. In 1918, the Army & Navy in Victoria Street, previously only seeking the patronage of officers of the armed services, opened its doors to all; in the Strand, the Civil Service Stores had a book department in 1920.

The shop primarily associated with books in the public mind however was none of those already mentioned, but Foyle's, of Charing Cross Road. The brothers William and Gilbert Foyle, aged nineteen and seventeen, failed their civil service examinations in 1904 and discovered there was a market for secondhand text books. They sold their own from the kitchen of their parents' house in Hoxton, turning over £10 in their first year. Next they rented premises for 5s. a week in Islington, before moving to others in Peckham at 10s. Soon after came the first shop in Charing Cross Road and in 1929 the Lord Mayor of London officially opened new five-storey premises at one corner of Manette Street, facing the older shop opposite. William's son Richard and daughter Christina joined the business and the latter inaugurated in 1931 the series of literary luncheons which continues today. Authors talk about their books and sign copies for members of the public who are delighted to pay for their lunch *and* buy books. Christina Foyle also started the book clubs previously mentioned.

In this period Foyle's mixed secondhand with new books and attracted customers who knew there was a good chance of finding what they wanted if they rummaged among the vast accumulation of titles on shelves and floors. Also attracted were those who like the Foyle brothers wished to sell their old books.

Lower down Charing Cross Road, opposite Zwemmer's, was, from 1910, a small shop plus a basement workroom run by Cyril Beaumont who specialised in books on ballet and the dance. Some he not only wrote and published, but even handprinted himself in the cellar. He was the complete bookman — author, printer, publisher, critic, bookseller and, frequently, his own delivery man as well. There is a graceful tribute to him in Osbert Sitwell's *Laughter in the Next Room.*

Specialist shops also included Luzac & Co, already thirteen years old when H.B. Knight-Smith became its proprietor in 1903, taking charge of its bookselling and publishing activities in orientalia; and the Poetry Bookshop, which opened at 35 Devonshire Street, off Theobalds Road, Holborn, in 1913. The latter was Harold Monro's creation, as much a *salon* for poets and intellectuals as a shop. Sadly it was never far from financial failure, and ended in a back room in Great Russell Street in 1935.

Meeting places were also provided in the twenties by other booksellers. One was Charlie Lahr's Red Lion Bookshop which could accommodate no more than four or five people at a time. Lahr came from Germany in 1904, never took out naturalisation papers and was, therefore, interned during both wars. He specialised in first editions and published early work by H.E. Bates, Rhys Davies and Liam O'Flaherty; also an unexpurgated edition of D.H. Lawrence's *Pansies.*

Across the Thames at 89 Bermondsey Street, Ethel Gutman opened a bookshop in 1921 with the object of bringing 'the love of books and the allied arts' into the lives of the working men and women of Bermondsey. She opened in the evenings and sold books on the instalment system for as little as 1d per week. She organised play-readings which led to the formation of a local repertory theatre, and published a quarterly review to which eminent authors contributed. She died tragically young in 1925 and five years later her successors closed the still flourishing shop.

The gap left by the closing of the Poetry Bookshop was partially filled by David Archer's opening of a similar shop in Parton Street, off Red Lion Square. He also published many poets for the first time but made no profit from them. An eccentric without business acumen, he spent his inheritance in supporting poetry, which he himself did not read. He preferred thrillers but claimed that he could recognise the poetry in people.

In 1917 William Jackson Bryce opened in High Holborn but moved in 1931 to the corner of Museum and Little Russell Streets in the shadow of Allen & Unwin. Very much so because Stanley Unwin rescued the shop when a receiver was appointed. In his autobiography Sir Stanley affirmed it would have been a tragedy if Bryce's services 'and those of his quite outstanding colleague, I.P.M. Chambers' had been lost to the book trade. Chambers, always determined to become a bookseller, brought a unique wit and the highest standards of personal service to his occupation. In later years he recalled Bryce putting one of the shortcomings of bookselling into a nutshell. He had asked for 5s. per week rise. 'No,' said Bryce, 'the shop cannot afford it. Your reward will be in the hereafter.'

Back into Charing Cross Road and Miller & Gill, which started in Cambridge Circus, then moved to No. 94 almost opposite Foyle's. Such was the service then offered to customers that Eric Norris, a junior assistant in 1925, remembers running to trade counters to get books whilst customers waited in the shop. A neighbour of Zwemmer's was 'The Bomb Shop' at No. 66. The name derived from the socialist-anarchist leanings of its owner, Mr Henderson. In 1934, Eva Reckitt, daughter of a rich industrialist, bought it and re-named it Collet's. Although not privy to acts of violence herself she took the shop to promote the sale of progressive literature, becoming a natural supporter of the Left Book Club, and later of Penguins. Collet's also became sole agents for many Soviet-bloc books which some officers of the P.A. later saw as a hindrance to the establishment of good trade relations with other British companies.

In the West End, Heywood Hill's elegant Mayfair emporium, with a Queen Anne bow window, opened in Curzon Street in 1937. His future partner, Handasyde Buchanan, then worked in the nearby shop of Michael Williams. Hill, joined by Buchanan at the end of the war, established a market for current new books, and a rare book department of distinction.

In 1931 Frank Ward opened the 'first modern bookshop' in London at 3 Baker Street. He challenged the image of the traditional bookshop, with window displays built up to obscure the inside of the shop from the street (examples are still extant) and its sanctified air of an old, dusty, ill-lit library. His shop had light oak shelves, fitted carpet and its window was low and open.

Three years after Eva Reckitt started, another woman bookseller made a humbler beginning in Store Street, Bloomsbury. Una Dillon had a science degree and had worked for the Central Association for Mental Welfare when she started her small shop at the age of thirty-five on £800 capital. Two years later she pursued her students and academic customers at London University to Cardiff, Leicester and Knebworth House, Hertfordshire, when the evacuation of 1939 took place. The Store Street shop survived the grim years that followed and her greater glories as a bookseller came later.

At Wimbledon, in the suburbs, Harold Cook took over the Hill Bookshop in 1935; and on the edge of Greater London, bookshops in Enfield and Banstead warrant mention. Don Gresswell, a mechanical engineer, purchased a stationer's and tobacconist's in Enfield in 1938 and soon learned to stock Penguins and other books. In the same year Irene Babbidge and Evelyn Folds-Taylor opened the Ibis Library in Banstead, and provided a small book-selling department in a shop which was to become very well-known to the trade. There were many others. The selection may seem invidious but I hope it is broadly representative.

For the statistical record, according to the Post Office Directories, the number of booksellers in the Greater London Area was approximately 400 in 1914, and roughly the same number at the end of the war. In 1919 the list took up some five columns against four-and-a-half, but some entries were overlong, Beazley's of Belgravia, for instance, taking up a quarter of a column and claiming they could 'supply any book wanted'. Ten years later this was altered to 'can supply *the* book wanted'. In 1929 the figure for all booksellers was nearer to 500 and remained so in 1939, but these lists are not entirely accurate and include a number who traded only in secondhand books.

It is less easy to record even as approximately the wages paid to managers and assistants. In 1927 a fifteen-year old at a Pall Mall bookshop received 12s. per week, which had risen to £1 by 1935. No wonder the recipient and many others who worked in bookshops changed sides, and became publishers' reps.

Bookselling:
Scottish, Welsh, Provincial

Bowes & Bowes, of Cambridge, because there has been a bookshop on its site in Trinity Street since the sixteenth century, claims the distinction of being the oldest in the United Kingdom. (It was bought in 1843 by the Macmillan brothers who brought nephew Robert Bowes down from Scotland to learn the business.) Nevertheless, John Smith of Glasgow has the oldest continuous heritage, with its name unchanged since the founder set up shop on the north side of Trongate in 1751. Glasgow then had a population of about 20,000 and Trongate was near its western border. Smith, youngest son of the Laird of Craigend, was twenty-seven when he became a bookseller (he was previously a soldier) and thirty when he opened the first circulating library in Glasgow. His shop has not remained on its original site but it has kept the founder's name although the Smith line ended in 1849. A limited company was formed in 1909, ending the partnership between the sons of David Watson and John Knox, two ex-apprentices who had succeeded the last Smith. John M. Knox succeeded his father David James Knox in 1927 and saw the company through the lean thirties when the loss on books and stationery in one twelvemonth was made up by the profit on the manufacture and sale of medical instruments. At Smith's they had long been accustomed to diversification. In their early days they had dealt in tobacco, snuff and tea. Although times were hard, there were still newcomers. John B. Wylie, an assistant at Smith's, broke away in 1935 and set up independently with the practical support of ten customers who each, on his opening day, deposited £100 against future purchases.

In Glasgow also, by 1900, were W. & R. Holmes and the Grant Educational Company, and later came Alan Jackson who ran the Western Book Club from his neo-Renaissance building in West George Street, supplying books to those outlying areas of Scotland too thinly populated to support bookshops.

Frederick Bauermeister, with experience in Hanover, Paris and London, set up as a foreign bookseller, displaying a sign reading AUSLANDISCHE-BUCHHANDLUNG, but moved to Edinburgh in 1924.

Edinburgh was rich in bookshops, as in publishers, with Robert Grant (1804) John Menzies (1833) and James Thin (1848) the cream of the cream.

Menzies built up the wholesaling side of the business which was also much concerned with magazines and developed along the lines of W.H. Smith, whilst Thin's became the leading academic booksellers, although with formidable competition once Bauermeister had moved across from Glasgow. The first James Thin died in 1915, aged ninety-two. Amongst other Scottish booksellers of long standing were Bisset's and Wyllie's of Aberdeen, and McDougal's of Paisley.

In Ireland, which became a republic in 1921 but remained linked to the book trade of Britain through membership of the Associated Booksellers, there were in Dublin James Duffy (1830), Charles Eason, to whom W.H. Smith II had very properly transferred his business when he became Chief Secretary for Ireland, Browne & Nolan (printers, 1827; publishers and booksellers, 1870) and the Association for Discountenancing Vice and Promoting the Knowledge and Practice of the Christian Religion (founded 1792). The A.P.C.K., as it became known, pioneered schools for both Protestant and Catholic children, though no child received religious instructions without the parents' permission. In religion-rent Ireland, these firms and others sold books in the Republic and Ulster, for much of the time under exceptionally trying conditions.

In the Principality of Wales Lear's of Cardiff started in 1887 as a small theological bookshop in the Royal Arcade, though destined for bigger things. In the neighbouring town of Swansea there was A.R. Way; in Aberystwyth from 1903 Galloway & Morgan, and in Bangor, after 1919, Galloway & Hodgson. But Wales was not a prime bookselling area for the very good reason that except in the south it was sparsely populated, and in that industrial south there was massive unemployment.

It was Basil Blackwell, perhaps the most favourably situated but least provincial in outlook of all British booksellers, who saw no future for his kind in any non-university town with a population of less than 40,000. In *The Book World,* Blackwell succinctly denounced the seven deadly paradoxes of provincial bookselling. The better the bookseller, he averred, the less likely was he to survive, because he carried a representative and unreturnable stock and spent too much of his time in unprofitable research. A draper selling children's books at Christmas reaped the reward of quick turnover and was not expected to have any knowledge of books. Another paradox illustrated the inane practice of offering better terms for journey orders (those taken by representatives on their quarterly or half-yearly calls) than for repeat orders for titles which sold quickly.

Blackwell's itself, founded in 1879 by Benjamin Henry Blackwell, prospered well enough in Oxford (where Alfred Mowbray had opened in Cornmarket Street in 1858), and was the means of saving others. Basil Blackwell joined his father in Broad Street in 1913 and continued the tradition of publishing poetry and books in other fields as well as being the leading bookseller to both town and gown. In 1920 he acquired the Shakespeare Head Press and two years later formed Basil Blackwell & Mott, to separate his general publishing from his bookselling. A.S. Mott, who had been with him at Merton, he described as a substitute brother for the one he never had, and a friend to lean upon when needed, just as in 1929 the descendant of William George of Bristol leant upon him when his eighty-two-year old business was ailing. Blackwell's backing ensured its survival. He also acquired a non-controlling interest in his near neighbour, Parker's shop in Broad Street, and on the eve of the second war he bought F.A. Wood, of Oxford. His work for the Associated Booksellers has been mentioned. A colleague who joined him in 1932, Henry Schollick, also combined his working day as bookseller/publisher with voluntary duties for the Association, believing that 'a man must serve the trade he lives by'. Blackwell and Schollick became two of the best-loved personalities of the book trade and although they plied their trades under conditions more advantageous than many others enjoyed, they did not withdraw from the world beyond Oxford. Nor did they neglect their companies while playing leading parts in trade organisations. Men of prodigious energy, they successfully contrived to combine both tasks.

In Cambridge Ernest Heffer developed the business which his father William had started in 1876 as a small post office and stationers, with a few books, at 104 Fitzroy Street. By 1900 it was established in Petty Cury and printing was added to its activities with the purchase of the Black Bear Press in 1912. Reuben Heffer, representing the third generation, joined Ernest in 1931 by which time the Cambridge bookseller, trading on the oldest bookshop site in the land, had become Bowes & Bowes, and how many changes of name that represented since the original William Scarlett is not known. Deighton, Bell & Co had also suffered changes of name since its establishment at 13 Trinity Street in 1700. Both firms absorbed others between the wars but not Gustave David, whose small shop in St Edward's Passage (and his stall in the market place) were taken over when he died in 1936 by his son Hubert.

Perhaps the most significant new provincial business in the first half of the century was that of Hudson & Woolston. It opened in New Street, Birmingham in 1906 when Ernest Foster Hudson, who had sold books at Saltburn-on-Sea in Yorkshire, of all unlikely places, and Walter Percy Woolston, with whom he worked at Combridge's, began a brief three-year partnership. Woolston then went off to Nottingham to trade under his own name, and Hudson remained in Birmingham, marrying a member of his staff, who produced him three (bookseller) children. The 1913 *Kelly's Directory of Birmingham* lists seventy-nine booksellers, twenty-nine of whom also rated as publishers, although branches of George Newnes and the Temple Press were two of them. By 1939 approximately 100 booksellers were recorded and Hudson was advertising in Kelly's, rather grandly, as 'The World's Booksellers, Wholesale and Retail ...' The figures for both dates include branches of W.H. Smith, Boots Booklovers' Library and the old-established firms of Cornish (c. 1790), the Midland Educational Company (1870) and Combridge (1887).

When he broke with Hudson, Woolston took another partner for the first year and traded as Sinclair & Woolston. After the Armistice, he planned a chain of shops but had second thoughts after opening only two. He then concentrated on supplying libraries. His trading neighbour in Nottingham was Boots Pure Drug Co which prospered not only as manufacturing and retail chemists, but also as commercial librarians and booksellers. They grew rapidly in the inter-war years and operated about 460 libraries within their stores by the early 1940s. The oldest bookselling firm in the city was that of Sisson & Parker which dated back to 1884 when the manager of the S.P.C.K. depot, Charles James Sisson, took over financial responsibility for his branch.

Elsewhere in the industrial North and Midlands conditions were not as good for bookselling or for any other trade after 1918. In Durham, a university city, the House of Andrews, opened in 1808, survived; in Middlesbrough, on Teesside, Boddy's, founded in 1904, was almost alone in surviving the depression, as was Hill's in nearby Sunderland. In this region only the toughest and luckiest made out. In Newcastle-upon-Tyne life was marginally less severe. The small store of Mawson, Swan & Morgan (1878) got by as did T. Robson Dring, who dared to buy the long-established Book Room connected with the Methodist Church in Savile Row, and develop it along general lines. In southern Yorkshire Alan Ward, son of an industrialist and brother of Frank Ward, opened in Chapel Walk, Sheffield in 1929, and also took a small shop in Leavygreave, close to the (literally) red brick university which then had only 800 undergraduates. Neither shop showed a profit until 1942. W. Hartley Seed, a longer-established Sheffield bookseller, also weathered these years, and the S.P.C.K. opened a branch in 1936.

In Leeds, where Henry Walker had opened in 1837, B.L. Austick started in 1928, and Mowbray's of Oxford and London took over Richard Jackson's in the same city in one of several attempts to sell books in Yorkshire. At Hull, Anthony Brown's (1860) kept going with enormous educational contracts in all school equipment and a large export trade, but across the Humber in Grimsby the successors to Ernest Gait (also 1860) had a thin time whilst doggedly continuing to offer books for sale in the smaller fishing port. In York, in 1906, T.C. Godfrey founded a new and antiquarian business in Stonegate, in the narrow complex of streets near the Minster.

In the larger cities bookselling was protected from the worst effects of the depression because sufficient middle-class non-manual workers remained in employment. Sherratt and Hughes (1896) enjoyed supremacy in Manchester and took an extra shop in 1905. J.D. Hughes, in charge of bookselling during the whole of this period, had a prodigious memory which appeared more formidable than it was because he took the trouble to enter into a day book the details of every purchase made by his customers, some of whom preferred to shop out of hours because they disliked crowds. For them he opened on Sunday mornings, and by appointment in the evenings. Cornish, the Manchester bookseller for whom both Sherratt and Hughes had worked, declined. Unwilling to pay a greatly increased rent, he moved into a side street where, after his faithful old customers had died, no new ones sought him. His business was absorbed into Kendal Milne's department store. Meanwhile, William Henry Willshaw had opened in John Dalton Street in 1920 where he remained until 1946 when Frank Gabbutt, who had started Seed & Gabbutt in Blackburn in 1907, bought him out.

In Liverpool, Henry Young's (1848), A.E. Parry's (1879), Philip Son & Nephew (1834) and a branch of Cornish's were all active in Edwardian times and, except for the latter, for long after. They were joined in 1929 by Charles Wilson who took over other local businesses. Lancashire became a stronghold of library supply. James Askew's were already at Preston in 1913 and were listed in Kelly's as publishers as well. The market increased in the early twenties, when the county libraries opened, and the Holt-Jackson Book Company at Lytham St Anne's began in the early thirties. By 1939 it was turning over £15,000 p.a. and employing two representatives, one of them being F.T. Bell, ex-Foyle, ex-Mudie, who was to manage the business after the war.

One of the shops sold to Charles Wilson was that opened in 1935 by H.J. Elsley and his wife who left Liverpool to base their developing chain on Chester, then served primarily by the old-established Phillipson & Golder which survived until 1970. The Bookland group, as the Elsley shops became known, will be mentioned in a later section.

In the Midlands again, G.J.T. Collier opened the Church Bookshop in Coventry in 1921, having learned his bookselling at Rugby, mostly at George Over's. Over's is a shop with a lengthy lineage and really needs the attentions of a trade genealogist if such a paragon exists. Over already owned another bookshop when he took over the business instigated by Arnold of Rugby, and he ran both until 1935. After his death in 1937 control passed to C.E. Pearce who had been with Warren of Winchester.

East Anglia and the East Midlands were starved of both bookshops and good libraries in the early thirties. This inspired Basil Donne-Smith, a Stoneham's manager, to start Countryside Libraries in 1935. It was an enormous success catering for the book-hungry in twenty-five outlets in Hertfordshire, Bedfordshire, Northants and neighbouring counties, and across the Thames in Kent and Surrey.

Another who pinned his faith on 2d libraries was Christopher Barclay who had a travelling library in Surrey in the mid-thirties and later helped to form Pelican Bookshops which had three branches by 1939.

In the South, always more protected economically than the North and the Midlands, many old-established businesses survived without undue difficulty. In the whole of this period Wells' was open at Winchester, King's at Lymington, Wheaton's at Exeter, William Smith's at Reading. The list could be much longer but there is little to record about them of general interest. It is publishers, on the whole, who make book trade history because of the authors and the series which they publish. Booksellers' awareness and initiative are factors in the process of bringing a book to the reader, but it would be tedious to relate how many or how few copies of every worthy book individual booksellers were responsible for selling. Two of them, with whom this chapter ends, did rather more, proportionately to their size and situation, than most. Both operated on the Kent-Sussex border. Their names are Thomas Rayward and Elise Santoro.

Rayward, a miller's son, left school at thirteen and joined Goulden & Curry, booksellers and stationers in Tunbridge Wells High Street, in 1905. The book department was then only a small adjunct of a business whose headquarters in Canterbury boldly advertised in *Kelly's Directory* for 1913

PIANOFORTE MANUFACTURER

BOOKSELLER

AGENT FOR ORDNANCE MAPS

3d in the 1s. discount for cash off books in stock.

So much for the Net Book Agreement even after the Times Book War.

At Tunbridge Wells the book department was not developed until 1919, when Rayward returned from the war in which he lost an eye. His health was otherwise unimpaired, and he set himself the task of selling books to the people of Tunbridge Wells and district. His department spread into the whole of the first floor, apart from the library at the rear. The actual space it occupied was far from ideal, but had the advantage of being on several levels with short flights of steps and an occasional cubbyhole to delight the browser. But the shelves went up to the ceilings, there was little open display space, and no concession to modernity.

Rayward had a flair for buying, and the customers came to accept his recommendations. An assistant reported that he would sometimes start the day by placing on the counter a volume which had been too long in stock.

By closing-time, invariably, he would have sold it. Tom Rayward was both shy and yet, to some, intimidating. He had a charm for women customers which made him a master of the soft sell but he did not abuse this attribute because he had high literary standards. As a buyer he took little notice of what travellers had to say but made up his own mind, quickly and unalterably. He learned his bookselling on the shop floor, read widely and had a wealth of anecdotes for his chosen customers who were, according to Marcus Crouch, ex-Kent county librarian, also his friends. But he would never visit their homes, despite pressing invitations, from feelings of social inferiority. This information came as a surprise to some who often haunted his book department but never dared approach him, dealing instead with Miss Elizabeth Woodhams, who was the model of all a bookseller's assistant should be. Helpful, serious and understanding, also a very good businesswoman, she remembered the subjects in which her customers were interested and brought new publications to their notice if they had over-looked them. She and Tom Rayward, working harmoniously, gave Tun-bridge Wells, a town of 35,000 – not 40,000 – inhabitants, the sort of bookshop which every town and suburb ought to have. Neither became rich except in the knowledge of what they had given to booklovers.

Elise Santoro would not have bought the Book Club, Crowborough, had she been aware of Rayward's authority and standing in Tunbridge Wells, only seven miles away. The Book Club was started by Miss Lea in 1932, in what she called a cultural desert – the lovely, undulating countryside to the north of Ashdown Forest. She took an old cottage in Crowborough's Broadway, and commenced wooing the locals. After a year her health broke and she sold to Miss Santoro and her partner, Miss Frampton, neither of whom had any experience of trading in books. Thirty years later Miss Santoro still believed that stockholding booksellers created their own read-ing public, and by then she had the proof. She and Miss Frampton bravely tested the theory and established a library delivery service over an eight-mile radius, opening branches in neighbouring small towns.

The immediate pre-war period brought some formidable women into bookselling – Una Dillon, Eva Reckitt, Christina Foyle. Miss Santoro's achievements, regardless of her sex, were those of a pioneer. Crowborough is a country town with a population even today less than Sir Basil's stipulated figure. Then, even taking its catchment area into consideration, there was a shortfall. The same was nearly true of Tunbridge Wells. The total purchases of books during the reigns of Miss Santoro and Mr Ray-ward might well have contributed less than the cost of a second-hand com-puter system to a publisher today but their approach to bookselling, born out of a love of literature, remained remarkably unsullied, and that cannot be said of some whose standards wilted a little in the pursuit of a comfort-able livelihood.

1939-1950

War and Peace

Compulsory national service was introduced in June 1939, three months before the declaration of war, and it eventually left few but the old and the unfit in most publishing offices and bookshops. Air raids brought loss of life and property, also dislocation of trade. War risks insurance as in 1914-18 had to be borne once again, paper was rationed and rose drastically in price and many important books went out of print for the duration and longer.

Yet under wartime conditions the book trade grew to know itself better. Statistics collected by the P.A., at Geoffrey Faber's instigation, proved that a total of 30% of home-produced books were sent abroad, figures which surprised many publishers and were of vital importance in the fight against the imposition of a purchase tax on books. According to *The Bookseller,* in February 1940, the figures also indicated that the percentage of export business usually increased in proportion to the size of the firm. It was evident that a trade depending so much upon export, with the extended credit which that involved, needed a healthy home trade to back it, so that the wartime trend towards increased reading amongst most sections of the population was doubly welcome.

Cooperation is more readily undertaken during war than in peacetime. The P.A. report for 1939-40 noted the benefits of collective action and, while it never suggested that all who published should be forced to join the Association, it did, justifiably, point out that non-members received rewards gained for and by members, a potent argument dear to all who believe in closed shops.

Continuity of paper supply was the trade's main concern throughout the war, but in the early period when there was little military action there was also a preoccupation with whether or not to evacuate from London. Civilians tended to drift back home to the cities when the expected bombing did not happen. Most publishers stayed put in the first place, a mistake for which they paid dearly, and the two largest wholesalers never, apparently, thought of leaving the capital. Harry Batsford and some of his staff left for Malvern; Macmillans strengthened their basements for use as shelters, Miss Dillon pursued her teachers and students to various addresses in the country and the Students' Bookshop moved to Cambridge. Other booksellers could not leave their town centres so they remained open for 'Business as Usual', and for those who were neither bombed nor burned out of existence the war years were not unprofitable.

Plans for the official training of booksellers' assistants were interrupted and the annual Conference became centred on London. There was, otherwise, little immediate change for booksellers. Christina Foyle's literary lunches occurred as usual. At one, in November 1939, Dr Benes, the exiled president of Czechoslovakia, and H.G. Wells spoke to more than 700 people, their speeches being broadcast on the Home and Overseas programmes. Four years later, at a Society of Authors meeting, Wells was to call for the burning of all textbooks when they became ten years old, a curious demand to make whilst they were in short supply.

The phoney war ended in April 1940 when the Germans invaded Denmark and Norway – of more immediate concern to publishers was the announcement that books would be subject to paper rationing. The allocation to publishers was fixed at 60% of their consumption during the twelve months to August 1939. The percentage fluctuated with the fortunes of war but the principle remained. Later the so-called Moberley Pool was introduced to supply paper for what were deemed essential books which provoked some fears of a hidden censorship – absurdly since new publishers were permitted to purchase on the open market, an anomaly which led to the birth of many imprints, some of them unashamedly offshoots of existing publishing houses bound by the quota rules.

The fight for a larger allocation of paper was overshadowed by the threat of purchase tax. The Chancellor of the Exchequer, Sir Kingsley Wood, a politician of exceptionally thin credentials even by the standards of the Chamberlain administration, refused to recognise that books were in any way different from boots. Stanley Unwin wrote a letter to *The Times* to point out that purchase tax was not being levied on food for the body, so books, which were food for the mind, should also be exempted. In a war for freedom of thought, the sale of books in which man's highest thoughts were enshrined should not be hampered by taxation. Kingsley Wood, like the woman who said she didn't want a book for Christmas, thank you, because she had one already, retorted that there were sufficient books in the country to be getting along with. He reckoned without Unwin and the P.A., under Geoffrey Faber, which called upon the Archbishop of Canterbury, MPs, academics and authors to keep up the pressure. Belgium, Holland, Luxemburg and finally France fell. The remnants of the British army were brought out of Dunkirk, but the energy of those fighting the proposed tax on books was undiminished. It was a peculiarly British situation. Europe was disintegrating around them, at any moment those concerned for books might be fleeing from the Gestapo, but they were able to concentrate on this issue. And they won. It will seem extraordinary to many now that time was found to organise public meetings against a tax on knowledge but who will doubt that it was correct? Wood unexpectedly caved in, the matter was not debated by Parliament, the concession was made without further argument. Perhaps someone showed the Chancellor a book and he thought he should own one. The campaigners held a celebratory lunch.

It was the last joyful occasion for some while. The long hot summer was ending and, in September, the blitz broke upon London and many provincial cities. The effect of the prolonged bombardment was summed up with typical Shavian wit. 'The Germans have done what Constable's have never succeeded in doing. They have disposed of 86,701 sheets of my work in less than twenty-four hours.'

The climax came on the night of 29-30 December when Paternoster Row and the surrounding streets were nearly all demolished. Longmans could supply between five and six thousand titles on 28 December but only twelve on the following Monday. Whitaker's were burned out, with all their records, but even so *The Bookseller* appeared on 2 January 1941, as usual, in Geoffrey Faber's phrase, 'without a hair out of place'. Simpkin's premises and total stocks were destroyed, a disaster from which the trade never completely recovered.

The City bookseller, Hubert Wilson, writing under the pseudonym Petrel, described the desolation in a memorable article in *The Bookseller*:

It is the eve of the new year – and the hub of the English book trade lies in smoking ruins. Such a scene of destruction I have never seen or imagined ... With many others Simpkin's, Whitaker's, Longman's, Nelson's, Hutchinson's and, further afield, Collins and Eyre and Spottiswoode, are gutted shells. In their basements, on Monday afternoon, glowed and shuddered the remnants of a million books. Gusts of hot air and acrid smoke blew across the streets, and around the outskirts of the devastation played the jets from the firemen's hoses.

This would have been bad enough by itself. But these famous houses, and the streets in which they stood, marked only the boundaries of a scene of destruction so complete, so utterly irretrievable that it held me spellbound. Nowhere were pavements or road surfaces to be seen. From Warwick Square on the west to Ivy Lane on the east, from the Row nearly to Newgate Street, there lies now an undulating sea of broken yellow bricks. As I picked my way gingerly across from brick to brick, hot gouts of sulphurous fumes from buried fires seeped up between my feet; desultory flames played in the remains of a rafter here or a floor joist there, and on either side the smoking causeway fell sharply away into cavernous glowing holes, once basements full of stock, now the crematories of the City's book world. I looked around me in what was Paternoster Square and recognised nothing but a pillar box, the top beneath my feet; there was nothing left to recognise. Here and there half a wall still stood in dangerous solitude, two or three stories high, giving form and significance to the desolation, and that was all. I was quite alone (for I had found my way in through a passage unsuspected by the police) and no living thing was to be seen.

Others whose premises went that night included Ward Lock; Sheed & Ward (a Roman Catholic publishing house started in 1926); Sampson, Low; Bailey Brothers; and Stoneham's bookshop on Ludgate Hill where the gold lettering on the spines of charred books temporarily survived the blaze, gleaming eerily amongst the burned remains.

In Coventry, Collier's bookshop was destroyed, and in Liverpool, both Philip, Son & Nephew's and Henry Young's. Provincial cities suffered more than once but London was under almost continuous air attack for many months. Cassell's, in La Belle Sauvage Yard, who escaped the great fire raid, were obliterated the following spring and during the same alert, a quarter of a million books were lost through incendiaries at Harrap's, in High Holborn, although the building itself remained mostly intact. Jones & Evans' shop in Cheapside was gutted. Hodder & Stoughton, who had taken over evacuated school premises at Bickley, in Kent, were bombed out there as well. The list could be much longer.

Amidst this chaos the demand for books increased, and those booksellers whose shops were unharmed found themselves in the novel situation of being rationed by publishers. They also discovered that almost anything would sell. New books were printed under wartime economy regulations; page margins were meagre, the paper quality usually poor and the use of small typefaces essential. Yet sales rose. Book Tokens also prospered, solving the gift problem for thousands, and introduced the book-buying habit to sections of the population previously unaccustomed to it. Nothing seems to concentrate people's minds so effectively on appreciation of the arts as a total war – although not all the literature disseminated could be termed art.

The British Council and the P.A. agreed a scheme under which publishers supplied books on sale or return to customers in the Balkans and elsewhere, and the Council then bought any that were returned. The percentage was low and John Hampden (ex-Nelson's), who became head of the Council's Books Department in 1941, judged the scheme a success. When the European market collapsed almost totally under the Nazi occupation the scheme was tried in South America and elsewhere, enabling British publishers to keep a foothold on traditional markets. In Canada, however, the public tended to buy the more attractive-looking American editions of books of British origin.

As the war went on there were long periods of comparative inactivity when business was not accompanied daily by screaming sirens and the descent of high explosive, and in 1943 there were two important centenaries. One was commemorated in Charles Morgan's *The House of Macmillan*, a small-crown volume which recorded that Harold Macmillan resigned his directorship on joining the government in 1940 and that Lovat Dickson was elected to the board soon after. Macmillan collaborated with O.U.P. to produce a single-volume edition of Tolstoy's *War and Peace*, for which there was a greater demand than ever before. They were also faced with the problem of finding sufficient paper for reprints of Margaret Mitchell's *Gone with the Wind*, a not especially distinguished epic of another war, which was backed by the arrival of a long-heralded Hollywood film. The first printing was a cautious 3,000 but the reprints soon added a nought, and the largest was 100,000.

A Batsford Century, edited by Hector Bolitho, ignored all wartime restrictions, with its quarter-binding in leather, hundreds of illustrations, some in colour, and generous margins. According to the P.A. report for 1942-3, all producers of books were required to sign the Book Production War Economy Agreement before receiving their paper allocation, yet Harry Batsford achieved this lavish volume without apparently incurring penalties. Batsford spent the war divided, Mr. Harry and some of his staff remaining in the west country, the others enduring the perils and inconveniences of unexploded bombs in the Mayfair offices.

One of the finest publishing ventures of the war was the Britain in Pictures Series produced by Adprint Ltd for Collins. It was the inspiration of Walter Neurath who, like Horovitz, had been a publisher in Vienna when Hitler marched in. The series was edited by W.J. Turner, each volume consisting of 48 pages, with 8 colour plates and 12 to 20 black-and-white illustrations, between thin boards. The aim was to represent the British way of life; in *The Observer* of 21 March 1941, Viola Garvin wrote, 'These books manage to distil "the glories of our blood and state" and with neither vanity nor pomp to make clear to ourselves, as well as the rest of the world, the full and serious nobility of our heritage.'

George Weidenfeld, a refugee, was employed by the BBC during the war but found time to bring out a magazine called *Contact*, to which was attached a small publishing imprint. André Deutsch from Budapest commenced his publishing career in 1942 with Nicholson & Watson where he was frustrated by not being permitted to buy Orwell's *Animal Farm*. He was not alone in this. Jonathan Cape wanted the book and would have bought it had not a senior official from the Ministry of Information informed him that the government would find publication a severe embarrassment in its relations with the Soviet Union. The book went to Fred Warburg (and André Deutsch started his first imprint, Allan Wingate) but by then the Allies had won the war and relations with Russia were fast deteriorating anyhow.

Of the many imprints established during wartime, or just before, one which endured into the 1980s was Macdonald & Co, said to have been founded by T.T. Macdonald in 1938. It was taken over by the west country printers Purnell who in 1943 used it for a novel, sensational in its time, *Forever Amber* by Kathleen Winsor. Like *Gone with the Wind,* this work has become a household name. It is not clear, since wartime paper allocations were based on immediately prewar turnover, how Macdonald got their share because they do not appear in Whitaker's for 1940. Perhaps they rated as new publishers? Certainly they got off to a good start and we shall hear of them again.

Other new wartime imprints included Hollis & Carter; Edmund Ward; the Brockhampton Press, run from Leicester by E.A. Roker; and Ladybird Books (but see page 67) in a format which remained standard for over forty years. All four became absorbed into large groups.

The year 1944, by which date there was reason for supposing that His Majesty's Stationery Office was in no danger of becoming Staatsverlag, saw the birth of two paperback imprints which were to cock snooks at Penguin in the future. They were Pan, started as an independent subsidiary of the Book Society, and Panther, founded by Hamilton & Co of Stafford. Paperbacks in those days were still poor relations of hardbacks although the importance of Penguin was recognised by the fact that it was deemed necessary to exempt one of the three Lane brothers (Allen) from national service. Richard and John joined the navy; John did not return which cast a permanent blight on Allen. Penguin made its contribution to the war effort in food for the mind not least through *Penguin New Writing,* an occasional review which brought solace to many an intellectual on active service. *New Writing* was complemented by the volumes issued by the British Publishers' Guild, formed by a consortium of publishers to produce other paperbacks of quality.

A specialist publisher who began by printing 2,000 copies at 1s. of a booklet about the Southern Railway was Ian Allan, who was ineligible for war service. He worked for the duration in the Public Relations Office at Waterloo Station and built the foundations of a new prosperous specialist list.

There were also some new bookshops. One, the Pelham at Havant, Hampshire, Irene Babbidge opened in 1941, another, a branch of S.P.C.K., started in Salisbury in the same year. In 1943 W. Hartley Seed's, of Sheffield, the oldest established bookseller in the city, was sold to the Duffields who were, perhaps, encouraged by the turning tide which had at last brought profit to Alan Ward.

In Paris, in 1940, there were four bookshops selling English books, three with British managers – W.H. Smith, Brentano's and the Galignani Library.

The managers of the first two escaped before the Germans arrived; F. Moulder, of Galignani, did not. Imprisoned for a time, after his release he was forbidden to sell any book published after 1870. Moulder, although in fact ill, continued to trade in books published after that date, under the counter. Sylvia Beach, owner of the fourth shop, Shakespeare and Company, spent six months in a concentration camp but survived.

After the destruction of Simpkin's, a group of publishers, headed by Sir James Pitman, took over from the Miles family and formed Simpkin Marshall (1941) Ltd. Stoneham's Bookshops were sold to Hatchard's. At first the revived Simpkin's was run from Book Centre (a distribution company mainly owned by Pitman) in the North Circular Road but premises were later found in the basement of a block of flats in the more conveniently situated Regent's Park area.

The final joint trade effort of the war was the creation of the National Book League out of the old National Book Council. It was a cause especially dear to the hearts of Geoffrey Faber, Stanley Unwin and Sydney Goldsack, sales director of Collins, who wished the League to involve the book reading public as well as those concerned with writing, printing, publishing and bookselling. John Hadfield, then serving with the British Council in the Middle East, was recalled to become the first director. The brave new book world lay ahead.

The fighting was over but austerity was not. The new Labour government of 1945, committed to creating a welfare state, was forced to continue rationing many commodities, including paper. In one bleak post-war winter the book publishers' quota was reduced to 60% of 1938 consumption. Strikes and shortages hit the nation, and in 1946 J.G. Wilson reported that five out of every six requests for books had to be met with a regretful 'No'. Alan Steele, ex-bookseller and publisher, returned from a Japanese prisoner-of-war camp to Butler & Tanner, printers, to find long delays in production. In *The Author* he wrote that when his firm were given a manuscript by a publisher, twelve months must elapse before they could deliver printed copies, such was the paucity of manpower and raw materials. Shortage of strawboard hampered exports which were also affected by continuance of the War Economy Standards. Urgent recommendations had to be made to the Board of Trade for permission to improve upon the sad 'utility' appearance of so many British books. The plea was heard but it was not until 1949 that paper rationing ended.

The boom period when almost all that was published could be sold was soon over. Stock in publishers' warehouses and on booksellers' shelves began to accumulate unhealthily once more, so that there was an inevitable renewal of the demand for 'sale or return'.

New titles proliferated. In 1945, 6,747 titles were published, as against

14,904 in 1939, but by 1949 there were 17,034 new books, though it was not until paper rationing ended that large reprint programmes for involuntarily out-of-print titles could be planned.

Turnover rose from just over £10m in 1939 to almost £27m in 1946, and by 1950, this figure had risen to £37m, of which 30.7% represented exports. Yet the percentage of exports in the immediate postwar period did not catch up with the 1939 figure so that the home market remained as important as ever. The large increase in the figure for the latter was partly due to higher prices, reflecting rising overheads, and it was this aspect which troubled the trade then, although the emphasis was to shift to worry about prices rising too slowly.

Membership of the P.A. rose from 124 in 1939 to 214 in 1945, and 272 in 1950. Penguin Books did not become a full member until 1950, and Hutchinsons, who had withdrawn in 1942, returned only in 1952 when Walter Hutchinson died.

The Associated Booksellers also gathered new members (there were 2,400 in 1945) which brought protests that there were too many bookshops, the belief being that if anyone new tried to share in the cake there would be fewer slices all round. Miss Hilda Light retired from the secretaryship in 1946. Two years later, when Bruce Hepburn, ex-Blackwell's, took over from her successor, the name was changed to the Booksellers' Association of Great Britain and Ireland. Both P.A. and B.A. had offices at 28 Little Russell Street, under the eye of Stanley Unwin, and Book Tokens were also accommodated there. It is a pity that such propinquity did not bring about an amalgamation though that was never likely because publishers were increasingly preoccupied with the export market in which only a minority of booksellers dabbled. The P.A., which had been bombed out of Stationers' Hall, needed more space and moved into the north side of Bedford Square. The B.A. went to Buckingham Palace Road in 1952, and Book Tokens went with it.

Members of both trade associations felt that somehow the wartime prosperity must be won back. Manifesting this, Sydney Goldsack, at the 1947 A.B. Conference, denounced the 'general bickering' characterising the joint bookseller-publisher session and proposed the formation of a committee to discuss terms of supply. As a result fifteen publishers and seventeen booksellers met on a cliff top in Rottingdean, Sussex. Their deliberations led to the formation of the 1948 Book Trade Committee which sat for four years and, after a further two for digestion and printing trade gestation, produced a document of pulverising tedium running to 94 pages plus a further 76 of appendices and index. Some of the recommendations appealed as sound sense to a few, perhaps to a great many, but neither the P.A. nor the B.A. had any power to command its members to accept them. They could only persuade, cajole and exhort. Everyone had a remedy for the ills of the trade; the difficulty lay in getting uniformity of views on anything except the Net Book Agreement.

A useful step was taken by the Associated Booksellers in devising the Booksellers Clearing House in 1947, to start a simple method of settling most publishers' accounts by one monthly cheque. Not all schemes were as clear-cut. Book Tallies, an idea of Harold Raymond's for extending the Token principle to appeal to a child's collecting instinct, did not catch on, possibly because it became liable to purchase tax. The National Book Sale, recommended by Conference in 1949, did better, though it was not as attractive to small booksellers as to the buyers in the department stores whose management were geared to offering bargains. However, it received sufficient support from all quarters to become a lasting feature of the book trade year.

Publishers were alerted by their Association more urgently to the Frankfurt Book Fair which replaced, in importance, the fair held annually before the war at Leipzig, now in the eastern part of a permanently divided Germany. The West, which was on the threshold of economic revival, needed a meeting place where the publishers of the world could unite. It ought to have been found in London, or elsewhere in Britain, but the German book trade was better organised, and attracted those who wished to display their wares to the Rhineland city of Frankfurt.

The Society of Young Publishers was formed in 1950, reflecting the post-war determination of the new generation to do better than their fathers. It provided a regular platform for new entrants to the trade though their speeches recommending cures for the ills of publishing had often a nostalgic flavour. The perennial subjects were brought out and aired – the need for more and better bookshops; broadening the market; cooperative advertising; and the death of fiction (surely one of the most protracted in the history of the world).

At official level, the desire to remain in touch manifested itself in the creation of more and more committees, in imitation of what was happening elsewhere. In 1945 the P.A. had representation on fifteen committees, some of them formed at its own instigation; by 1950, the figure had doubled. The process of identifying work and industry with groups of people talking round a table reflected mid-twentieth century society, when almost everyone confused the two.

The book trade was caught in the dilemma of the Western world – trying to make democracy work because no one had thought of a better system. Fortunately, within particular firms, individuals still ruled. Books, usually, were not written by committees, bought by them, nor read by them either, except when twelve good men/women, and true, were required to decide whether or not one of them was obscene.

Once wartime restrictions had been shed over-production became alarming. As early as 1947 the Hon. Andrew Shirley, manager of the Times Book Club (where, under his successor, books *were* bought by a committee), complained that publishers, like the rest of commerce and industry, were bringing out more titles in order to pay the overheads incurred in producing past titles.

Television returned, after the enforced closure of the war, and there was immediate alarm about its possible effect on the sale of books. The book trade displays a death-wish in the face of each new invention. Usually it has been wrong. Television had a marked effect on the book trade but it did not kill it. It savaged the cinema, the commercial libraries and the provincial theatre but it brought increased sales to the book trade. It enlivened the offices of literary agents and the rights departments of publishers' offices but it certainly did not kill the book, and some of those most concerned with its continuance in a positive, profitable style were not backward in understanding the new post-war world in which they, happily, survived. Collins and Longmans both became public companies. Other, smaller firms, recognising the demands of death duties, turned their partnerships into limited companies. Similar transformations took place in bookselling amongst the more stable practitioners but on the retail side it was still possible to remain small and viable. The capital required to run even a medium-sized bookshop on a good site in a prosperous town centre was in no way comparable to that needed by a general publisher of even small aspirations. That was so in 1950 and doubly in 1980.

The sum needed to start a medium-sized publishing company during the 1950s was said by Sir Geoffrey Faber to be £50,000, at the least. Some ignored the advice but succeeded. In 1980 they would need to have been that much shrewder and luckier on the inflated equivalent. Probably less literate, as well, than a Faber, a Gollancz or a Blackwell.

In considering the changes of the last thirty years it is more than ever necessary to be aware not only of technological advances but of the patterns of social change which have affected publishers and their customers. Mercifully, there is still scope for personal enterprise, but we shall see in the pages which follow how increasingly difficult it became after 1950 for the individual not to become a sacrifice on the corporate altar.

1950-1980

New Patterns

The centre of London publishing was, by 1950, in and around Bloomsbury which in a sense was proper because the British Museum is at its heart and to the B.M. (now the British Library), by law, goes one copy of every book and pamphlet published.

In 1950 the majority of trade and educational publishers still maintained warehouses in the capital and also trade counters, some of which opened on Saturday mornings. (In Oxford, Blackwell's was open for a full six days.)

The drift westward had resulted partly from the bombing, although Cambridge University Press had opened its purpose-built publishing headquarters in Euston Road in 1938. Later, Longmans settled in Clifford Street, Mayfair; Collins in St James's Place; Blackie in William IV Street, nearly opposite the undisplaced Chatto & Windus. Eyre & Spottiswoode were now in Bedford Street, Covent Garden, close to Henrietta Street where Nelsons temporarily shared Duckworth's premises. Along the block were Baillière, Tindall & Cox and the dishevelled but unbombed Gollancz offices. Chapman & Hall had left this same fruit-and-veg-scarred thoroughfare to join Methuen, with whom they had already amalgamated, in Essex Street, Strand. The Publishers Association had settled into Bedford Square, so had the Whitaker family business though lacking a complete run of *The Bookseller* since fire had consumed their files. Cassell remained in the City in St. Andrew's Hill whilst their splendid new offices were being built in Red Lion Square. The undisturbed Bloomsburyites included Heinemann, Hamish Hamilton, Michael Joseph, Allen & Unwin, Faber, The Bodley Head (though sadly moribund) and Evans Brothers. Robert Hale had departed for the Old Brompton Road, Kensington, from Great Russell Street which remained a centre of bookshops gathered near to the Museum – Luzac, Grafton, Kegan Paul and Probsthain.

Most publishers mentioned in the previous section were still active, many from the same address, and most were still independently owned, as private limited companies, except Chatto & Windrus, still a partnership.

There were many new names, some of which have survived the last thirty years without selling out – George Weidenfeld & Nicolson, Thames & Hudson, Andrew George Elliott, William Kimber, Dennis Dobson – and many which have been perpetuated within groups – Rupert Hart-Davis, MacGibbon & Kee, Hollis & Carter, Max Reinhardt, James Barrie, Nicholas Kaye and Edmund Ward. Others have all but disappeared into the mists of mergerland – John Lehmann, R.H. Rockliff, Hammond & Hammond, Max Parrish – their names retained only for technical reasons.

Penguins was a sturdy fifteen-year old. Pan had become the second largest paperback imprint, but Corgi, Panther, Sphere did not yet exist, while Fontana was a name given to seven 3s. booklets on the Collins list.

In bookselling, as in publishing, there were new names, some of them still familiar – Norman Lucas of Altrincham, Cheshire; Carter & Wheeler, of Slough (but gathered unto W.H.S. in 1981); in London, The Economists' Bookshop and Louis Simmonds, who had promoted himself from a barrow in Farringdon Road to historic premises in Fleet Street. Simpkin Marshall was still the principal wholesaler to a trade accustomed to transact many of its daily purchases through a middleman, and it is with its demise in 1955 that this survey of the main trends of the last thirty years commences.

Few events affected the trade so radically. Simpkin's stocked (partly on consignment) sufficient supplies of all important publishers' lists to meet daily single-copy and small stock orders from booksellers, and acted for certain small publishers whose books were available only through them. They also boosted their sales by putting travellers on the road to persuade booksellers to buy in bulk through the wholesaler instead of the publisher. They were thus placed in the position of working both for the publisher, by syphoning off his unwanted single-copy trade, and against him by competing with his reps. They had, as well, departments for wholesale export which buttressed publishers against small, long-credit orders from overseas, and for remainders. They were expected to be the middleman *par excellence* performing numerous tasks which publishers have since found it more expensive to undertake for themselves. And they would be there today had their suppliers been willing to allow them a more generous margin on which to operate.

The re-floated Simpkin Marshall (1941) Ltd carried on until 1951 before being sold to the Czech-born Captain Ian Robert Maxwell M.C., who moved out of the makeshift premises in Rossmore Court, St. John's Wood, into a warehouse in Marylebone Road which, with a splendid indifference to its instant-coffee associations, he grandly named Maxwell House. He expressed confidence in Simpkin's future and his name became a byword for dynamic action executed with panache. By 1954 however he was in difficulties and consultations took place at the P.A. headquarters. Simpkin's were buying at between $33\frac{1}{3}$% and 40%, and selling at 25% or, for quantities, $33\frac{1}{3}$%. The margin was inadequate, particularly in view of the extra service expected of reporting on non-available items, and there was an estimated deficit of £475,000. Macmillan's, petitioning for a compulsory winding-up against the wishes of a majority of creditors who wanted a voluntary liquidation, had their demands upheld on 2 May 1955. In the same month, the name, goodwill and Maxwell House, together with the export department and other adjuncts, were purchased by Theodore Cole, then managing director of Hatchard's. But Simpkin's never operated again as a wholesaler for the home trade despite various schemes for a 'single-copy house'.

Maxwell, who later dropped Ian in favour of Robert, and Captain for Mr, concentrated on building a publishing and bookselling empire and winning himself a seat in the House of Commons.

Piers Raymond, son of Harold, and a director of Chatto & Windus, campaigned to save Simpkin's and was rare among publishers in understanding what its end would mean in economic terms. He formulated a plan for a non-stockholding wholesaler but other publishers would not accept it. J. Neilson Lapraik, managing director of Book Centre, favoured a single-copy house on the Dutch Boekhuis pattern working alongside a central clearing house for orders, but this did not commend itself to publishers either – especially after booksellers had made it clear that they would not accept a discount of 25% plus a carriage charge.

Simpkin's thus had no successor, the export department went to Wyman's and the creditors received only a small dividend. The immediate effects were alarming. Publishers were inundated with tiny orders from booksellers, the cost of servicing which made for instant resentment on both sides. Yet the fault lay clearly with the publishers who, when wholesaling of a less comprehensive nature became an important part of the trade structure in the seventies, sensibly, if sometimes grudgingly, gave realistic discounts.

After 1955, a few smaller wholesalers, such as Gardner's of Bexhill, continued to operate, as did W.H. Smith in London and, later, Swindon, but neither they nor anyone else attempted to fill the gap left by Simpkin's failure, which hastened the introduction of the computer. Then, automation was still reverently regarded as a means of emancipating workers from unnecessary drudgery, and as leading to a shorter working week. In fact, the working week was curtailed to an average thirty-five to forty hours confined to five days but many people put the hours they had gained not into creative leisure for which publishers increasingly catered in their lists, but into working overtime at higher rates of pay. Nor did automation make working life more efficient, perhaps because computer operating demanded greater intelligence than had been bargained for.

The 1955 edition of *The Shorter Oxford English Dictionary* describes 'compute' as 'now rare' and 'computer' appears only as a sub-entry as 'one who computes; *spec.* one employed to make calculations in an observatory, etc'. Few, if any, publishers had observatories in 1955; by 1975 few operated without the use of a computer and many owned one.

Computers quickly established themselves as the universal excuse for things going wrong, which they did every single working day because those who fed information into them were human. Before automation errors were more easily perceived but when the computer input was incorrect mistakes of wild comicality occurred. For instance, the sales manager of a small company, thrilled to receive an order from Australia for 500 copies of a book, sent his instructions to Book Centre on processing it. He was less pleased when the entire consignment was delivered to his cramped office, invoiced to him personally at £750. Nor were booksellers amused when opening parcels to discover anything between 10% and 50% of them revealed errors, the rectification of which added to everyone's overheads. The resulting correspondence should have produced huge profits for the monopolistic post office which regularly put up its charges, whether or not it was making a loss, thus further contributing to the ever-increasing price of books.

Nevertheless, the volume of book trade business which grew from £37m in 1950 to £644.2m in 1980 could not have been handled effectively without either computerisation or slave labour. Penguin Books in 1971 received an average of 2,838 orders each week for single and multiple copies of over one thousand titles, and invoiced and despatched them within seven days. At Book Centre in 1970 the lists of 120 publishers were invoiced and despatched through the Publishers' Computer Service, and the books on another thirty lists were invoiced, making a combined annual turnover of £21.5m.

Yet, as late as 1980, Mrs Elsie Bertram, who breathed new life into wholesaling in 1968, sent out 8,505 *handwritten* invoices, totalling £1,720,000, in the four months before Christmas. And any invoice clerk who made a mistake paid a £2 penalty. Mistakes seldom occurred. Mrs Bertram would have nothing to do with the computer, nor with teleordering (see page 214), a further extension of automation which caused lengthy controversy in the trade in the last years of this period.

A world war taught publishers the need for statistics. The computer became the means of achieving vital figures at the touch of a button. Computer operators replaced invoice clerks, or alternatively the work was farmed out to Book Centre or another publisher. Then, as property values soared in inner London, the often crummy premises in which despatch and trade departments had worked became ripe for development. New legislation laid down standards of employment which were difficult to meet in some of the Dickensian hovels occupied by publishers who began to move to the country, to new towns and purpose-built accommodation. Gone, very soon, were most of the old retainers who had been with their firms since they left school, and who had spent their working lives sitting at high desks writing out charges to booksellers. Unemployment was already growing in the sixties but it hardly affected London, so that replacing these faithful, underpaid servants was difficult and expensive. The machine, theoretically at least, was more efficient and cheaper.

Individuals who spent a lifetime with a company had memories which were of practical use every day but modern workers tended to move from firm to firm in search of more interesting or better-paid work, so their memories became less valuable. The computer remembered numbers rather than words so International Standard Book Numbering was introduced in the 1960s. Librarians had been accustomed to Dewey for many years, gramophone record companies dealt in letters and numbers — never in song or opera titles — so the book trade followed suit, because the computer demanded it, and all ethnic, political, linguistic and temperamental differences were overcome in a remarkably short time. Every book was given a number recognisable to every computer, joint publications were given two because, incorporated into every ISBN, were some digits denoting the publisher. It was hoped that booksellers would start thinking of books as numbers and Penguins even produced a numerical monthly list but it did not become popular. ISBNs appeared with increasing prominence in advertising and on the spines of books. 1984 seemed uncomfortably close and those who held the old-fashioned belief that a title and an author were simpler to remember than nine or ten digits were clearly due for sacrifice to the machine.

At the publishing end there was exasperation when orders were received written on scraps of paper and postcards, or typed on order forms of varying dimensions, bearing individual demands about delivery and charging. The result was P.A.C.H. (Publishers Accounts Clearing House) which was introduced by Walter Harrap and others in 1958, and provided a simpler form, carbonised to five copies, one of which could be used by the publisher as an invoice, for ordering up to ten different titles. It was adopted by many booksellers who thus gained preferential terms from the eighty-four publishers who accepted it by September 1958. P.A.C.H. was killed off abruptly in 1971 mainly because it was not acceptable to the computer, and because a standard form had come into use, but no progress was made in persuading publishers to standardize their invoices, which came in fifty or more different sizes, from narrow vertical to squashed landscape.

A striking consequence of the computer age was the proliferation of unnecessary bumf (a word *not* excluded from the *Shorter Oxford*). Before automation, publishers complained because wholesale exporters demanded five or six copies of every invoice but once computerisation got under way it was customary for a book to be wrapped in so much documentation that extra packing was scarcely required. No wonder publishers protested about viciously rising overheads, to combat which surcharging was introduced, and became a new area of contention between publishers and booksellers. However reasonable it seemed to some on both sides that publishers with extensive popular lists should charge for servicing small orders to large stockholding booksellers, this did not answer the problem for publishers with modest-sized lists dealing with one-room booksellers, or even for small publishers supplying larger booksellers. Many felt that the cost of servicing an order should be built into the price, though many more did not.

Individual booksellers, as early as 1956, instituted their own surcharging of members of the public for whom they performed the service of obtaining any book in print but this procedure was not made easier when occasional publishers advertised their wares as 'available from all good booksellers' at a stated price. In consequence the tradition, emphasised in the fight for better bookshops, that booksellers must be willing to obtain any book or pamphlet published by any institution, society, underground press or religious sect, grew thin as the century progressed. (Vaughan's of Tottenham Court Road, London, proudly proclaimed on their shop fascia in the 1940s and '50s SPECIALISTS IN ALL BOOKS; is it significant that Bill Vaughan went into publishing?) The attitude of booksellers hardened.

Terms gradually improved after 1958. Some publishers – Collins for instance – recognised that by simplifying them they could also reduce their overheads; others continued to create their own eccentric conditions, even after the inauguration of the Charter Group of Booksellers in 1964.

Terms of supply was one problem; the rise of a breed of faceless credit controllers, another. Their approach was impersonal and often crude and endangered the goodwill established between the sales department and customers. An absurd situation often arose where a salesman would persuade a bookseller to take fifty copies of a book which he might expect to sell in six months, but the credit controller threatened to stop supplies if payment were not made in 30 days. This was further aggravated as more publishers elected to be invoiced through the Publishers' Computer Service so that the largest account any bookseller had to pay each month (until 1977) was that of Book Centre. As it is the largest bill which is usually delayed longest, accounts therefore were frequently 'stopped', though sometimes, unjustly. It was not uncommon for notices such as this, from the Sheffield booksellers, W. Hartley Seed in August 1971, to appear in the trade press:

> We would like all publishers to know that we do not and never have owed Book Centre any money. Book Centre have apologised for stopping the account following a stupid computer error, but nevertheless parcels are still being held up, and orders are being returned.

It happened to all booksellers, so that it ceased to be a disgrace if one's account were stopped, only an annoyance, which further hindered the flow of books from publisher to the reader. When Book Centre ceased to service publishers outside the Pitman Group, Heinemann and Dent and others took over their function, but by then sales directors had gained some control over the accountants and could intervene on behalf of their cherished customers.

For booksellers near or in London the problems of distribution were at first eased by the continued existence of some trade counters from which stock could be collected. These, however, grew fewer each year as more publishers moved their warehouses into the country.

Trade counters had existed for as long as publishers had sold to each other and to booksellers. In London the public got the books they wanted quickly (sometimes, as we have seen, actually waiting in the shop whilst a runner fetched them) and the publisher was saved from delivering them. Booksellers' collectors were always an underprivileged minority, trudging about the City and Bloomsbury, through all weathers, with heavy bags slung over their shoulders. One, working for William Jackson (Books) Ltd in Southampton Row, earned £2 10s. per week in the late forties, but his employer, Frederick Joiner, did not expect him to live on this, because as an ex-collector he knew about 'doubling-up'. If two or more collectors had single copy orders for the same publisher who offered only 25% on one copy but $33\frac{1}{3}$% on two or more, then orders were pooled to obtain a third-off cash paid, and the difference split between the operators. There would be 1s.3d on each 15s. book for each collector, which at that time meant several cups of tea or a pint of beer. The system enabled the bookseller to underpay his collector but it did not improve terms.

Most trade counters closed as overheads rose and it was argued that if better service were offered from country-based warehouses there would be no ill-effect. In reality it rarely was. The general closure also coincided with an upgrading of the role of collector who now drove, in company car or van, around the counters still open. Many came from far away in the provinces and the amount saved for the publisher in packing materials and labour was immense. At any hour of the business day several booksellers' vehicles were outside Collins in York Way, King's Cross until it closed down in 1975, because the site was worth £3m. Yet many London booksellers know today that they and Collins lose sales because Collins' stock is now all kept in Glasgow.

The handful of counters remaining open was kept busy and between those who manned them and those who called there grew up a relationship which was valuable to both sides and to the bookbuying public. Exemplifying the best was Heinemann's in Gower Mews, behind the north side of Bedford Square. Here collectors were welcomed by George Chapman and Pat Morris, through a barrage of two-finger typing, with items of good-humoured badinage. George and Pat were previously to be encountered in the early forties down the area steps of 99 Great Russell Street, where they operated until their editorial and sales colleagues moved off to Mayfair. In Gower Mews the wide knowledge they had of the lists which they sold was ever-helpful to visiting booksellers. They acted as salesmen, giving useful tips about new titles which were catching on, and about 'dark horses' on the back list. Almost certainly the last of their breed, they provided a personal, efficient service which booksellers whose careers started after their retirement will not know about. Tim Manderson, sales director for many years, had the sagacity to understand the value of a London trade counter, and insisted on its retention. So did Norman Askew, of Cape. They stood almost alone.

British-Owned Groups

At Great Russell Street, in addition to handling the Heinemann list, the trade counter held stock for Peter Davies, the Naldrett Press, The World's Work, and others in a group soon to include Rupert Hart-Davis and Secker & Warburg.

Rupert Hart-Davis, who had failed to come to terms with his pre-war mentor Jonathan Cape, started his own list in 1946 but was soon complaining that too many bestsellers too quickly had ruined him. (It was not a lament that Cape himself or Victor Gollancz would have made.) Fredric Warburg has described in *All Authors are Equal* how he and his colleague David Farrer orchestrated their cry for help.

Under the Heinemann umbrella Warburg prospered, Hart-Davis did not. The latter was an enthusiast for poetry and minority fiction but had learned in his years at Bedford Square the importance of middle-of-the-road literature. He found it in J.H. Williams' *Elephant Bill,* Heinrich Harrer's *Seven Years in Tibet* and Gerald Durrell's *My Family and Other Animals.* Warburg had as sound a training at Routledge under Stallybrass. When he built his first list, he allowed his idealism full play, but he also watched for the lower-middle-brow bestseller. Yet he, like Hart-Davis, although more experienced at being on his own, sought sanctuary at about the same time.

History records that the Secker & Warburg list survived triumphantly in the Heinemann tent, and that the Hart-Davis imprint was sold to Harcourt, Brace of the U.S.A., who not so long after disposed of it to the growing Granada empire in the U.K. Rupert Hart-Davis retired from publishing to enjoy a literary career; Fred Warburg went on discovering authors until his official apotheosis as president of the company in 1971. By then he had utilised the freedom from financial worry to introduce numerous continental and Japanese novelists to the British public, as well as many indigenous works, not least of which were the novels and short stories of Angus Wilson, a writer who remained loyal to the list for more than thirty-five years. Wilson also gave good measure to the National Book League, of which he was chairman, the Society of Authors and the Arts Council, bodies for which he worked conscientiously and voluntarily. (Many publishers and booksellers also gave their time and services but authors do not enjoy regular salaries.)

Heinemann's, having been the saviours of Warburg and Hart-Davis, found themselves in urgent need of resuscitation in the late fifties. In the immediate postwar period they had enjoyed many successes — Boswell's *London Journal,* for instance, the manuscript of which had been discovered at Fettercairn, and Douglas Hyde's *I Believed,* the testimony of an apostate communist who turned Roman Catholic. They had reaffirmed their role as major fiction publishers. Graham Greene became a bestseller; Nevile Shute flowered, Georgette Heyer bloomed; Maugham and Priestley went into standard editions. There was a D.H. Lawrence revival, celebrated in an ill-produced uniform edition, mercifully long out of print.

The details of what drove Heinemann near to collapse are not clear. Certainly they were under-capitalised and it was a City company which bailed them out. W. Lionel Fraser, chairman of Thomas Tilling, was a self-made tycoon and a man of culture who had to make his own agonising reappraisal about purchasing the Bloomsbury publishing group not long after he had backed it. McGraw-Hill, of America, attempted a takeover and some of the details of their abortive move, never leaked at the time, can be found in the volume of Fred Warburg's memoirs to which I have already referred.

In 1961 A.S. Frere resigned as chairman, and with him, his deputy H.L. Hall. A. Dwye Evans (son of Charles) became managing director, and, one year later, chairman, when Charles Pick moved over from Michael Joseph (via an abortive attempt to take over Jonathan Cape). He brought with him his own 'discovery', Monica Dickens, and Richard Gordon, and settled in to revitalise a rich backlist. Editor James Michie however left Heinemann for the Bodley Head, and took Georgette Heyer and Graham Greene whose next book was dedicated to Frere.

John le Carré, a rising star, was attracted to Heinemann from Gollancz, but left for Hodder & Stoughton, after two books. To the analyst of British publishing in the sixties it was not clear what Heinemann had gained in real terms. What they retained was more easily recognisable – Galsworthy, Maugham, Priestley, Noel Coward and others, and, especially, Kahlil Gibran, whose *The Prophet,* an insipid item of religiosity in pseudo verse, was first issued in 1925, and remained the largest selling book on the backlist for fifty years. Gibran became a cult author. In a survey carried out by the *Times Educational Supplement* in the early seventies, *The Prophet* was voted into the top ten by students on a campus survey.

Galsworthy did not become essential reading for students but he reached a new public when *The Forsyte Saga* was televised by the BBC in a 26-week serial, repeated twice, and also shown in many other countries including the Soviet Union. 150,000 copies of Galsworthy's epic, in its various volumes, were sold by Heinemann during the years of the television exposure (c. 1970) and a million and a half of the nine Penguin volumes – a statistic impressive enough to convince even the most pessimistic that television had not killed the book.

The greatest success of the Heinemann Group, however, lay elsewhere. In 1946 a young man returned from the forces, opting for publishing rather than politics, to revive the educational department which had been discontinued during the war. Alan Hill was given a tiny office in Great Russell Street but so small a share of the paper allocation that he was able to produce only twelve titles in three years. When rationing ended, he spread his wings and, concentrating on English and science at secondary level, developed a list which within twelve years became a separate company in its own offices. After twenty years, Heinemann Educational Books Ltd had established subsidiaries in Australia, New Zealand, South-East Asia, East and West Africa, and Canada. In 1971 a holding company was formed for all the H.E.B. companies and in 1978 a subsidiary called Tinga-Tanga was set up to market foreign books in the U.K. Tinga-Tanga is Swahili for windmill, the Heinemann colophon. The New Windmill series, shortened versions of contemporary works edited for young people, was one of H.E.B.'s greatest successes. Another was the Drama Library started by Edward Thompson, one of an ever-increasing team who remained loyal to Hill over a long period. It was rare for any senior member of staff to leave. Expansion was so rapid that promotional opportunities were always occurring and there was an excitement in working for Alan Hill who conducted the entire operation with a cheerful, missionary zeal, as an exhilarating adventure into publishing. It took him regularly to all parts of the world but especially to Africa where he was once accused, at an airport, of being a Biafran mercenary. (Nigeria was then in the throes of civil war.) It was a story he loved to relate and embellish. In 1979, by which time he was managing director of the Heinemann Group, H.E.B. moved into Bedford Square. He retired officially a few months later, except for remaining chairman of the Nigerian company, and A.R. ('Tony') Beal and Hamish MacGibbon took control of the mission into the difficult eighties, which soon saw Hill back as managing director of Heinemann Computers in Education Ltd, with MacGibbon as *his* chairman.

Fred Warburg handed over the managing directorship of his company in 1971 to Tom Rosenthal who had achieved success at Thames & Hudson. That company, however, had no fiction list, nor were any of its shares for sale. Warburg was looking for a successor since his long-standing partner,

Roger Senhouse who still had a holding in the company, had died and there had been a suggestion from Graham C. Greene, at the time he was negotiating a link between Cape and Chatto, that Secker & Warburg should join them. Behind the approach lay Greene's conviction that a quality list such as Secker & Warburg's should not be allowed to founder although it was losing money. Perhaps this made Tillings protective, so Rosenthal was hired and offered the Senhouse shares. He began at once to exercise a flair for creative publishing, working closely with Warburg's surviving senior colleague, David Farrer, who had been with the firm since 1945, having previously been barrister, journalist, tutor to an Indian prince, private secretary to Lord Beaverbrook, and censor in the wartime Ministry of Information. Such diverse occupations made it fitting that he should eventually become not only editorial but also, and concurrently, sales director, an unusual combination of duties. In 1979-80 when the changes referred to above occurred he was already over seventy years old, and gave up sales and regular office attendance to edit from home. In the early eighties the group was restructured in three tiers, at the top of which was the Heinemann Group of Publishers, of which Charles Pick was managing director and Michael Kettle, of Tillings, chairman. Below this were William Heinemann International Ltd, Heinemann Educational Books International and Heinemann Distribution, all of which had Pick as chairman. Then came the actual publishing houses, with Rosenthal chairman of both Heinemann and Secker & Warburg, and Beal chairman of H.E.B.

In the late seventies the Heinemann Group made two other purchases of significance. Ginn & Co, originally an American company which opened in London in 1901, had had several owners on both sides of the Atlantic, and had become associated in the minds of generations of teachers and schoolchildren with primary school textbooks. It was a sensible purchase (for £1.7m) in that it complemented the H.E.B. list, although it continued to operate independently. The other acquisition for the lesser sum of nearly £600,000 was of Kaye & Ward, two small lists which had been combined when purchased by the printers, Straker's, in 1955. Kaye specialised in sports and topographical titles, Ward in juveniles. The purchase of Kaye & Ward nicely augmented The World's Work list owned by Heinemann since 1933.

Publishing, and subsequently bookselling, followed the national and international pattern in becoming group-minded. In some cases individual firms could not obtain sufficient capital to finance growth; in public companies the alternative to being gobbled up was to strike first. In the case of Cape and Chatto & Windus, later joined by the Bodley Head, the merger took place, according to one spokesman, to make the companies less susceptible to American takeover. There were those who considered it made them more vulnerable. The poet William Plomer was neutral:

Said Jonathan Cape,
'We've got a new shape.'
'Ship-shape,' said Chatto,
'We're in the same *bateau*.'

It is easy to understand why Graham C. Greene (nephew and namesake of the novelist) wished to link Secker & Warburg with Cape, of which he was managing director, and Chatto & Windus. All three were medium-sized quality publishers whose lists showed a strong literary bias. After Secker & Warburg had been secured within the Heinemann group, there were discussion with Faber & Faber, André Deutsch and others, but the one who joined was Max Reinhardt, owner of the revived Bodley Head, which had already taken under its wing several other companies. A services company (Chatto, Bodley Head, Cape) was set up in the mid-seventies to administer sales, accounts and distribution for all the imprints, but editorially the three remained independently in their own offices around Bloomsbury and Covent Garden.

Chatto & Windus had stayed a partnership until 1953 with Harold Raymond its senior luminary; in 1954 Ian Parsons became chairman. The trade responsibilities and management of the Hogarth Press had been taken over in 1946 when John Lehmann left Leonard Woolf for the second time, to start his own imprint, but the stoical Mr Woolf remained in editorial command of his small and ever distinguished list to the end. The educational company of Christophers was acquired in 1954 when Bertram Christian died, though later sold to Granada, by which time Oliver & Boyd's juvenile list had been purchased. C. Day Lewis became literary adviser in 1946, later joining the board on which he remained after he had become Poet Laureate. Norah Smallwood rose to become a director with not only editorial flair but a deep concern for maintaining high standards of production. She later became Chairman, but there were losses when Piers Raymond left for Methuen, and Peter Cochrane became a printer.

To the list itself dazzling new names were added – Iris Murdoch, Richard Hoggart, Laurie Lee, Margery Allingham (from Heinemann); others stayed constant from pre-war – Aldous Huxley, William Faulkner, V.S. Pritchett, Laurens Van der Post (a Hogarth Press author); and the connection with poetry was always evident. Ian Parsons himself paid close attention to the verse on the list and edited among other anthologies one of First World War poetry – *Men who March Away* – for his own trade list in 1965 and also, in hugely greater numbers, for a Heinemann Educational edition. The Chatto over which he had ruled, and which changed little when Mrs Smallwood took over, was highly personalised, a type of medieval court, eccentric, cultured, autocratic and bristling with life and tension. The offices were second only to Victor Gollancz's in their shoddiness but the books poured through them until the merger with Cape's sent all but advance copies to far-off Grantham.

Parsons, however, remained joint chairman, with Greene and Max Reinhardt, of the holding company which was the superstructure of the group and his dynamic presence enriched the scene right up to his sudden death in 1980. At his secular funeral service a favourite Thomas Hardy poem, *Regret Not Me*, was read, but those who knew him could not but regret. He was a towering figure in the trade – president of the Publishers Association and of the Society of Bookmen, member of the Stationers' Company and the first publisher to Sussex University. He lived expansively, cared passionately about the books he published and wrote personal letters to booksellers to promote them. He was the wittiest of after-dinner speakers (also the one who worried most to get the right words and express them with brevity), loved travel, cricket and wine, and gave a creditable impersonation of Renaissance man.

Chatto & Windus's offices changed little during the whole of this period. Ronald Cortie, who joined the firm as a young rep in 1951, remembers the gentleness of Harold Raymond, the only prospective employer who had ever risen to greet him, ask him how he was and invite him to be seated. And who listened attentively whilst the eager applicant expressed his enthusiasm for books and reading. Cortie also remembers the dandified figure, with cigarette holder, who turned out to be the invoice clerk, and a gruff packer who asked him if he wanted any bets placed. 'No money in books,' he said. 'We all makes it out of 'orses.'

In 1979 Hugo Brunner, who had already spent some years at William IV Street before hiving off to Oxford University Press, returned as managing director, and, on Norah Smallwood's retirement in 1982, became chairman.

At the end of the war Cape's, nearly seventy years younger than Chatto, were still led by their founders. Jonathan Cape had always been inclined to a take-it-or-leave-it attitude in his dealings with booksellers, who had no alternative but to take it when the book in demand was published only by Cape. Wren Howard also remained aloof from them and to some extent from his own juniors. Only the readers and editors – the historian Veronica Wedgwood, Daniel George and William Plomer – were permitted to know what was in the forthcoming spring or autumn list. It did not occur to either Cape or Howard that it was any business of their underlings to know what was to be published until the time came to sell it. Michael Howard, Wren's son, sought to alter this patriarchal approach and persuaded Jonathan that there would be value in holding in-house meetings. In this he had the support of Norman Askew, the new London rep and later sales manager, whose tricky task it was to woo booksellers away from their reasonable belief that Cape's were stingy. That he succeeded was due to his utter integrity to both his customers and his company. He never oversold and took endless trouble to help those who were prepared to promote Cape books.

The fifties was a marking-time period, after initial post-war successes with American novelists Ernest Hemingway, Irwin Shaw and Herman Wouk. *The Wooden Horse* was rejected but other war books proved lucrative. H.E. Bates moved to Michael Joseph, William Golding was turned down. And Cape and Howard were getting old. The former outlived three wives and bore the disappointment of his son David's deciding to quit publishing and return to the army. There was not to be a second generation Cape-Howard partnership, and Michael's active participation did not last long beyond his father's death in 1968, by which time a new team was in full command.

The renaissance began in 1960 with Tom Maschler's appointment as an editor. He had been with Deutsch, MacGibbon & Kee and Penguin, had chaired the Society of Young Publishers, edited an anthology, *Declaration*, and became identified with new strains in literature. Two years later, and already a special director, he survived a *coup d'état* when three directors of Michael Joseph, with the backing of Allen Lane, made an offer for Jonathan's shares. The company's financial adviser, William Balleny, who was also Cape's executor, advised the Howards to accept. The offer was refused because the intending newcomers would not have Maschler to whom the Howards remained loyal. Sidney Bernstein, later to form his own group, bought a minority interest and, a few months later, Graham C. Greene, then sales manager at Secker, became another special director.

Maschler and Greene – later chairman and managing director – proved as brilliant a team as the founders. Cape's, under them, rocketed through the sixties and seventies with numerous successes in fiction and non-fiction, in children's books for which Maschler showed an unexpected flair and in wallets of documents on historical subjects, called Jackdaws. They also inherited the spy-thriller writer Ian Fleming who sold phenomenally in their editions and in Pan's. Popular science provided another source of revenue, so much so that Desmond Morris, the zoologist author of *The Naked Ape*, had to flee to Malta for long periods to avoid paying away too much of his royalties in tax. Fleming, with the same thing in mind, sold himself to Booker Brothers, an international company, who already 'owned' Agatha Christie, and who were to become the donors of a prestigious prize (see page 183).

In the first partnership Howard was the one who participated in trade affairs; in the later one it was Greene. He became president of the P.A., chairman of the National Book League and worked hard for Public Lending Right for authors. One of his contributions to the list lay in memoirs by or biographies of politicians, usually those on the left. His father Sir Hugh Carleton Greene, an ex-Director General of the BBC, was already chairman of the Bodley Head.

We left the Bodley Head in the doldrums into which it had been cast for most of the years since Allen Lane had disposed of it (see page 56). It was sold in 1957 by the Unwin-Howard-Taylor triumvirate to Max Reinhardt who was financed by merchant bankers in the City. They had backed his small personal imprint which published a few books of quality each year and also his purchase of H.F.L. (Publishers) Ltd which had a lucrative line in law and accountancy textbooks. Reinhardt had also revived the Nonesuch imprint, bringing out a four-volume Shakespeare for coronation year, 1953, and bought Putnam (1962), which included Bowes & Bowes Publishers (as distinct from the bookshop); Nattali & Maurice; T. Werner Laurie and Hollis & Carter.

Putnam was owned for several years by Roger Lubbock, of the distinguished family of Liberal politicians. He published Caitlin (widow of Dylan) Thomas's autobiography, *Leftover Life to Kill*, and the early novels of bookseller Martyn Goff. Max Reinhardt had in Judy Taylor a children's editor who made the juvenile list one of the best in contemporary publishing. When she had established that over many years, she moved on to general books, becoming deputy managing director, a post she held until her semi-retirement in 1980, a few months after marrying the author and ex-publisher Richard Hough. Hough had given her her first job in the publicity department of the Bodley Head in 1951 when he was the general manager for Unwin, etc. Judy Taylor was one of the first seven women to be elected to the Society of Bookmen, in 1972, and also the first woman to be elected to the Council of the P.A. (1973).

Graham Greene, a transfer from Heinemann, benefited the Bodley Head. In addition to novels, he gave it two volumes of autobiography, written in his best dry sherry style, in one of which he describes how as a boy he stole books from W.H. Smith at Berkhamsted. (If W.H.S. buying policy has been on the ball he has amply repaid them.) Reinhardt also published Solzhenitsyn, Chaplin's *Autobiography* and the revised edition of Kobbe's *Complete Book of Opera,* a standard work bought with Putnam. His acumen led to the publication of quite the best of all the many splendid books on Venice, J.G. Links' *Venice for Pleasure*. This came about when Max Reinhardt was planning his second marriage. Links, a friend, gave him notes to assist the newlyweds in their enjoyment of his favourite city on their honeymoon. Reinhardt was so delighted when he used them as a field-guide that he commissioned the book which has been reprinted several times.

Chatto, Bodley Head & Jonathan Cape are now a formidable British-owned publishing group with a sales department and trade counter in Bow Street, near the Opera House and almost opposite the police court. It upholds much that is of the best in our native publishing tradition.

The Granada Group grew out of another small conglomeration, owned by a left-wing property tycoon, Howard Samuel. He made an unexpected offer for the MacGibbon & Kee list in 1956. It was accepted and MacGibbon joined the Curtis Brown literary agency where another former publisher, Graham Watson, was a senior director. Samuel appointed Reg Davis-Poynter, who had had bookselling experience and had also worked for H.F.L. (Publishers), general manager, and a Heinemann rep, David Harrison, sales manager. He then became acquisitive, purchasing the Staples Press (mainly dental and business management books) and Arco, a young list which was used as the basis for a popular series of instructional books on a wide range of subjects. In 1961 Samuel was drowned whilst on holiday in Greece. He left £10,000 to Harrison and £15,000 to Davis-Poynter who negotiated through Arnold, later Lord, Goodman, a sale to Sidney Bernstein, a film and television magnate. It was Goodman who suggested to Bernstein that he should buy Jonathan Cape's shares. When the bid to buy Cape's outright failed, he put Bernstein on to Harcourt, Brace who in 1963 wanted to dispose of their recently acquired Rupert Hart-Davis and Adlard Coles lists. Thus began the Granada empire. The Adlard Coles sale was noteworthy in that it reversed the trend which had seen the transfer of so many businesses from east to west across the Atlantic. Next came Panther Books and another paperback range, Mayflower, founded in 1948 to represent American educational publishers in England. David Harrison resigned in 1969, followed soon after by Davis-Poynter and Samuel's original chief editor, Tim O'Keeffe, both of whom started their own imprints. Alewyn Birch left Heinemann to succeed Harrison and stayed to become managing director and oversee further purchases both educational (from Blond and from Chatto), general (Paul Elek), and technical (Crosby Lockwood). The general side became known as Hart-Davis, MacGibbon Ltd; the Staples imprint was merged with that of Crosby Lockwood; Panther, once a very downmarket paperback imprint, took on a certain gloss when a deal was done with Cape and Chatto which slashed gaping holes in the Penguin backlist. (Interestingly, by 1980, some titles were returning to Penguin.) In 1979 group turnover rose by 22% to £10.03m, and pretax profit by 25% to nearly £1m.

We saw in Chapter Eight that Purnell, the west country printers, acquired in 1939 the newly-founded publishing firm of Macdonald & Co. After the war other imprints were added – Max Parrish, John Lehmann and Sampson, Low, Marston & Co, publishers of *Jane's Fighting Ships.* Wilfred Harvey of Purnell let the publishing part of his empire coast along under a competent team until he helped to create the British Printing Corporation, when three of his long-serving directors quit. James MacGibbon, who had not long remained a literary agent, joined from Gollancz; but huge losses on partworks forced a reorganisation on the book publishing side. MacGibbon left; Ronald Whiting, who had arrived in 1971 to reorganise Jane's, became M.D. of what was later Macdonald & Jane's; Tom Boardman, whose father's firm had been absorbed years before, was placed in charge of the educational division; and a year later Anthony Cheetham was hired to start Futura Publications. There was rapid expansion on all fronts during the rest of the seventies resulting in a further realignment which merged Macdonald and Futura, with Cheetham M.D. and Whiting chairman, while Jane's became a separate company.

There were years of enterprising publishing during which Whiting deliberately took Macdonald into the big time, bidding successfully for such mass-market novels as *The Thorn Birds,* and, through a music list created by editor Penelope Hoare, attracting the memoirs of Yehudi Menuhin. Whiting had done most jobs in publishing, from repping to editing and sales management. He had given his name to two short-lived lists. One, Ronald Whiting & Wheaton, became the property of Robert Maxwell when he bought Wheaton, a Devon printer; the other, Rapp & Whiting Ltd, was run down when Georg Rapp, who provided the capital, had a coronary. When Jane's, which Whiting had revived, was sold off to Thomson in the cash crisis of 1980 it was a bitter blow to him. The Group had made a loss of £11.3m in 1980 and internal relations in the publishing companies were soured by continuing trade union disputes. During 1981 Maxwell gained control of B.P.C. and became Chief Executive, renaming it B.P.C.C. Soon after, Whiting left and by the end of the year Cheetham and many others had also gone. Whiting joined Hamlyn at Feltham; Cheetham, backed by a Hong Kong group, set up a new hard and paperback company.

After his failure to make Simpkin Marshall profitable Robert Maxwell concentrated on building up his Pergamon Press which grew out of Butterworth-Springer (see below) and published textbooks, encyclopaedias and scientific journals from its headquarters in Oxford. Its ramifications were wide and Maxwell was a true son of his time in grasping all that he could lay hands on, which was by no means all that he desired. He failed to buy Butterworth and the *News of the World* but succeeded with Wheaton's, The Religious Education Press, the Aberdeen University Press and various bookshops. In 1964 his political ambitions were taken a step forward when he was returned as Labour Member of Parliament for Buckingham, a seat he lost in 1970 by which time he had also been ousted from the Pergamon board as the result of a highly publicised takeover bid by the American Leasco Systems and Research Company the year before. Dealing in shares was suspended and a Board of Trade enquiry instituted. In 1969-70 the company lost over £2m and in the following year the auditors reported 'we have not been able to obtain all the information and explanations we require'. By then Maxwell had returned as a non-executive director and 'super salesman and ideas man'. In 1971-2 the situation improved; in 1976 profits rose sharply to over £2m and payment of dividends to shareholders was recommended for the first time for years. Maxwell related the increase in profits to the low value of sterling, an opinion he would not be able to hold a few years on. In 1980 in an interview in *The Bookseller* he spoke contemptuously of the British approach to work and survival. Booksellers however did not always find that the Pergamon Press were much different from other companies whose delivery was slow or erratic, and whose staff were prone to make mistakes.

In August 1980 it was announced that Pergamon had signed a 10-year agreement with the Soviet Union giving it access to a database, to be used 'in an abstracting service covering all fields of science, technology and engineering . . .' Maxwell was not a man to avoid the implications of modern technology, in which he differed from many in the book trade.

The battle for Butterworth mentioned above was a struggle between two powerful men, and it was Paul Hamlyn who won it on behalf of the International Publishing Corporation (I.P.C.).

Paul Hamlyn, an assistant at Zwemmer's bookshop, inherited £300 in 1946. He registered Books for Pleasure as a company, bought up remainders and used department stores as his principal outlets. He serviced the stands he put into the stores and allowed returns. In the early fifties he started to publish his own books, printing them for cheapness in Czechoslovakia. Restless and energetic, he developed in several directions at the same time, buying up foundering imprints at home, extending his remainder operation to the United States. He took warehouse premises in Spring Place, Kentish Town, London, N.W., hung the whitewashed brick walls of his own office with colourful paintings, and set about proving his belief that the great British public would buy books if they were attractively presented and sold at bargain prices. Speaking to the Society of Young Publishers in 1960 he said that most people were terrified of going into bookshops and that, to change this attitude, new outlets must be found. Translating his words into action, he did no harm to existing booksellers whose shops were brightened by the very appearance of his products (always excepting the shoddily produced Czech art books). Young people in publishing were eager to work for him because to do so was stimulating and exciting. The editors thought up their own books, then Hamlyn and his salesmen literally flew round the world selling them and buying others. He was joined in 1959 by Philip Jarvis who, when book buyer for Boots, had become notorious for insisting that books could be sold like soap. Certainly some books could and it was on those that the Hamlyn company concentrated – mass appeal volumes about cookery, gardening, needlework and other crafts, and many series of younger children's books. Original publishing and importations became more important than remainders. Hamlyn always displayed an enthusiasm for art books, earning the praise of no less a person than Anton Zwemmer for the Landmark series launched in 1968. By then the companies he had created had become the property of

I.P.C. to whom he had sold out for nearly £3m in 1964, retaining his job in the deal.

At I.P.C. Hamlyn became head of a publishing division which included earlier acquisitions, Odhams Press – together with Newnes, Pearson, Country Life, Collingridge, and Dean's Rag Books – and Hulton's annuals. The organisation moved to Feltham (near London Airport) but Paul Hamlyn himself remained at the centre of power in the *Daily Mirror* skyscraper overlooking Fleet Street. When his immediate superior, Cecil King, was ousted it was revealed that he, Hamlyn, owned more shares in I.P.C. than any other individual. In 1968, after the successful battle for Butterworth, two groups were formed, Hamlyn for the popular books, Butterworth for legal, scientific and technical, the latter including Ginn (later sold) and Temple Press (acquired through Odhams-Newnes). However, the distribution machine for this huge empire soon created nightmares for the sales staff and booksellers and in 1968 a loss for the whole book division was recorded, despite a massive turnover. In the autumn floods of the same year hundreds of thousands of Odhams books were washed away and had it not been for the enterprise of Elsie Bertram and her son Kip, many trade outlets would not have been supplied with Hamlyn Group books for the Christmas trade. They mounted a wholesaler operation to cope with the crisis and, to this day, a great many retailers buy all their Hamlyn books from them.

Within the group there were sackings and resignations. It was rumoured that eighty or so accountants were being employed to correct the work of the computer, and that vast stocks of popular titles which the machine had deemed out of stock were found. Kenneth Stephenson, who had won a name for himself as an expert on distribution, was brought in as a consultant and stayed to become chairman two years after Paul Hamlyn's departure in 1970. The warehouse was moved to Wellingborough in Northamptonshire and the new managing director, Hugh Campbell, began a policy of rationalisation.

Paul Hamlyn subsequently joined another newspaper empire, that of Rupert Murdoch's News International Ltd, remaining there as joint managing director for about a year before buying from them the imprint of Octopus Books, and becoming a book publisher again. Some hoped, now that he was a millionaire, that he would test his market theories on more traditional types of books – fiction, poetry, general literature. He did nothing of the sort and his first Octopus list could easily have been mistaken for a typical month's Hamlyn output. It was enormously successful and by 1979 Octopus was claiming to be 'the largest trade hardback publishers in the United Kingdom'. Later that year a joint company was formed with Hachette, of Paris – La Compagnie Internationale des Livres. There was one important change in the Octopus operation. It did not supply retailers direct; all business went through wholesalers. And it is not quite true to say that he overlooked fiction. In 1976, in conjunction with Heinemann and Secker & Warburg, he launched a series of omnibus volumes of the works of notable contemporary or near-contemporary novelists – a catholic selection ranging from Kafka through Maugham to Dennis Wheatley. They were greeted by the press as a major breakthrough and sold well; but they were no more of an innovation than Allen Lane's Penguins in 1935. Like Penguins, they were marketed so vigorously that they captured the imagination of the public. Like most of Paul Hamlyn's ventures they were successful, but it must be said that had all publishers adopted Hamlyn's style of publishing there would have been no Kafka to reprint in omnibus form, no Maugham either, not even a Dennis Wheatley.

The talents of Kenneth Stephenson were later to be exercised in reorganising Butterworths. Following the death of Stanley Shaw Bond in 1943 a substantial holding in the company was sold to Hambros Bank in order that estate duties could be paid. Bond had ruled the company autocratically for most of the century; now it was the turn of a City solicitor, Hugh Quennell, to take command, although he did not even have an office in the Butterworth building. A scientific company was formed in 1947 as the result of government prompting and a link made with Springer Verlag which, at that time, had not got permission to trade outside Germany. Springer became associated with Robert Maxwell, who sold its publications once it was allowed to export again, and continued its alliance with Butterworth, with a new company incorporated in 1949. It was short-lived for the reason given by an executive of the British firm who said 'Butterworth-Springer worked more to the advantage of Springer than Butterworths'. Robert Maxwell bought the Butterworth interest for £13,000 and renamed the company Pergamon Press. He did not reappear on the Butterworth scene until 1967 when he made his much-publicised takeover bid. By then the company with its overseas subsidiaries was one of the largest properties in publishing but was being managed like an old-fashioned family business. I.P.C., who thwarted Maxwell, were interested in acquiring it because, apart from the book divisions, Butterworths were strong in legal and technical journals; perhaps, also, because Paul Hamlyn relished a battle with Maxwell.

In 1972, four years after the takeover, Stephenson became chairman of Butterworth and the reorganisation began. Editorial, sales and accounts were moved to Borough Green, in Kent, and the offices in Kingsway retained for legal publishing. Gordon Graham was hired as chief executive to succeed Stephenson who never claimed to be a publisher but was a splendid organiser, a catalyst in other similar situations. The ebullient Mr Graham divided his week between London and Borough Green. His experience of international publishing through his twenty-two years with

McGraw-Hill was invaluable to Butterworth. He also achieved the distinction of bringing the austere legal and technical giant marginally into general publishing by contracting with the Master of the Rolls, Lord Denning, for two semi-autobiographical works which had a popular appeal.

Other British-Owned Groups and Companies

Longmans prospered in the fifties and early sixties. Mark Longman joined the company before the war and he and his second cousin, Thomas Michael, became directors in 1947. Thomas later left to start Darton, Longman & Todd, a mostly theological list, Mark stayed to become vice-chairman in 1962 and joint chairman the following year with William Longman, who was by then eighty. The sudden demise of Kenneth Potter led to the promotion of John Newsom, sometime senior education officer for Hertfordshire, and whose name was given to the official government report on secondary education, *Half our Future*. Newsom became a working director in 1957 and organised the move of the warehouse and, later, the editorial offices to Harlow New Town in Essex.

School and university textbooks were always a dominant feature of the vast Longman organisation, whose trading profit approached the £1m mark as early as 1963, but general books were not ignored. Sales of novels by Mary Renault or James Gould Cozzens may have looked relatively puny beside those for Eckersley's *Essential English for Foreign Students,* but they were welcome properties, as were the poems of Stevie Smith and the travelogues and memoirs of Gavin Maxwell, although the latter had a tendency to involve himself and his publisher in lawsuits. His *Ring of Bright Water*, however, the story of his pet otter, had massive sales without drawing repercussions from the animal world, if one discounts a Scottish bookseller's being bitten by the beast, a fact of which Ross Higgins was inordinately proud. There was also a continuing association with the Trevelyan family, G.M.'s superb *English Social History* selling steadily from its first appearance in 1944, in various editions, some illustrated.

Longman's independence ended in 1968, when the 244-year old company accepted a bid by the Financial and Provincial Publishing Company of between £16-17m. Mark, the last of the family still active in the company, remained chairman, and Longmans became the chief publishers in a group which already included the medical houses of J. & A. Churchill and E. & S. Livingstone and the general and educational list of Oliver & Boyd, all acquired by the *Financial Times* (F.P.P.C.) earlier in the decade. Later in 1968 Constable Young Books were bought and amalgamated with the Longman juvenile list, and the Oliver & Boyd children's titles were sold to Chatto. In the following year consultations began between Mark Longman and Allen Lane to find a formula for the merging of Penguin's with the Longman group, to avoid an American takeover of either, and sufficient agreement had been reached by the time of Sir Allen's death in 1970 for the union to be proclaimed on the day after he died. It was a fitting alliance at one level because the first Thomas Longman, like Lane, was a Bristolian.

The Longman tradition of serving the trade was much upheld by Kenneth Potter and Mark Longman, both of whom became presidents of the P.A. and chairmen of the N.B.L., whilst Sir John Newsom was a member of so many committees and public enquiries that the strain involved undoubtedly contributed to his early death in 1971. In the following year Mark himself died, after years of illness courageously born. He had no sons and was said to have known that the general list in which he took particular pride was to become part of the Allen Lane imprint. The Pearson Longman group could not be thought of as a family business, and there was no room for sentiment in perpetuating one name when another seemed more suitable. The name Longman was retained for the massive educational and technical list.

There were other rationalisations. The juvenile list also went over to Allen Lane, becoming known as Kestrel Books, although Ladybird, purchased from Wills & Hepworth in 1971, remained a separate entity. The medical imprints of Churchill and Livingstone were brought together.

Group sales were enormous, nearly £88m in 1980 in the three book divisions, of which Longman (70% export) accounted for £45.7m, Penguin £36.1m and Ladybird £5.9m, with a total profit from book publishing of £9.03m. Tim Rix, who was appointed chief executive in 1976, after eighteen years of service, was optimistic about the future, believing Longman had achieved the right balance in its international operations. Rix became president of the P.A. in 1981.

Ladybird Books had a remarkable publishing history. The price of this series of small, thin books remained at 2s.6d from the end of the war until 1971. How the publishers achieved this can only be explained by strictly rationalised production, soaring sales and ever-increasing print runs. It was a series no bookshop could do without, although orders were not often solicited by representatives. After the change of ownership, which was intended to increase sales world-wide, the price often went up, reaching 50p by 1981.

The Penguin story after the war will be told in the chapter on paperbacks.

The Collins line, happily, did not die out. Supreme amongst them was 'Billy', W.A.R. Collins, who enjoyed his finest hours in this period, making the pace for his fellow publishers, leading the team which took the turnover past £42m in 1976, the year of his death, and leading it very much in the traditional style of a cricket captain, paternal but understanding, knowing in detail what each and every one of his eleven was capable of. Commenting on one of his reps who had called on me twenty years previously, he said, 'X has left us now. We sent him to Australia. Did quite well, not quite our style.' (Pause.) 'But a splendid left-arm spinner.' His then central London traveller Trevor Moore recalls one evening trying to get his car out of a traffic-clogged St James's Place. Hearing angry hoots Billy Collins leaned out of his top flat window, took in the situation at once, descended and sorted out the jam. 'You go back! You go forward! Left arm down' and then in an aside to his rep, 'Jolly good sub order from Harrods this morning'.

To the end of his life the arrival of each post was an exciting event, which might contain a new typescript with great potential. He encouraged and cajoled his team on five continents to greater effort and enjoyed his publishing, often with a boyish enthusiasm.

Under Billy the list had one enormous seller after another – Eric Williams' *The Wooden Horse*; Chester Wilmot's *The Struggle for Europe*; Desmond Young's *Rommel*; Boris Pasternak's *Doctor Zhivago*; *The Leopard* by Prince Lampedusa; *The Phenomenon of Man* of Teilhard de Chardin; Joy Adamson's Elsa saga in several volumes – the roll is long and impressive. There were some failures as well but he dismissed them. Apart from individual titles there were new series; the New Naturalist Library, the Companion Guides (amongst the most readable and reliable ever published), and the Pocket and Field Guides to Birds, Flowers, the Sea Shore etc. The Fontana paperback imprint was also launched and in due course became a serious competitor to Penguin and Pan, the latter of which was partly Collins owned.

Billy Collins went on believing in the saleability of hard-backed fiction long after some of his competitors had begun to retrench. His novelists ranged from Simone de Beauvoir, Rose Macaulay, Rosamond Lehmann and Bryher to Agatha Christie, Alistair MacLean and Hammond Innes.

Dr Zhivago fell into his lap through the purchase of the Harvill Press which had been started in 1946 by Mrs Manya Harari and Mrs Marjorie Villiers who concentrated on introducing European writers to the English market, rather as William Heinemann had early in the century. Another acquisition was Geoffrey Bles which was bought, together with its managing director, Jocelyn Gibb, in 1953. This brought Collins the work of C.S. Lewis, both his theological treatises and his popular Narnia novels for children.

Inevitably in so large an organisation there were many deaths and entrances. In one period of a few years Sydney Goldsack (sales), Ronald Politzer (publicity) and W. Hope Collins (M.D.) died. The chief editor, R.T. Smith, retired in the sixties. By then Sir William (the sword fell on him in 1970) had brought in his son-in-law Philip Ziegler who as well as editing wrote excellent history for the list. When he took time out to write the official biography of Lord Louis Mountbatten, Christopher Maclehose, who had previously joined from Chatto & Windus, became editor-in-chief. Lady Collins also played a busy role as editor of Fontana religious books but the top job on the book side went out of the family for the first time when Ian Chapman, who succeeded Goldsack in 1959, became deputy chairman in 1976.

Three years later reorganisation placed all the book companies in one group and the manufacturing and stationery divisions in another. That year, 1979, Collins announced a loss of £255,000, which led to the sale of a recently acquired United States company, and of the freehold in St James's Place. In 1980 it recovered with a pretax profit of just over £2m. Expecting greater profits in the future, an investment trust trebled its holding of ordinary shares to take almost 8% of the voting capital. A few months later the trade was astonished when it learned that Jan Collins, Billy's son, had arranged to sell his shares, along with other family holdings, to Rupert Murdoch's News International. He was instantly replaced as chairman by Ian Chapman who waged an intense campaign to retain the company's independence. His leading authors backed him, advising shareholders not to sell to Murdoch, with whom amicable agreement was reached in August 1981. News International was left holding 42.45% of the ordinary shares and was allocated two directors. Whilst the negotiations were taking place Lady Collins, who had backed her son, left the board.

Collins was one of the first of the major publishers to recognise the need for larger discounts and to offer 35% all round for general books, with additional bonuses for Charter and other booksellers. After Goldsack's death the smartly-trained reps were allowed with discretion to take returns from booksellers. The reps were controlled by a brigade of sales managers and field sales managers, who often hunted in packs, with trainee reps tagging along too. They were given regular sales drill in London and Glasgow by the chairman, sales director and others. Some did not stay with the firm but other publishers often placed great value on having a man who was Collins trained.

In 1966 the Scottish house of Blackie & Son sold to Collins their printing works and bindery at Bishopbriggs, Glasgow. Blackie proceeded on traditional lines through much of this period, the directors quietly pursuing their policy of issuing children's books for the reward and educational markets and technical volumes on various subjects. Then, in 1975, three years after the death of the ex-chairman, W.G. Blackie, it became group-minded, buying the total shareholding of Intertext Publishing Ltd which was strong in children's books through Abelard-Schuman Ltd. It also had academic and technical strength, partly through Leonard Hill, an imprint dating from the 1920s which had a strong agricultural flavour. Abelard-Schuman had acquired distinction during the time it was American-owned and managed by a young German, Klaus Fluegge. Fluegge settled in London and later started the Andersen Press in which he had a majority holding, although Hutchinson also had an interest.

A.B.P. are familiar initials to the book trade in the 1980s. The names of all its publishing components would have been equally recognisable at any time earlier in the century. Associated Book Publishers included Methuen, Eyre & Spottiswoode, Chapman & Hall, Sweet & Maxwell, Stevens & Co, Spon, Tavistock Publications and W. Green.

Methuen had been a public company since the death of the founder's wife in 1928 and had owned Chapman & Hall since the thirties. After the war Stanley Unwin sold his shares, commenting later in his autobiography that he could have controlled the company had he wished. J. Alan White, the managing director, was more concerned that it should not be controlled by a non-publisher and negotiated with the Crosthwaite-Eyre family. In 1954 Eyre & Spottiswoode and Methuen joined forces, shortly to become A.B.P. In 1962, the law publishers Sweet & Maxwell with its allied company, Stevens, were added. Spon had come under the wing of Eyre & Spottiswoode; Green and Tavistock followed later in the decade.

Readers of *The Bookseller* became accustomed to regular announcements of changes in the management structure of A.B.P., and sometimes also of subsidiary company's names. The adult general list, after some years as Eyre Methuen, became plain Methuen, the name also associated with plays, children's and educational books. Chapman & Hall was the technical academic imprint, Tavistock that for sociology, while Sweet & Maxwell remained firmly imprinted on massive legal tomes. It is less easy to decide whom, amongst the horde of directors, managers and executives, to mention. Certainly John Burke who was the first managing director of A.B.P. after Sweet & Maxwell had joined it. A barrister, he was trained in publishing at Butterworth, started a legal list for Hamish Hamilton in 1937, found his paper ration too meagre for survival and so moved to Sweet & Maxwell in 1942. He was succeeded as managing director of A.B.P. by another barrister, Peter Allsop, who later became chairman (1976) in place of Maurice Maxwell. Allsop also took on the presidency of the P.A. during the crucial time of the American Justice Department's Suit (see page 171). During the inevitably complicated legal proceedings it was hugely beneficial for the P.A. to have a president who was also a lawyer. A third name I shall mention is that of Michael Turner who not only survived all the numerous changes, after his appointment as a director of Methuen in 1961, but rose higher with each realignment, becoming group managing director and later chief executive when Allsop found chairmanship of the world group sufficient to undertake. Turner deserves mention in another capacity for a niche he made himself in book trade history in a series of Society of Young Publishers' revues. His double-act with Desmond Elliot (see Arlington Books) as Rosenkrantz and Guildenstern (Publishers of Good Books) Ltd, was such a hit that it outlived the years when the revue was staged and was revived as a cabaret act on other occasions. So it was appropriate that Turner in his real publishing role should have presided over a list which was strong in contemporary humorists.

Methuen also published the translations of the French strip cartoonist for children, Hergé, whose *Tintin* volumes (of which Michael Turner was part-translator) became as popular as older favourites for the young – *Babar, Winnie-the-Pooh, The Wind in the Willows*. In publishing playscripts they competed with Faber and Heinemann, they also put into paperback the Arden Shakespeare, a series remarkable for the fact that the footnotes sometimes left room for only a line or two of text on a page, and introduced University Paperbacks, an 'egg-head' series based on their extensive backlist in such subjects as history, psychology, science.

Chapman & Hall, once heavily dependent on Dickens, again became a one-author list with Evelyn Waugh dominating the literary side in merit and sales. The long-held Wiley concession in technical books was lost when the American company set up its own organisation in England.

Eyre & Spottiswoode had a moment of glory in the history of fiction when Maurice Temple Smith bought for them John Braine's *Room at the Top*. It became an instant success, its *zeitgeist* hero being readily recognisable as a contemporary figure both fascinating and repellent. Temple Smith later left to start his own imprint and, as he put it, to commence publishing at 9.30 a.m. daily instead of at 5 p.m. after all the committees, without which large groups cannot operate, had been adjourned. In 1981, he sold out to East West Publications, which was owned by a Dutch wine merchant, L.W. Carp, who had already acquired the Words and Music chain of bookshops and Wildwood House.

Charles Hammick, an ex-regular army officer, decided whilst recuperating in hospital from a heart attack to try his luck as a bookseller. His first shop opened in Farnham, Surrey in 1968. One year later he received the Ronald Politzer Award, from the Publishers' Publicity Circle, for 'significant services in the widening of book interest and ownership'. By 1975 he had opened another four shops and also started a cash-and-carry wholesaling operation which did business even on Sundays, so that frustrated booksellers who could not get their orders serviced quickly enough by the publishers' new technology could spend their leisure hours driving into the Surrey jag-belt to replenish their stocks. In the same year he became responsible for managing Sweet & Maxwell's bookshop in Chancery Lane, London. His expansion had been backed by A.B.P., at Michael Turner's instigation, and in 1979 he sold all his shares to his financers, at the same time remaining chairman and managing director. In 1980 he suffered a setback when he had to close down his cash-and-carry wholesaling because the computer didn't know how to take money, but added to his ever-growing chain of shops by opening in the new Covent Garden shopping complex on the site of the fruit and flower market.

In 1980 Hammick's bookshops turned over £3.36m – A.B.P. as publishers made a pretax profit of £1.71m on a turnover of £35.8m.

Not all public companies in publishing were as large as A.B.P. or Collins, but it was only a minority of firms who sought a quotation for their shares on the Stock Exchange. Most publishers and booksellers learned to form themselves into limited liability companies in order to protect the firms they had started or inherited, but to 'go public' involves meeting conditions laid down by the Stock Exchange, and undergoing investigations into the firm's stability, for the protection of investors.

Two established companies with strong family connections went public in this period – Routledge & Kegan Paul, and A. & C. Black. When Routledge shares were publicly quoted for the first time in 1967 they were hugely over-subscribed (as were not some of the learned R.K.P. titles offered to booksellers). Within two years, however, with the cost of expansion and the move of their warehouse to Henley-on-Thames, Routledge had cash problems which they resolved in a deal with Crowell, Collier-Macmillan who subscribed some £350,000 for loan stock convertible into ordinary shares in 1974. Before that date, however, the financial situation had eased and Routledge bought back a majority holding. They were not, though, with their large publishing programme, out of trouble and they turned in pretax profits of only £241,000 in 1980, having paid bank interest of over £100,000 in that year.

The Routledge list continued to be distinguished by libraries of books on the social sciences, education and literature. Fiction was abandoned after a quarrel with Madame Simenon but returned to, of all times, in the late seventies. Poetry was never entirely neglected, nor was lexicography, either run-of-the-mill or specialised; Eric Partridge's compilations of slang, collo-quialisms and other byways of the English language earned large sums for the once-struggling proprietor of the Scholartis Press. And also for R.K.P. The Kegan Paul premises in Great Russell Street were sold to the Souvenir Press and the shop transferred to Store Street, where until an abrupt closure in 1976 it remained as part of a general academic shop. Norman Franklin was the only member of the family on the board in 1980.

A. & C. Black, which went public in 1965, moved out of long-occupied premises in Soho Square to almost equally elegant new quarters in Bedford

Row in 1975, having transferred its trade department and warehouse to Eaton Socon, near Huntingdon, in the same year. It remained in the forefront of primary school book publishing with large sales of history textbooks by R.J. Unstead and with a successful music list. Black was particularly well-known for its increasingly popular annuals, including *Who's Who, The Writers' and Artists' Yearbook* and the *Public and Preparatory Schools Yearbook*. It also specialised in books on ballet and angling, and in the seventies launched The Fishing Book Club.

The Blacks continued to play their part jointly with others from outside the family. Jack (J.B.) Newth celebrated forty-five years with the company in 1970, and retired some three years later, a few months before his death. He was a tower of strength to the Book Trade Benevolent Society and the P.A., both of which he served as president. David Gadsby, who also wrote for the list, followed Newth as joint managing director, sharing that position with Charles Black, who was also chairman. In 1981 part of the Pitman trade list was purchased.

A third company which went public in 1979 was not generally so well-known to the trade. The Haynes Publishing Group had a turnover of £5.27m in 1980-81, and a pretax profit of £779,000. Based in Yeovil, Somerset, it specialised in do-it-yourself car and motorcycle maintenance books.

When Walter Hutchinson died in 1950 he was the subject of an unflattering obituary notice, occupying a whole page of *The Bookseller*, above the initials of its editor. Edmond Segrave referred to his 'uninhibited capacity for self-glorification' which was manifested in a circular distributed to the trade at the end of the war. In this Hutchinson told, 'with pardonable pride, the story of the greatest achievement in publishing history' which was the vital contribution of £1,000 a day towards the cost of the war his companies had made to ensure the survival of the book trade. Segrave said that to many of his fellow publishers Hutchinson was a figure of fun, but that his unpredictable rages made him an object of terror to those whom he sacked without warning. A few days after his suicide a petition was filed to put his company into liquidation, a firm of electricians having tired of waiting for payment for work carried out at Hutchinson House, a mansion off Oxford Street which 'Mr Walter' had transformed into a National Gallery of British Sports and Pastimes. The electricians were paid and Mrs K.H. Webb, who had worked closely with Hutchinson for many years, helped to administer the company until Robert Lusty was attracted from Michael Joseph's to become managing director, reputedly at a vast salary (for the book trade), a watertight contract and a chauffeur-driven Bentley. His first action was to install order. He gave the group an all-embracing new colophon, that of a bull. All the companies which Walter had acquired, and no one knew quite how many, were accustomed to perform autonomously, with the result that three or more of them produced books on the same subject at about the same time. Bob Lusty sorted out this tangle, settling all the sporting books on Stanley Paul, the romantic fiction on Hurst & Blackett, crime on John Long, and so forth. He also resumed the normal practice of dating his books. The warehouse in Ireland Yard was vacated, so was Walter's Museum in Stratford Place. The trade department removed to Tiptree in Essex, the offices to Great Portland Street. The list was weeded and nursed back to strength. Harold Harris, an *Evening Standard* journalist, joined as editorial director and was a right-hand man to Lusty in refurbishing – or rather creating – an image which would appeal to literary agents and their clients. They were rewarded by gaining Arthur Koestler, Brendan Behan and Stalin's daughter, Svetlana. Later came Frederick Forsyth and a series of novels, beginning with *Day of the Jackal,* which placed him and his publishers in the big-time again. Robert Lusty was appointed deputy chairman of the BBC board of governors, for which he received a knighthood, and became the publisher whom journalists always wished to quote. He retired as M.D. at the end of 1972 and handed over to Charles Clark, a Penguin editor of high standing. In 1978 the company was sold to London Weekend Television under whose auspices (and with Clark now chief executive) it attracted more major authors to its list. Despite this, in 1980 there was a pretax loss of £2.3m, some of it due to the strength of the pound in foreign markets, although in 1981 there was an improvement.

By then Hutchinson had acquired Barrie & Jenkins, itself the amalgamation of almost as many companies as Walter Hutchinson had acquired during his lifetime. Some, like Herbert Jenkins and the Cresset Press, had a distinguished heritage. Jenkins, which went on indefatigably publishing P.G. Wodehouse, but not much else of note, was acquired by Barrie & Rockliff in 1965. Rockliff had been successful with a series of theatrical books. Cresset went to Barrie when Dennis Cohen retired.

Another commercial television company, Harlech, entered publishing in 1978 with the purchase of Frederick Muller Ltd from the Australian Consolidated Press. In the following year the small Blond & Briggs list, started when Anthony Blond left his own imprint in the hands of its American owners, was acquired and it appeared that yet another group was in the making.

The Pentos group had its origins, on the publishing side, in 1969 with the purchase by the First National Finance Corporation of Marshall, Morgan & Scott, a religious list founded in 1859 which had the attraction of being a public company. The man behind the purchase was Terry Maher, an accountant who believed in the philosophy of diversification and who enjoyed taking over businesses which were basically sound but lacked dynamic management. He hired Frank Herrmann, who had had experience at Faber, Methuen and Nelson, to build up a publishing empire. Ward, Lock was added and later World Distributors of Manchester. Until then the Lock and Shipton families had continued to own and manage Ward, Lock, which existed mainly on its backlist – Red Guides, Mrs Beeton's cookery books etc. World Distributors, run by John Pemberton, dealt not only in children's books but in toys and stationery as well.

In 1971 an investment banking company was formed and Pentos came into being, with Maher as Marshall, Morgan & Scott's chairman. Pentos bought Ward, Lock from First National and then branched out into bookselling. In nine years thirty-four shops were purchased including the Hudson chain, in Birmingham and elsewhere, and Dillon's. The three children of E.F. and Elsie Hudson had expanded the family business by enlarging the New Street shop and by opening branches in the universities of both Aston and Edgbaston. Pat, John and W.G. (Barry) Hudson remained directors on three-year contracts, and under Pentos expansion was intensified. Medical and art bookshops were opened in Birmingham, branches were started in Wolverhampton and Coventry, an existing bookshop bought in Loughborough. In 1980 an even more ambitious takeover added Brown's of Hull to the group within a group.

Dillon's bookshop which we left in small, bomb-damaged premises in Store Street became the largest in London. When London University returned to Bloomsbury Una Dillon had already moved across Store Street to larger accommodation. Assisted by Veronica Whatley, she was laying the foundation of departments specialising in education and Africa, the latter prompted by attendance at the shop of so many students from that continent. The solution to her expansion problems came from the University itself which bought an empty block at the corner of Malet Street and Torrington Place and invited Miss Dillon and another bookseller to run it in partnership. When this plan did not mature she was asked to go it alone which, encouraged by Mrs Whatley, she did and was given a minority shareholding in a new company with capital of £11,000. Ten years later Dillon's University Bookshop was turning over £600,000 and held stock valued at £115,000. The gross profit was 24.1% which reflected the poor terms given on academic books by most publishers.

In the year of Una Dillon's retirement when she was succeeded by Peter Stockham there was a staff of 109, many of them occupied in a large mail order department. Branches were opened at the Queen Mary College in the Mile End Road, at Wye Agricultural College in Kent, on the university campuses at Canterbury and Nottingham, and elsewhere. Cyril Mercer administered these shops as development and marketing manager until his resignation in 1973. A year later the new general manager, Michael Seviour, a London bookseller of wide experience, also resigned. There was much unrest amongst the staff, who channelled their grievances about low pay and working conditions through a trade union. Kenneth Stephenson became chairman and, with his growing reputation as a company doctor, began to sort matters out. Stockham resigned from the board in 1976, some branches were closed and, in 1977, the sale to Pentos was arranged. R.Grant Paton, a Glasgow bookseller, was appointed managing director (a position confirmed only after it had been approved by the union!) and recovery slowly began, although in 1980 there were still disputes about pay, and some working to rule. Paton's difficulties were accentuated when publishers began to stop the Pentos account because it was said, in some cases, that the company were taking several months to pay instead of the stipulated thirty days. In the same issue of *The Bookseller* (January 1981) when this was announced, there was an article about Terry Maher's further acquisitions – Sisson & Parker's of Nottingham; Hodges, Figgis of Dublin (which led to the opening of other shops in Eire); the Pilgrim's Bookshop, Canterbury (later closed when better premises were found).

In 1980 the bookselling and publishing side of Pentos made a trading loss of £312,000 on a turnover of £29.5m and it was reported that the bookselling side made some profit but that publishing made significant trading losses. Ward Lock Educational has since been disposed of.

In this section I have referred to the principal groups in British publishing still under native ownership; in the next I shall deal with foreign-backed organisations. One company, of historic origin, W.H. Allen, moved between British and American ownership on three occasions so that it properly belongs in neither chapter. But as it is still at the time of writing part of a U.K.-based operation, it is included here. It will be recalled that Mark Goulden, a journalist, revived the eighteenth-century imprint in 1940. He ran it for twenty-one years before selling to Doubleday, of New York. Seven years later he bought it back, only to re-sell it to the Walter Reade Organisation of America in 1970. A few months later it returned to British ownership when the theatrical group, Howard & Wyndham, purchased it for approximately half a million pounds. During all these changes Goulden retained editorial control until he retired, aged eighty, in 1976. He published much fiction, British and American, and developed a line in popular showbiz biographies. Howard & Wyndham bought other book properties such as the Grant Educational Co, of Glasgow (1972) and Hawthorn Books, through its American subsidiary (1977). Within two years it had sold both, and was recording dismal results. In the eighteen months to the end of 1980, there was a pretax loss of £1.09m. W.H. Allen also had to cope with author alienation when, in the summer of 1980, they were blacked by the Writers' Guild which sought to protect inexperienced authors without agents. The company's mainstay was its retail jewellery division. Commenting, *The Bookseller* noted that 'one very valuable sector is (its) series of Made Simple Books'. A few months later this was sold to Heinemann, and there was no Mark Goulden to arrange a re-purchase. He had died in May.

It can be said that W.H. Allen's changes of ownership represent one aspect of the international nature of publishing. A more creative aspect can be found in the skill with which some companies published for an international market. In the field of general trade books, two remarkable individualists were pace-setters.

George Weidenfeld's wartime arrival in Britain has been noted. In 1949 he started a publishing company bearing his name and that of Nigel Nicolson, younger son of Harold Nicolson, and he quickly became one of the most vigorous figures in world publishing. After a modest start, publishing children's books for Marks and Spencer to retail, Weidenfeld (always the dominant partner) found fresh capital, and expanded as forcefully as any Collins or Methuen of Victorian days. By 1968, he was issuing 250 titles a year under his own imprint or that of Arthur Barker, which he had absorbed and still retains for sports and other non-literary books. For a while he had an educational list which he sold to Granada in 1969; and there were always books of academic distinction on his list. But, basically, he was a general publisher with an interest in the international market. He became well-known for his personal marketing tactics at Frankfurt where he invited others to breakfast for selling sessions rather than coffee and rolls.

A senior colleague for some years was the ex-bookseller and Penguin editor, Tony Godwin, who developed an unexpected talent for making authors appreciate him. Distinguished indeed were some of those who lamented his going, as go he had to, when he had spent too much Weidenfeld money, but most of them have remained with a company which has captured an enviable proportion of the literary market.

Weidenfeld played a miniscule part in trade affairs. His company belonged to the P.A. but he was not of its Council. He was never on the executive committee of the National Book League or the Book Trade Benevolent Society; he was not elected to the societies to which other leading publishers belonged. But he was not a loner. He gave parties in his Chelsea house to the highest (or almost the highest) in the land. He was knighted by premier Harold Wilson, and later ennobled by the same politician. He was interviewed in and on the media, but he remained aloof from the trade. Not, though, from his colleagues who respected him and to whom he delegated much responsibility. A cultured man with a strong sense of being European, he could be seen as a late twentieth-century William Heinemann, drawing on the continent in which he was born to bring forth much that was valuable in literature. He drew also on his Jewish connection, publishing work that was relevant to the modern state of Israel, and also to the holocaust of the forties.

He was unfashionable amongst leading publishers in not joining in the committee world of Bedford Square; also in moving his offices to a part of London in which there was scarcely a bookshop – Clapham High Road,

S.W., where the absence of an immediately convenient restaurant was made up for by a directors' dining room in which the fare was delectable. He was astute, as always, in foreseeing the recession of 1980. He watched with apparent equanimity his managing director, Christopher Falkus, go and did not replace him, making other appointments from within and declaring himself 'minor-recession-proof'. At the start of 1982, however, John Gross, editor of the *Times Literary Supplement*, joined Weidenfeld as deputy chairman and publishing director with responsibilities for buying books and authors for the group and co-ordinating its programme.

Walter Neurath started in the same year as Weidenfeld. He took a Highgate bookseller, Trevor Craker, as sales manager, and used Constable's for representation and distribution, but the tail was soon wagging the dog. Constable travellers had to decide whether to stay with their parent firm or move over to Neurath's exclusive employment. Most chose Thames & Hudson which built up a list at lightning speed without overlooking quality. The emphasis was at first on art, then on anything good of its kind which came into the office except fiction, although the early books of Edward Blishen's which they published were not strictly autobiography. The market was international, as was implicit in the name of the company. It was only possible to issue certain types of books demanding a high standard of illustration, in colour or black and white, if a big print run could be ordered with the illustrations printed for several editions simultaneously. Neurath and his colleagues had a perfect understanding of the formula and they continued to exploit it long after his death in 1967. He left a widow and a son, Thomas, who became managing director; but the editorial inspiration behind some books, Tom Rosenthal, left in 1970 to manage Secker & Warburg. Thames & Hudson survived his departure and new books continued to pour forth, serviced as expertly as ever by the most efficient of trade departments at Aldershot.

Weidenfeld acolytes, a senior one of whom had been at Thames & Hudson, maintained that it was too costly to establish their own warehousing. When challenged with the example of T. & H. they replied that that company did not have to cope with continual bestsellers. At T. & H. there were those who said they were handling them all the time.

Foreign-Owned Groups

Rumour held that Roy Thomson was not aware when he bought Illustrated Newspapers Ltd that the purchase included the publishing house of Michael Joseph. Thomson was certainly not a literary man yet it is unlikely that he would have created a world-wide newspaper empire without paying attention to detail, but whether his entry into book publishing was accidental or not, once involved he became expansionist.

Michael Joseph sold out to Illustrated Newspapers in the mid fifties to finance his expanding list. Robert Lusty, who had managed the business during the war, returned to Hutchinson's at the end of 1955, and when Joseph died in 1958 Charles Pick and Peter Hebdon, two salesmen who had been with the company since its early days, became joint managing directors. They ran it devotedly for several years until the Thomson takeover, which alarmed them as much as the sale to Illustrated Newspapers had disconcerted Lusty and others. Their attempted bid for Cape has been noted. Pick went to Heinemann, Peter Hebdon returned to Joseph's where he became increasingly involved in the higher management of the Thomson book empire which absorbed Nelson, Hamish Hamilton and George Rainbird. The extra responsibilities and taxing overseas travel which this necessitated undoubtedly led to his death in 1970 at the age of fifty-three. He was not made for a conglomerate having learned his craft from an independent publisher, but he was supremely confident and energetic in managing the growth of Joseph's. He built up the subsidiary imprint, Pelham Books, which took the company into the sporting world. It was traditional practice for books by leading sportsmen to be ghosted by professional writers. Pelham carried the operation a stage further when it published a ghosted novel by a famous sportsman.

A major Joseph success of the sixties was a delightfully illustrated volume, *The Concise British Flora in Colour,* compiled by an elderly clergyman, H. Keble Martin. Published when what was designated pornography was flooding the bookshops, its huge success was refreshing to many. Fiction remained important, as did guides to various parts of the country sponsored by Shell, the petroleum company which subsidised a great many titles, only some of which went to Joseph. But the greatest success of all came with *The Country Diary of an Edwardian Lady* which was published in 1977 and had sold 1,445,500 copies by 1980. The first print was 148,000. Some bookshops placed it amongst their top Christmas sellers for two and even three years. It came to Joseph via the west country 'packaging' firm of Webb & Bower. Managing directors came and went in the decade following Hebdon's death. The offices were moved to Bedford Square and the last link with the founder was broken in 1981 when Michael's third wife, Anthea, died.

Nelson, the second Thomson acquisition, was also directed by many different hands and its image as a general publisher was first blurred, then lost. The classics, which had never enjoyed such huge sales as Collins' or Dent's, were discontinued and, after several changes of policy, the company came to concentrate on school and technical books. Nothing similar happened to Hamish Hamilton who retained personal control of his list during his lifetime as a condition of the sale to Thomson. Although he relinquished the managing directorship in 1971, 'Jamie' Hamilton was still active ten years later and much esteemed by his colleagues and authors as was shown in the privately circulated book, production of which was kept secret from him, compiled for his eightieth birthday in November 1980.

In the late forties Hamilton was responsible for an outstanding series of reprints – The Novel Library. They had varyingly patterned designs on the dustjackets and bindings which blended when placed together on a shelf, and they were impeccably printed. The size (foolscap 8vo) made them a joy for the traveller or armchair reader, and it is sad that they were allowed to go out of print. However, Hamilton never seemed to care much for establishing a backlist, although many of his books had long lives, and the very first, Graham Robertson's *Time Was*, was still in print in 1981. His authors included Alan Moorehead, Albert Camus, Jean-Paul Sartre, Georges Simenon, Nancy Mitford, L.P. Hartley and J.D. Salinger, whose *The Catcher in the Rye*, published in the U.K. in 1951 with mild success but critical acclaim, became perhaps *the* seminal novel of an era. It bridged two generations and when the Penguin eventually appeared teenagers were affronted to learn that an earlier generation had previously 'discovered' it. Hamilton's passion for music was expressed in many volumes by or about distinguished pianists, conductors, singers; his belief in Anglo-American cooperation in works of political commentary by John Gunther, J.K. Galbraith and others. A strong children's list was built up by the author, Richard Hough, and greatly developed by Julia Macrae until she left to start her own imprint with American backing. Her successor's lead title in 1980 was a story by the Prince of Wales, the profits of which went to charity. (One can't help thinking he had an unfair advantage over professional authors.)

George Rainbird, the fourth member of the Thomson Group, created books at the request of other publishers, or suggested subjects to them. He started in 1951 when he produced for Billy Collins a large format, colour-plate edition of Thornton's *Temple of Flora*, following it with the *Album de Redouté* and other splendidly printed and bound volumes. He went on to concentrate on creating fine books from original material which he published in limited and in standard editions. The former, priced between fifteen and one hundred guineas, sold out; the latter, seven-to-ten guineas, did not. In 1966 he sold to Thomson. Joined by John Hadfield and Edward Young, he began designing quarto volumes which were recognisable as Rainbird books. Each season there would be three or four. The authors did not receive as high a royalty as from their other books because the illustrations were realistically regarded as being as important in sales appeal as the text, but they enjoyed an international sale, the American and German markets being especially important. Rainbird's did not have their own sales organisation, except for foreign rights, and distributed through the publishers whose books they produced. Each year they took on trainees whose year's apprenticeship included working with a printer for a few weeks, and in a bookshop for two months.

Packaging, as it became known, was an idea which appealed to publishers because it cut their in-house overheads although some found they could produce Rainbird-style books themselves and did. Significantly, by 1980 Rainbird was planning titles aimed specifically at the home market.

Meanwhile all the companies had been made subsidiary to a parent holding company, Thomson Publications, which was itself part of the International Thomson Organisation with worldwide ramifications in journals and books, and also diversifications into other industries. In 1979 I.T.O. profits were £172m to which books contributed only £2.3m. Through Times Newspapers Ltd, which Thomson also owned until 1981, prestigious publications such as *The Times Atlas* also became part of the book empire and were distributed through Hamish Hamilton.

The ties between Macmillan, New York, for long a separate entity, and its London parent grew weaker after the war and eventually disappeared. The American company opened a London office and the British Macmillan started the St. Martin's Press in New York in 1952. In the sixties there were various takeovers by the American company which became known as Crowell, Collier-Macmillan Ltd. In 1968 it bought Studio Vista and Geoffrey Chapman (a young independent Roman Catholic list) and in 1969 Cassell's, all of which had already absorbed a number of others.

To understand the evolution of Studio Vista it is necessary to keep a cool head. The Studio, which had been a family business under the Holmes' since 1893, was sold to Edward Hulton in 1957; two years later it was bought by Odhams Press, which was taken over by I.P.C. in 1963. I.P.C. sold what was then known as Studio Vista to the Rev. Timothy Beaumont who, five years later, disposed of it to Crowell, Collier. (Edward Hulton, a magazine publisher, started *Picture Post* in 1938, and branched out into books in 1949. Even after the sale to Odhams he retained one imprint, Hulton Educational, until this was sold to Kluwer in 1979.) During Beaumont's ownership of Studio Vista, when his cloth precluded him from seeking a seat in the Commons, there was a deliberate policy of publishing for creative leisure, to which end David Herbert, with a previous career in bookselling, teaching, paperback publishing and the theatre, built a splendid list. When Beaumont became a Liberal peer Herbert went to Rainbird (in 1972) and moved on to start The Herbert Press in 1976.

Cassell's fortunes after the war relied much on Winston Churchill who provided them with six volumes of war memoirs, a four-volume *History of the English Speaking Peoples* and a sumptuous illustrated version of the latter called *The Island Race*. His sales were phenomenal, there were queues in Charing Cross Road when the first book of memoirs was published, and it was entirely fitting that he should be invited to lay the foundation stone of Cassell's new building in Red Lion Square, Holborn, opened in 1957. Other authors, Nicholas Monsarrat and Alec Waugh for instance, provided bestsellers; more such as Ernest Raymond, of longer standing, exemplified the loyalty which existed for so long between Cassells and its authors.

Desmond Flower, head of the company during its buoyant post-war years, saw the establishment of an Australian branch, as well as the purchase of George Blunt, library suppliers, and Ballière, Tindall & Cox. He survived the American takeover for longer than his deputy, Bryen Gentry, who within a few months left to start his own list.

Geoffrey Chapman, an Australian lawyer, was independent for only eleven years during which time he flew to Rome to bid successfully (against Collins and others) for the late Pope John's memoirs. He took over Duckett's Bookshop in the Strand and, after he had sold out himself, purchased for Crowell, Collier the map specialist publishers, Johnston & Bacon. (Johnston had been Geographer Royal to Queen Victoria and the firm dated back to 1826; Bacon's (1861) bought it in 1944, and sold it to Morrison & Gibb, Edinburgh printers and binders.) Chapman was left to manage his own imprint which was still alive in 1980. By that date Crowell, Collier had bought the Woolston Book Company, major library suppliers based in Nottingham, and Claude Gill's bookshop in Oxford Street.

Many reorganisations left Crowell, Collier operating separately from the British companies it took over, but through Collier-Macmillan Distribution

Services Ltd it retained a close connection with the library suppliers, Woolston and Blunt. The parent company, Macmillan Inc, of New York, turned a net profit of $22m in 1978 into a net loss of $56m the following year, with, inevitably, repercussions in England. In 1981 it was announced that the Cassell-Studio Vista division would withdraw from general publishing apart from dictionaries and the Berlitz travel guides and phrase books. Later the Gill bookshops were sold. They had been run as American-style stores on six sites in Greater London, emporia which operated not on the traditional lines of bookselling as a service but on the impulse-buy super-market principle. In 1982, Macmillan of New York sold the Cassell Group to C.B.S.

The Phaidon Press remained in Britain after the war but following its founder's death in 1967 became first American-, then Dutch-owned. During Horovitz's lifetime it was a small, quality list issuing very few titles each year. Kenneth Clark said of it, 'Phaidon were responsible for the first exciting art books to appear'. When it became part of a group, production was stepped up and it was not possible for the same detailed, loving care to be given to each new title although the standard remained high. There is the usual takeover story to tell. Horovitz's daughter and son-in-law, Harvey Miller, stayed for only three years with Frederick A. Praeger, Inc, the new owners, who were themselves a subsidiary of Encyclopaedia Britannica. In 1974 the Dutch firm Elsevier, whose English company had been established in 1939 and revived in 1947, bought Phaidon, moving it from London to Oxford three years later. In 1981 it changed hands yet again when those who had managed it for Elsevier became the owners.

Mills & Boon looked in the direction of Canada, not the U.S.A., when they felt the need to become international. This was rational because, since 1967, Harlequin Enterprises of Toronto had taken the rights of some of their romances, the survival of which into a world bereft of ciculating libraries was unforeseen. Indeed the generation of Boons then running the firm had already taken steps to broaden their list. In 1955 their first general book for twenty-five years was published, and more followed. John Boon also bought the old established Allman educational list in 1961, thus giving a third string to the bow. But things did not evolve as expected. The commercial libraries, victims of the spread of television and the rising cost of books, closed rapidly thus depriving Mills & Boon readers, who were not book buyers, of their favourite romances. The company received touching letters from thousands of them and reacted positively to retain its market. The romances went into paperback and M. & B. readers learned to buy them not only from newsagents and railway bookstalls but from quality bookshops. A survey undertaken by the book trade's market researcher-in-chief, Dr Peter Mann of Sheffield University, discovered that some M. & B. readers were highbrows who read romances for relaxation.

By 1981 the market was so buoyant that Mills & Boon almost alone amongst publishers faced the year with increasing optimism. Their editorial director, Heather Jeeves, was quoted in *The Daily Telegraph* as saying that 'in 1981 we shall sell a million copies in hardback before going into paperback' because their readers had now become habitual buyers of books, purchasing as many as five per month in some cases. The educational and non-fiction general list was sold off to Bell & Hyman. Harlequin-Mills & Boon, as it had become, confidently placed all its eggs in one basket again, and prepared a massive advertising campaign on television. *The Observer* decided to investigate the phenomenon, and a snide piece appeared, making superior fun of the whole business. Asked to comment, Paul Scherer, the managing director, refused. *The Observer* had never reviewed an M. & B. romance. Why should he risk being mis-quoted? Oxford University Press were less stuffy. They bought seven M. & B. titles for an E.F.L. series. M. & B. later diversified into the thriller market.

No publisher of his generation played a more active part in trade affairs than John Boon who was president not only of the P.A., but also of the International Publishers Association, and a member of many missions to the book fraternities of other lands.

Also in the romance market were Robert Hale which never gave up general books. In some years their output of titles was the largest in British publishing.

In addition to the foreign-owned groups there had long been U.K. branches of American, Australian and French companies. Of these McGraw-Hill, active in Britain since 1909, had such connections on all other continents that it constituted a group in itself. In 1963, Gordon Graham, a Scot who had lived and worked in the United States and the Far East, where he wrote for a McGraw-Hill journal, was appointed managing director of the U.K. company. In due course, as British-based international sales manager, he became responsible for Europe and the communist countries, a 'territory' which was expanded in 1971 to include West Africa and the Middle East. But in 1974 it was all over. The Atlantic, as Graham put it to a friend, became too narrow. Few lasted as long as he as ambassadors for American companies.

Another American company was Prentice-Hall Inc., which acted as agents for other publishers, including some university presses. Its terms to general booksellers were poor by British standards as were those of John Wiley, an immensely successful scientific and technical publisher with world-wide ramifications and which, as we have seen, set up its own British base after several decades of being represented by Chapman & Hall.

Obtaining books from American publishers who were not represented in the U.K. was an exasperating operation for British booksellers who undertook the task, often involving weeks or even months of waiting, and unless exchange rates and bank charges were calculated accurately, it could result in a net loss. A number of companies sold through T.A.B.S. (Transatlantic Book Services Ltd), the American Book Supply Co, or Roger Lascelles, who specialised in travel guides. Many American university presses tended to be represented by O.U.P. or C.U.P., although some – Harvard and Yale for example – had their own London offices; others joined the American Universities Publishers Group Ltd.

Harper's, which became Harper & Row in 1962, continued to be represented in the U.K. by both staff and stocks; the Heath Company of Boston, for which Harrap long had the agency, set up at Farnborough, Hants, in 1970, and the R.R. Bowker Company, proprietors of *Publishers' Weekly*, and which was later owned by Xerox, opened a London subsidiary for a while. There were many other American-owned companies, some of which will be dealt with in the chapter on paperbacks, but a comparative newcomer to their ranks must be mentioned here. That is Mitchell-Beazley Ltd, which became part of the huge American Express empire late in 1980 when the surviving founder, James Mitchell, sold his shares for an estimated £1m. He was also given a long service contract. His is a remarkable success story. After publishing experience at Constable and Nelson's, where he met John Beazley, a small list for the international market was planned. They started in 1969, financed by George Philip, with two lavish atlases, followed by a book commissioned by the late Shah which they sold to the Iranian government for over £100,000. There followed a stream of handsome slip-cased volumes on wine, trees, gardening, astrology, all designed for the coffee-table, and another of slim pocket-sized manuals on similar subjects. John Beazley died of cancer aged only forty-four in 1977; quality production was crucial to Mitchell Beazley's success and this was his department. Mitchell gave lavish parties to launch most of his major titles at some of which he read doggerel composed by himself. One rather bizarre occasion occurred at the Savile Club when he threw a dinner for the American publisher of *The Joy of Sex*. The rules of the club at that time did not allow ladies to be present.

The fortunes of the Australian company, Angus & Robertson, fluctuated during this period. The publishing side ceased to represent Australian university presses in Britain in 1973 and closed down its London production department in 1980 by which time the bookshops in Australia (twenty-nine of them) had been sold to the British exporter, Gordon & Gotch, who reported a large loss on them. The Australian bookselling scene was by then in some confusion. Soaring rents and the abolition of price maintenance were the reasons given by some booksellers for abandoning their premises but there were retailers who insisted otherwise.

French interests in Britain were in Hachette, who gave up wholesaling in 1974 but maintained their bookshop just off Regent Street in London. The

Michelin Tyre Company, for long as justly famous for its guides as for its motor vehicle products, distributed its publications through the Dickens Press until 1973 when it set up its own sales department. The popularity of Michelin maps and guides spread rapidly as it became the custom for more and more British residents to motor in Europe. Other continental map publishers were Hallwag, whose agency went to Collins, and Kummerley & Frey, who supplied through wholesalers.

The most complicated story of ownership belongs however to Transworld, publishers of a successful paperback series, Corgi Books (see page 166). In 1977 Bertelsmann, a German publisher, bought 51% of the shares in Bantam Books of U.S.A., owners of Corgi which had passed through several hands. In 1980 it bought the other 49% from the Agnelli group of Italy through its Luxemburg-based associate. How many digits that added to the various ISBNs is not related.

Italy was also represented in the ownership of Orbis Publishing which was directed by Czech-born Martin Heller who had managed Purnell Partworks for B.P.C. Partworks had enjoyed a heyday in the nineteenth century and Orbis, started in 1971, succeeded in their revival where others failed. Magazines played a larger part in Heller's publishing than books which, nevertheless, were treated respectfully, with an eye to the up-market coffee-table owner.

Educational Publishing, University Presses

We have seen that British publishers began to open overseas branches before the end of the nineteenth century. Their number grew steadily in the first half of the twentieth, and after 1945 not only were more opened but separate companies were formed in Australia (which, after the U.S.A., had the largest English-reading public overseas, and was the biggest single export market for books), Canada, Africa and elsewhere. These subsidiaries usually began original publishing once they had become established as sales points for the parent companies' lists. This seething activity took place against a background of educational and political upheaval, especially in Africa. As new countries emerged out of the lost empires of the British, French, Belgians and Dutch, those who had led the clamour for independence now devoted part of their energies to spreading literacy, which meant a demand for textbooks both in English and the vernacular. Competition to dominate this more lucrative new market was not confined to rival British firms but became an issue between the U.K. and U.S.A. which had begun, during World War II, to break into the British publishers' traditional market. American publishers enjoyed a much larger home sale than their British counterparts, so exports tended to be icing on the cake rather than a means of making the whole operation viable, which was how it appeared from London. The Russians also sought to influence the new nations of the Far East by printing heavily subsidised editions of British books, in English, which they distributed at give-away prices. British publishers had to fight to persuade successive governments that books must also be helped if British influence and trade were to be maintained and increased. Too often government refused to intervene, at the same time as cutting down on British Council funds and causing that worthy institution to close some of its overseas libraries. It says much for the industry and initiative of our publishers that despite a general lack of official support they continued, at least up until the late seventies, to prosper in the export market, even finding spare time to slit one another's throats, as a change from those of the Americans and Russians. That they succeeded in overseas markets was partly because their product was a good one. Educational publishing improved not only in cash terms but also in quality and it was to promote educational lists that much foreign travel was undertaken. And there were times when one had the impression that the surest way of meeting everyone of importance in British publishing would be to take up residence in the arrival and departure lounges at Lagos, Nairobi or Singapore airports.

At home, the school book market was less encouraging, and expenditure did not keep pace with inflation. Thus many schools continued to use books first published before the war and bearing every appearance of having been printed and bound then, though in areas where local authorities spent more on books some schools were able to discard the tattered and disintegrating volumes, preserved by sticky tape and faith to last through the war, and replace them with up-to-date titles more attractively designed than most of their precursors.

Small wonder that educational publishers felt the need to form the Educational Publishers Council in 1969 to bring pressure to bear on government and local councils to spend more on books which in 1981 still accounted for less than 1% of total educational expenditure. One of the points they made was that some children being crammed for O and A Level examinations were learning geography from atlases published in the early fifties when Africa was still largely governed from Europe. And it was in Africa and Asia especially that educational publishers looked for the sales which they found so hard to increase at home. For several decades they never had it so good. During that long period when the pound was weak on the foreign exchanges and when all Britons were exhorted to export, textbooks – primary, secondary and tertiary – were pumped into the classrooms and lecture halls of the third world by enterprising publishers of long standing, and by newcomers, some of whom have already been discussed.

At Macmillan the family retained control, some giving their working lives to publishing, others dividing their time between Westminster and St. Martin's Street. The strong bias towards educational publishing was maintained. In the export field, Macmillan signed agreements with some new African countries, notably Ghana, to manage state publishing concerns, an action hotly resented by their competitors who saw in it a threat to sales of their own school books. Accusations, denials and dignified statements were issued all round and the storm was a long time dying.

Macmillan Australia became a separate company in 1967, another was formed in South Africa a year earlier. At home the importance of audio-visual aids and cassettes in teaching was recognised. The firm's continued record of being innovators may have been in Robert Maxwell's mind when he forecast, rather more than a decade ago, that in ten years' time only Macmillan, amongst British publishers, would remain independent.

The general list was also healthy in most categories. Several paperback series were launched and, with Collins and Heinemann, they came to own the popular Pan imprint. Other acquisitions included the technical list of Cleaver-Hume Press, M.H. Gill of Dublin which became Gill & Macmillan, and the Nautical Publishing Co Ltd. The solid Victorian building in St. Martin's Street, built to last a thousand years, was sold in 1965 and demolished for redevelopment. The warehouse and main office was moved to Basingstoke but a foothold was retained in London at Little Essex Street, where some management remained and, even, a few books.

The accountants were powerful in Macmillan long before they dominated other firms. Few, if any, booksellers were permitted to exceed the statutory thirty days credit, and warehouse space was costed down to the last square inch, prices being increased accordingly if slow-moving stock did not pay its way. Reconstructions of management were common. In 1980 three separate subsidiary companies were created to control accounts and administration, distribution, and information systems. The chairman of all three and of a further company controlling them, was N.G. Byam Shaw, none of whose co-directors at that level was a Macmillan. Those of the family who remained were directors of an even more exalted overall company. This reorganisation was announced to the trade as being 'in accordance with their general philosophy that expansion is best dealt with by delegation of readily identifiable operations to small specialist units within the corporate structure'. The word 'book' did not occur in the statement, but perhaps only because the actual product in that sense was looked after by three other companies, one general, one academic, one educational. There was yet another, Macmillan Film Productions Ltd – but it is outside the scope of this book.

More specifically concerned with the educational than the general market were other survivors from the nineteenth century. Edward Arnold and his successor, B.W. Fagan, believed that a publisher should be conversant with every aspect of his business and should not publish more books than he could, as a good midwife, deliver himself. Fagan died in 1971, having out-lived his senior colleague Thomas H. Clare, sometime chairman, whose responsibility was the strong medical list. (Clare's father was foreman packer to Arnold and his mother caretaker of the Maddox Street premises which continued to house the firm until 1972, when it moved first to Hill Street and then to Bedford Square.) Anthony Hamilton, chairman, and Bryan Bennett, vice-chairman, then guided Arnold to considerable expansion in Africa and elsewhere. Bennett was also much involved in trade activities, including a spell as chairman of the Book Development Council.

E.J. Arnold, a Yorkshire-based namesake, specialised in school books and formed a Scottish subsidiary in 1971 when it bought Holmes McDougall Ltd. Seven years later it acquired from Howard & Wyndham the educational contract division of Grant's of Glasgow and in 1980 the whole book operation was moved from Leeds to Cumbernauld, north of the border.

Arnold of Leeds, as the company was known by booksellers, was no more popular for the terms it offered to the trade than its near neighbour for most of the century, Schofield & Sims, of Huddersfield, who were massive suppliers of primary school books. This perhaps explained their poor export performance which by the end of the seventies accounted for about 5% of turnover, in contrast with Evans Brothers which exported as much as 75% of its output, much of it to West Africa. Evans changed course dramatically after the post-war boom in war stories like *The Dam Busters* in which it participated particularly successfully; under the guidance of Noel Evans who died in 1964, it returned to concentrate on its publishing for schools at primary and secondary levels in the U.K. and in Africa, and to build up a trade list in craft books and children's books, for which Robin Hyman, the managing director, and his wife Inge, wrote. Hyman spent much time abroad in Africa and elsewhere, developing Evans' exports, compiled a *Dictionary of Famous Quotations* for the general list and a school dictionary for Nigeria. He left to buy the George Bell list in 1977. In 1980 Lord Lever, a Labour minister under Harold Wilson, bought control of Evans.

George Bell still operated until 1977 from the gloomy offices on Portugal Street, Lincoln's Inn, which were purpose-built for them in 1904 and from which there emanated a strong aura of distinguished decay. There was, in fact, a fine publishing list lurking there, sufficiently so for the retiring chairman, Richard Glanville (a great-grandson of the founder) to be able to be selective about the purchaser he sought. He wished to see Bell's continue as an independent company rather than have it disappear into a conglomerate. Robin Hyman, having spent twenty years with Evans and seeking an imprint of his own, saw in the backlist not only such classroom perennials as Parr's and Durell's mathematics books but also desirable properties in many other directions, including crafts and chess. There was one especial plum in the definitive edition in eleven volumes of the *Diary of Samuel Pepys*, a work with which Bell had been associated since 1864. York House, Portugal Street was sold, the company re-named Bell & Hyman Ltd and offices were taken across the Thames, near Tower Bridge, an area not much associated with publishing but having the advantage of costing about £10 per square foot less in rates and rent than it would in Bloomsbury. In 1980, at the height of the recession, Hyman boldly bought the Mills & Boon non-fiction list, declaring that one should not wait for times to improve – precisely the

1920s philosophy of Victor Gollancz, by whose company his trade books were travelled.

Other established names in educational publishing range from the massive presses of Oxbridge to the relatively small James Nisbet, and University Tutorial Press, and the considerably larger Holmes McDougall and Ginn. Many general publishers, of varying size, continued to have healthy educational lists. Amongst those not already mentioned was John Murray who had a spectacular success with Mackean's *Introduction to Biology,* which set a new standard in large-format illustrated textbooks. Published in 1962 it sold three million copies in ten years, eight million in nineteen years and was translated into eight languages. Kenneth Pinnock was in charge of educational publishing, John Grey (Jock) Murray concentrating on the general list.

Jock Murray was a complete bookman, living with his work as much in his Hampstead home, where authors often stayed, as at his office, at ease equally with writers, other publishers and booksellers. He was as happy to turn delivery boy when his local bookseller sent a message 'Will you ask Mr Murray to pop twelve *Nudes* in his car for me?' as he was to be publisher of Kenneth Clark's book of that title. And many others from the same author, notably *Civilisation* (issued jointly with BBC Publications), which sold phenomenally in part because of the hour-long plug it received each week during its thirteen weeks showing on television. No new book had ever received such gratis publicity before.

In the autumn of 1968 Murray's, a limited company since 1951, celebrated its double century with a series of four parties at the Albemarle Street house famous for its Byron associations. Sir John Murray V had died in the previous year but not before another generation had come into the firm, Jock's son John. By 1980 his other son Hallam, having served an apprenticeship elsewhere, and indulged the family passion for travel, arrived to reorganise the warehouse, after a year in which Murray had, sadly, declared a loss.

Jock Murray's personal preoccupation during the seventies was the complete *Byron's Letters and Journals,* in eleven volumes, edited by Leslie Marchand. He also did fieldwork for further updating of Murray's *Handbook to India,* the only one of the famous Victorian guides to have remained in print.

At Harrap's the educational side became more important than the general. They pioneered audio-visual language courses, an extension of their pre-eminence in the field of French dictionaries and texts under the masterly editorial direction of Rene Ledesert. Walter Harrap remained in command until his sudden death in 1967. A man of many parts, always active in trade affairs, he also, when things got behind in his warehouse, would defy union regulations, take off his jacket and pack parcels himself. Enormously energetic, given to writing long letters to *The Bookseller* and personal correspondents, he never spared himself in promoting cooperation within the trade, and in furthering the family business. He was succeeded by another formidably likeable individualist, R. Olaf Anderson who handed over to Walter's nephew, Paull, in 1971; his son Ian resigned to become a bookseller in the same year. A projected merger with Litton Industries (U.S.A.) was called off in 1970 after a year of negotiation. The majority of shares remained in the ownership of the Harrap and Anderson families until the company was sold to Nicholas Berry and various trusts. In 1981, the building in High Holborn, which had withstood the Blitz, was sold and demolished. The offices were moved to Ludgate Hill, where Paull Harrap shared the managing directorship with Nicholas Berry until Berry became chairman and sole managing director at the end of 1981.

Anthony Blond, although not active for long in either general or educational publishing, made a unique contribution to the latter, when thinking over the possibilities of issuing textbooks. He was allowed to teach English at a school in Doncaster for a while, an experience which confirmed his distaste for current books on the subject. So he commissioned Emmens and Rowe to write new ones and launched Blond Educational as a subsidiary of the general list he had founded in 1958. The venture was successful but ran him short of capital. When he failed to raise backing in the City he sold out to Columbia Broadcasting System and Holt, Rinehart, of the United States, retaining the managing directorship for himself and the sales directorship for Desmond Briggs. There are those who believe that had he been less lavish in the advances he paid for general books he could have financed his own expansion in the educational market, but it was Blond's nature to move from one enthusiasm to another. Needless to say, the period of working for the American owners was barely the usual two years, after which he and Briggs broke amicably and started their own imprint, using their two names. When that was sold (see page 125) Blond took to writing.

In general and educational publishing, towered the mammoth Oxford University Press from which Humphrey Milford retired as publisher in 1945, being succeeded by Geoffrey Cumberlege, who had managed the Bombay and New York branches during his thirty-two years of service. When Cumberlege retired in 1956, John G.N. Brown, who started with the Press in 1937 and had also worked in the Bombay branch, and been sales manager since 1949, took over. At the Clarendon Press A.L.P. Norrington was succeeded as Secretary to the Delegates, in 1954, by Colin Roberts. Norrington then became president of Trinity College and gave his name to a magnificent extension to Blackwell's bookshop.

The size and authority of Oxford publishing expanded apace in the fifties and sixties and by 1970 reorganisation was overdue. Equally responsible to the Secretary to the Delegates were the Printer, the Controller of the

Wolvercote Paper Mill, the Publisher to the Clarendon Press, the Publisher to O.U.P., London, and President of O.U.P., New York. Below them were the heads of the cartographic and music department, and the managers of the overseas branches, seven in Africa, ten in Asia and one each in Australia, New Zealand and Canada. It was a formidable institution, publishing about 850 new titles each year and handling 600-700 titles originated by other university presses. 17,000 titles were listed in the 1970 catalogue and, at the Neasden warehouse, which was extended in 1961, there were usually three million volumes in stock. The annual turnover exceeded £13m. No wonder the Franks Commission reporting in 1966 on the University recommended a full enquiry into the Press and its relationship to the University. The result was the Waldock Report of 1970 amongst whose thirty-eight recommendations was one that senior executives of the Press should receive salaries comparable to those paid by other publishers rather than remuneration on a par with academics.

Ahead lay a decade of undiminishing activity and many problems, culminating in a loss for 1980-81 of £2.5m on the U.K. publishing side. There had been industrial unrest at Neasden over many years, an unhappy situation which it was planned to cure (in addition to providing more space) by moving to Corby in Northants. There were numerous changes at top level; George Richardson was appointed Secretary and chief executive in 1974; Brown, knighted in the same year, became Deputy Secretary to the Delegates in 1980 but left soon after to join Blackwell's. Robin Denniston, who had moved through various top jobs at lightning speed, and always in an upward direction, became academic publisher in 1978 and overlord of the Academic and General Division two years later; the other U.K. publishing division, Educational, was headed by M.A. Morrow. By 1979 it was reported that net profits were growing but so were problems, especially in Nigeria where the law obliged the Press to convert its branch into a Nigerian company, University Press Ltd, in which O.U.P. had a 40% holding.

So O.U.P. entered the ninth decade of the century in an unhappy state, with the price of its books leaping from one month to another, and with a heavy paring operation on the backlist overseen by George Depotex, an ex-sales manager who as a consultant had the task of selling thousands of volumes as remainders.

What was published during the whole of this time was usually exemplary and led to O.U.P. being as important to most booksellers as any of its competitors, and often more so, and not only for its ever increasing range of dictionaries, a newcomer to which was the *Advanced Learner's Dictionary* for foreign students which has sold some eight million copies in thirty-two years. *The Oxford Junior Encyclopaedia,* in thirteen volumes, came but, alas, went in the cuts, there were additions to the Companions series, the children's list was extended widely and had a hallmark of class, and there were unexpected general bestsellers such as the plays of Christopher Fry and the three-volume life of Trotsky by Isaac Deutscher. Another was A.J.P. Taylor's addition to the Oxford History of England, *English History 1914-45.*

Perhaps the largest bestseller was the new translation of the Bible. The New Testament, published jointly with Cambridge, appeared in 1961 and sold 4,700,000 copies by 1970 when the Old Testament came out under the same sponsorship. (Eyre & Spottiswoode had to be restrained by court order from printing it as well.) Few books have received better promotion than the *New English Bible* which by the end of 1980 had sold, excluding editions produced in the U.S.A., over two and a half million copies.

In 1966 Amen House in Warwick Square, with its section of preserved Roman Wall in the deep basement, had been vacated to allow for the extension of the Old Bailey. The London headquarters moved to an eighteenth-century mansion, once the town house of the Bishops of Ely, in Dover Street, Mayfair. In 1976 most departments moved from here to Walton Street, Oxford. Two years later the Press celebrated its 500th anniversary, an event the BBC recorded in a television film. At the end of 1980 O.U.P. employed in the publishing divisions 941 people in the U.K. and 1290 overseas, including the Nigerian company. In November of that year Robin Denniston, still academic and general publisher, became one of the two Deputy Secretaries to the Delegates. The other was J.Y. Huws Davies, who had charge of O.U.P. New York for many years.

That there was no serious rivalry between the two foremost university presses was shown not only by their joint sponsorship of the *New English Bible,* but also by the appointment of R.J.L. Kingsford to the Waldock committee. Kingsford was London Manager for Cambridge until 1948 when he succeeded S.C. Roberts as Secretary to the Syndics. R.W. David, who took over in London, followed him to the university city in 1963 and was replaced at Bentley House by Colin Eccleshare. This left Kingsford free to write his history of the P.A. The Cambridge managers in London all served the Association as president and in other capacities, Colin Eccleshare being a member of many official P.A. delegations to various parts of the world. He was wont to report on them verbally, and in writing, with a happy wit. He did not, however, take the road to Cambridge like his predecessors because in 1972 there was a restructuring which brought in Geoffrey Cass, sometime management consultant who had served a spell as managing director of Allen & Unwin, to head C.U.P.'s publishing division. Later he replaced David, who retired in 1974, as Secretary to the Syndics. When Bentley House was sold in 1977 Eccleshare also retired, and Cambridge publishing, always more strictly academic than Oxford's, retreated to its native city.

C.U.P. was slower to establish overseas branches than O.U.P. and its operations, at all levels, were less spectacular. It nevertheless maintained a tradition for fine production and scholarly work. Until the 1960s it issued only about 150 books each year but this had doubled by 1966 with the introduction of an extensive 'egg-head' paperback list which came to include many volumes of the New Cambridge Modern History and the New Shakespeare, edited by Quiller-Couch and Dover Wilson. C.U.P. also sponsored the School Mathematics Project, a series of textbooks designed to make maths more easily taught and learned. In 1967 the two great presses joined with Longmans and A.B.P. to provide a computerised mailing service, the inspiration of Michael Hosking, to teaching and research staff in the U.K. and Ireland in all institutions above secondary level.

The activities of the lesser university presses must seem puny by comparison but from Manchester, Liverpool, Leicester, Edinburgh, Bradford, Sussex and elsewhere there was a steady issue of worthy volumes. In London in 1948, the Athlone Press was formed by a resolution of the Senate and named after its then chancellor. It was sold to Bemrose, the printers, in 1979 at a time when they were still attempting to create a publishing empire. In 1981 Bemrose disposed of it to Brian Southam, whom they had appointed to manage it.

There was also the Open University, created by the Wilson Labour Government to encourage mature studentship in cooperation with the BBC. Those who took the courses worked at home and in them booksellers found a new type of customer, students who actually bought all the set books, who did not, as was the case with many teenagers, borrow or steal them. Those booksellers who became official local stockists, agreeing to keep all set books so far as publishing vagaries allowed, added appreciably to their business. Some even became regional stockists, wholesaling to local bookshops. Snags arose because of the waywardness of academics in selecting titles published by American university presses unagented in this country, or from imprints not generally known to the trade; but those in charge at the Open University, including the former owner of Putnam, Roger Lubbock, attempted to bring home to the dons the needs of the book trade. The O.U. also published its own manuals for certain courses.

Until the 1960s the BBC, as a publisher, was mostly concerned with booklets relating to particular radio programmes, and especially schools broadcasts. Some such books were put out at a loss on the grounds that they were essential accompaniments to what listeners heard. The development of television, however, not only spread the need for such material but led the Corporation into the general book field in competition with publishers. In the case of *Civilisation*, Kenneth Clark was contracted to Murray's so it was a joint publication; in most cases it was not. Alastair Cooke's fame stemmed from his broadcasts from the States for thirty years or more; it was reasonable that his *America,* written for television, should be the BBC's property. Similarly with J.N. Bronowski's *Ascent of Man* and Robert Hughes' *The Shock of the New.* Booksellers were not unhappy about this. A saleable book was a saleable book and BBC Publications for obvious reasons received far more publicity than any ordinary publisher could afford. By and large publishers took a swings-and-roundabouts attitude. There were so many opportunities on radio and television for exposure of their own books that they were resigned to competition from the BBC as publishers. The Beeb, as it was known, also tried hard with programmes about books. No entirely satisfactory formula was found for television – it being basically dull to seat a few people round a table to discuss literature – but the novelist Melvyn Bragg and the interviewer Robert Robinson have made notable progress. On Radio 4 Frank Delaney attracted a wide audience for his Bookshelf; commercial stations also regularly featured interviews with authors.

The growth of the new universities was responsible for an increased demand for technical books, which found other outlets through polytechnics and colleges of further education. Subjects hitherto unheard of by some booksellers became labelled sections in their shops. Cybernetics, automation, nuclear energy, plastics, business management, aerodynamics, computers and numerous other studies produced literatures of their own. Much was published by established houses such as Macdonald & Evans, which dated from 1907 when Alfred Macdonald, having declined the managing directorship of Butterworth, took Griffiths Evans as his partner and started on a capital of £2500. In 1964 the first M. & E. Handbooks were published, the birth of a series which extended to 100 titles by 1976. The company moved to Plymouth in that year, and continued to grow substantially.

The Technical Press, which grew out of Crosby Lockwood's troubles in the thirties when the last Lockwood sold a major part of his copyrights and stock to a new company so that his creditors, mainly his authors, should not lose, had another successful series. The Common Core books, started in 1957, sold a million copies by 1969. After the war the Press was bought by C.F.G. Henshaw and Oliver Stobart. At Crosby Lockwood, Humphrey Wilson, having succeeded his father, sold out to Granada in 1972.

The Cleaver-Hume Press, which its editorial director over many years, Paul J. Edmonds, claimed to be 'the only new sci-tech publisher of a purely traditional British character in the adventurous post-war years', developed apace in tertiary education and in 1964 came under the Macmillan umbrella. Pitman's, Nelson's and the Temple Press produced car manuals and other technical literature to do with vehicles two-or more wheeled, and at Griffin's (scientific and engineering publishers) the seventh generation in the person of James R. Griffin took over from his father, C.F. Rae Griffin, at the end of 1970. Blackwell Scientific Publications, a part of the large

Oxford-based empire, and run by Per Saugman, grew rapidly and opened in the U.S.A. in 1980. Its books and journals ranged widely across the whole medical and scientific spectrum.

The social sciences, with which the new universities were much concerned, also spawned thousands of titles, many of them giving headaches to booksellers attempting to classify them, the lines between sociology, education, psychology, philosophy etc, becoming considerably blurred. Routledge & Kegan Paul's list was heavy with books for this market which also attracted newcomers, some of whom survived.

Independents,
Old and New

Of the imprints founded in the nineteenth century and which remained privately owned, two grew prodigiously. One, Macmillan, has already been noted; the other, Hodder & Stoughton, has not. It could be said that Hodder's waited to make sure they had understood in which direction books, literature and public opinion were evolving before allowing an outsider, Robin Denniston, to conduct them into the latter half of the twentieth century; certainly the Hodder-Williamses and the Attenboroughs, the owners of Hodder & Stoughton, then transformed themselves into modern publishing moguls with immense alacrity.

The facts were that Hodder & Stoughton, a company of solid achievement and many bestsellers in educational and general publishing, but with a marked bias towards the conventional, suddenly in 1962 tacked in a new direction, taking on the other large general publishers in the grab for leading authors. It started, appropriately enough, with Anthony Sampson's *The Anatomy of Britain,* an analysis of home society which Collins, Macmillan and many others would no doubt have been happy to publish, given its author's standing in quality journalism. This was Denniston's breakthrough and he knew what he was doing because he had worked for Collins. The image of Hodder & Stoughton changed rapidly; by the time he left, just over ten years later he had, in John Attenborough's words, 'helped to rescue the firm from a fuddy-duddy Establishment image'. The company was in business for bestselling authors of fiction and non-fiction, and it attracted them. But it did not neglect the successful educational side although there was rationalisation of a singular nature when the *name* of University of London Press, acquired in 1910, was sold back to the University in 1974 for a token £10,000, yet the books remained with Hodder. Teach Yourself Books, under the guidance of Leonard Cutts until 1969, and many series on most aspects of the curriculum, as well as the agency for the Langenscheidt dictionaries, kept Hodder to the fore. Nor was the religious list allowed to vegetate. Denniston, a practising Christian like the ruling descendants of the founders, attracted authors and additional sales for the theological side of the list.

Brockhampton Press, a subsidiary company started in 1940, grew to become an important children's list under Ewart Wharmby, who operated from a light and airy office building close to Leicester University. By the time of his retirement in the seventies Brockhampton, as well as the old imprints of E.U.P. and U.L.P., were phased out and, within the new structure of the company, adult general books, juveniles, educational titles and paperbacks were grouped as individual entities. To the general side was added the important concession of lavishly illustrated volumes published by the Reader's Digest and Drive (a Digest/Automobile Association joint company). Although heavily promoted by their sponsors direct to individuals by post, these handsome editions became fast-selling items in most bookshops. To house all these activities a large office block and warehouse was built at Dunton Green, near Sevenoaks, on land purchased in 1972, and a London editorial foothold maintained in Bedford Square, to which they moved in 1976, being the last major publisher to abandon the traditional St. Paul's neighbourhood. In 1981, to the surprise of some, Hodder's acquired New English Library, a British subsidiary of the Los Angeles Times Mirror, which, along with their existing three brands, put them firmly into the paperback big time and took their total group sales for 1981-82 to over £25m.

Surprisingly, Hodder remained privately owned with Philip Attenborough, a descendant of Matthew Hodder, in command. In 1981 he became treasurer of the P.A. and in 1982 vice-president, posts which, as well as the presidency, his father John had held. His brother Michael took command of general publishing after Denniston had left, and, to complete the overall bookish image of a firm which could have been public, John Attenborough on his retirement wrote not only an excellent history of the company but also a novel about a family of not unsuccessful business people living in Kent. (The Attenboroughs lived in Kent.)

Hodder's were typical of many big publishers in their approach to selling. It was no longer sufficient to engage a rep, give him samples and send him off on the road to obtain orders. Seasonal conferences were held, attended by the sales and marketing staff and also by heads of other departments. Often the publisher's own offices were found to be too small for these events so hotel suites were hired and also bedrooms. Even the reps who lived near the conference centre were expected to abandon their homes for its duration. Togetherness was all. On several occasions Hodder chose Spain as their venue, it being argued that a hotel on the Mediterranean out of season was cheaper than one in London. Authors as well as staff were flown out to talk about forthcoming books.

Nothing as elaborate occurred at Allen & Unwin's, at least while Sir Stanley reigned, although even he took to throwing parties for booksellers and the press, which he did without a sign of his reputed meanness. Unwin was knighted not once but twice through some quirk of the honours system and continued actively in his business until 1968 when he died aged eighty-four. His son Rayner succeeded him and brought *his* son into the business some ten years later. Philip Unwin, Stanley's nephew, who was responsible for buying one of the biggest sellers of the fifties – Thor Heyerdahl's *The Kon-Tiki Expedition* – retired in 1970, dying in 1981. Stanley Unwin was said to have been lukewarm about *Kon-Tiki* at the beginning but as soon as his salesmen had convinced him that the book had quite exceptional potential he ordered a second impression before publication of 27,000 copies. Thereafter it was kept in print throughout the period of peak demand, for more than a year, with different printers and binders working on large reprints simultaneously.

Allen & Unwin also entered the egg-head paperback market early and, with their increasingly large social sciences list, came to issue cased and paper bound editions simultaneously. Under Rayner Unwin a trend observable in most companies, of making senior employees directors whether or not they had appreciable shareholdings, was reversed. By 1980 there were only three members of the board. The trade department had for long been at Hemel Hempstead in Hertfordshire where the books warehoused indicated a much greater degree of specialisation than in the company's previous history. This was deliberate policy, to provide books for the academic market against a known demand in order to weather the recession, rather than speculate in the general market, although as a paperback imprint the egg-head image was scrambled by the huge success of certain humorous titles concerned with graffiti. Would, it was wondered, Unwin accept this as writing on the wall? As with most firms there were redundancies at all levels, and especially the top. John Bright-Holmes, editor of general books for seven years, left in 1980 and later joined the Search Press, a Roman Catholic list which had taken over 238 titles formerly on the Burns & Oates catalogue. R.C. publishers were badly hit by a papal encyclical which did away with missals. Mrs Charlotte de la Bedoyere struggled to survive under the umbrella of Herder & Herder, of New York, a subsidiary of the German company Verlag Herder. When she broke from them she turned a £30,000 loss into a £17,000 profit in one year by broadening her list to include leisure crafts for which she found an instant demand. Associated with the Search Press for a while were Darton, Longman and Todd, a mostly theological imprint, which published the Jerusalem Bible, a version in contemporary English. Michael Longman was the last male of his line to work in publishing. He died in 1978.

Amongst the companies which started in the nineteenth century and which remained independent, or more or less so, were Dent, Constable, Duckworth, Batsford, Pitman and Warne. Of these Warne was a public company though its shares were not quoted on the stock exchange, and the two major shareholders in Batsford were Midland Bank Industrial Finance Ltd and Charterhouse Development Ltd; but neither was part of a group.

Until Cyril Stephens' death in 1981 the Stephens family continued to manage Warne's which moved back into Bedford Square in 1970 although not into the house occupied by the founder. For years the company appeared to coast along on its back list. Titles were added to the Observer series regularly and the Beatrix Potter stories spawned something of an industry. There were board games and book cases and then a flood of books about the author's life and art. Her journal was published, then a history of her writings and a fine biography by Margaret Lane. The management came to realise, however, that it could not live by rabbit alone and the removal to Bedford Square gave a new impetus to growth. The young Leo Cooper list, and the much older (1744) Seeley, Service imprint were bought in 1979 as one, together with the services of Cooper whose specialisation was militaria. Warne also bought Gerrard Publications which had a series of walks for motorists, and even for walkers. (Cooper joined Secker & Warburg some months after Stephens' death.)

The colourful Harry Batsford died in 1951 and was succeeded by his nephew Brian Cook, who changed his name at his uncle's request. Brian Batsford became a Conservative MP but being a man of prodigious energy he contrived to combine his duties, working as a publisher until lunchtime, then going to the House for the rest of the day, and sometimes the night. When he was appointed a government whip Sam Carr became managing director but the style of publishing altered little. Books entitled *Britain* or *England* or *London in Colour* continued to appear at frequent intervals. The authors varied, so usually did the illustrations but the subjects were dictated by the tourist trade. There were also series on battles and on everday life at different periods of history, and they made a successful early entry into the nostalgia market with many volumes of photographs taken in Victorian and Edwardian times. Brian Batsford, knighted in 1974, retired from both the board and from Parliament in that year, when there was a redistribution of the shares in the company with the object of maintaining its independence.

At Dent's the pattern for the first twenty-five years after the war was similar to that of other elderly companies. The Everyman list continued to expand and was put into paperback; there were new editions of the Encyclopaedia, some successes in children's publishing under Gwen Marsh, while one new author who did not fit naturally into the list made much money for it – the poet Dylan Thomas. Dent's reader Richard Church did not like the poems of the young Welshman but listened to the advice of Ralph Abercrombie and his brothers, and bought them. After Thomas's early death from alcoholism they sold by the tens of thousands, as did his radio play *Under Milkwood*. Curiously the success of Dylan Thomas did not lead to the building of a significant list of contemporary poetry.

A subsidiary, Phoenix House, was started in 1948 with John Baker given absolute freedom to publish what he liked, which included many books sponsored by Shell. Baker also continued to run the Reader's Union book club and became sales director of Dent itself until, in 1963, he bought the Richards and Unicorn Presses from Martin Secker and ran them as John Baker Ltd until his death in 1971. Dent's sold the book club to David & Charles (see below) in 1970, at the beginning of a decade when they divested themselves of much else including Aldine House, the freehold premises in Bedford Street, and, in 1980, their bindery at Letchworth. By then, under Piers Raymond who succeeded F.J. Martin Dent, grandson of the founder, as M.D. in 1977, a distribution organisation for other publishers was set up. In 1979, following losses in previous years, the net profit was only £24,000, partly due to the sixth edition of the *Everyman Enclyclopaedia* which was estimated to cost £300,000, but became a victim of inflation and ran up a bill of nearly £1m; in 1980 it was de-netted and sold to booksellers for £97.50 a set. Early in 1981 Piers Raymond resigned.

W. & R. Chambers, famous for even longer than Dent as encyclopaedia publishers, sold theirs, by lease, to Robert Maxwell's Buckingham Press, via Newnes, Odhams and Hamlyn, in 1966. A decade previously they had ceased publishing their *Journal* after 134 years. They remained healthily in the dictionary business, however, and added several new items in that category to their list, to challenge O.U.P. and others, and had the satisfaction of seeing their *Twentieth Century Dictionary* adopted as a reference work by the National Scrabble Club in 1979.

Pitman's remained large, mostly educational, publishers with R.H. Code Holland as publishing director for many years. Sir James Pitman, whose idea Book Centre was, left the company in 1964 to concentrate on popularising the Initial Teaching Alphabet which he had invented but which teachers were reluctant to use. Pitman's also had a medical imprint, and until 1981 when it was bought by Butterworth owned the Focal Press, specialising in photographic books. It was started by Andor Krasna-Krausz, a Hungarian who had worked in Germany for eighteen years. He sold out to Pitman in 1962 but continued to run Focal for them until 1978. At a retirement ceremony in Cologne he was described as 'having had more direct influence in the last fifty years on the art and science of photography than anyone else in the world'.

Constable, which remained in its Orange Street offices, was bought in 1962 by Ben Glazebrook, previously with Heinemann, and Donald Hyde, an American bibliophile. It then had a flourishing children's list under Grace Hogarth, but this had to go when she retired, not just for that reason but because Hyde had died and there were death duties to pay. Constable's did not grow as fast as some of their new competitors but they retained a reputation for high class biography, history and travel, in the last category building an excellent library of bulky pocket-sized walking guides. They had the Dover concession for most of this time, a rare case of an American publisher remaining with the same British distributor for more than a few years.

Duckworth's also changed hands, and offices. Mervyn Horder, who became a peer on the death of his eminent physician father, ruled over a small but valuable list from 1949 with the inestimable help of A.G. Lewis (manager 1923-50) who, perhaps extravagantly, claimed to have taught Stanley Unwin all that gentleman knew about publishing whilst they were together at Fisher Unwin's. The debt is not acknowledged in Sir Stanley's memoirs. Horder sold to Colin Haycraft who moved from Henrietta Street to eccentric premises in an ex-piano factory in Camden Town, north west London. Here, in a circular building with an office most easily reached by climbing the fire escape, he presided over a general list, the high prices of which often provoked discussion amongst librarians and booksellers. Visiting customers were sometimes chided by him for not selling more copies of the novels of Beryl Bainbridge whom Haycraft discovered. The lady herself was sometimes to be seen actually writing one of her books in the office, which Mervyn Horder continued to frequent. On one occasion they both stopped work and went to the piano to regale this author with a ballad. May there always be room for the Duckworths of publishing.

Sidgwick & Jackson was under the direction of J. Knapp-Fisher until 1970 when he sold to the catering industry magnate, Charles Forte. Sidgwick's had kept a low profile immediately after the war although for a while an S.F. list was built when that genre became suddenly popular. The image changed dramatically in the seventies when Forte installed Lord Longford, most of whose family were furiously writing for other publishers, as chairman, and William Armstrong as editorial (later managing) director. Together they aimed at the big time and attracted many celebrities, notably ex-prime minister Edward Heath who wrote volumes on music, travel and sailing, to promote which he toured the country ceaselessly, signing thousands of copies with the alacrity of a politician used to kissing innumerable babies. Signing sessions, which had always enjoyed a vogue at London department stores, became all the rage. Any publisher with a book by a famous sportsman, statesman or media celebrity, toured the country (even the world in the cases of Frank Muir and Joyce Grenfell) with his author in tow, sometimes selling huge quantities. At W.H.S. Brent Cross, another ex-premier, Harold Wilson, even got away with signing copies of his *The Governance of Britain* for the almost certainly tory-voting matrons of Hendon and Finchley who probably thought the word 'governance' was a misprint for 'government'. Wilson's wife Mary was even more successful with her verse which Hutchinson published and which drew crowds of eager buyers to signing sessions at Harrods and Selfridges.

Sir Ernest Benn died in 1954 and thereafter his family, who retained an interest in publishing, tended to care more for their journals and yearbooks than for the trade list. The latter had, as its centrepiece, the excellent Blue Guides and a children's list on which it was proposed to concentrate after a loss was incurred in 1980.

Benn's sometime managing director, Victor Gollancz, remained firmly in control of his company until his death in 1967, although he had by then suffered a stroke. For most of the period, he was active as ever in politics and publishing, also finding time to write books, some in the form of a diary to his godson, Timothy. When he died his daughter Livia took over, with John Bush, who might be described as the one who survived, as her joint managing director. They had the difficult task of convincing authors, some of whom had remained on the list because they were too terrified to tell V.G. they wished to move, that the Gollancz list would continue to be as positively promoted and sold as in the past. They kept their heads down for a few years and won through.

Those who did not stay at Henrietta Street make a very distinguished roll call. Hilary Rubinstein, V.G.'s son-in-law, discoverer of Kingsley Amis, whose *Lucky Jim* ushered the anti-hero into Eng. Lit.; James MacGibbon who brought the Russian dissident Solzhenitsyn's *One Day in the Life of Ivan Denisovitch*; Giles Gordon, an editor at Hutchinson and Penguin, and a novelist himself; John Gross, later editor of the T.L.S., and others. The list lost John Le Carré whose *The Spy Who Came in From the Cold* was turned into a best-seller months after publication thanks to a mention by Graham Greene in a Books of the Year column. Amis and Solzhenitsyn also moved to other publishers.

V.G., hurt by Le Carré's defection to Heinemann, commented, 'In my own good time I shall tell the whole story . . . an affair of the greatest import to every publisher in the land'. He never did; probably he forgot about it because, like Billy Collins, he was always alert for the next enthusiasm, which might be expressed in a jacket blurb starting in the usual place, then proceeding to the back flap (again not unusual) but after that taking off to encompass not only the entire back of the jacket but the whole inside of it as well. His colleagues could not always go along with his recommendations but he was a great publisher and held in affection by all who cared for people and apparently lost causes. It should never be forgotten that he, a Jew, was amongst the first to sponsor help for the broken German nation after the second war. His humanitarianism may not always have been apparent to his senior colleagues during the day-to-day hustle of business, but he was a big man in every sense, and widely loved.

V.G.'s voluntary work was done outside the book trade; Geoffrey Faber (who died in 1961) and his successors were very much involved in the running of the P.A. and other trade institutions. The growth at Faber's was controlled. In 1940, 177 new books were published; in 1950, 216; 1960, 268; 1970, 276; and in 1980 it dropped to 160. The staff grew from 109 in 1950 to 118 in 1980. As always the list reflected most categories of publishing, and was especially strong in poetry, even after the death of T.S. Eliot. The play library was much developed after Charles Monteith's purchase of John Osborne's seminal *Look Back in Anger,* and the immense popularity of Lawrence Durrell's *Alexandrian Quartet* encouraged the board to demonstrate that Faber had just the backlist for a successful paperback imprint, and one large enough to allow for frequent injection of new titles. They also found new authors, such as William Golding and Ted Hughes, to provide regular lead titles.

Peter du Sautoy, having previously been at the British Museum and in education, joined Faber in 1946 and rose to be vice-chairman in 1971. He brought in his successor, Matthew Evans, son of George Ewart Evans, a Faber author, and then a young graduate with bookshop experience at Dillon's. By 1980 Evans had proved himself acceptable not only to Faber but to the trade. He was chairman-designate of the National Book League and on the Council of the Publishers Association. By this time Faber was calling itself a group but, apart from a holding company of which one of Geoffrey Faber's sons was Chairman, its only other component was Faber Music, another of du Sautoy's enthusiasms, of which Benjamin Britten was a board member at one time.

Of those not already mentioned in detail one name stands out amongst the new publishers in this period and that is André Deutsch who, for thirty years, has weathered the takeover and merger storms, the economic climate of the late seventies and all the alarms and excursions of the international publishing world. His first book, 1950, was called *Books are Essential* and had contributions from the then pundits of the trade. Nothing could more have belied what was to follow because although Deutsch has always believed in cooperation between publisher and bookseller, and publisher and publisher, the rather fusty, *belles-lettres,* image evoked by that first book did not indicate in any way the determination and acumen which was to place him right at the top of his particular division for a long while. He sold shares to Time-Life of America but he soon re-purchased them; he was offered unlimited finance by a newspaper magnate to develop a new list but refused. To the party he held for the twenty-fifth anniversary of his imprint he invited everyone who had ever worked for him, plus those who had been offered jobs and turned them down. Scores of those who had left him after some disagreement, major or minor, attended that party without rancour. The number of ex-sales managers present was a subject for dispute; exsecretaries and editorial assistants moved about the buffet supper tables in bevies, those now distinguished in other fields of activity boasting of being in the class of '54 or '66. It should be mentioned, too, that colleagues of long standing were also present – Diana Athill, editorial director, and Nicolas Bentley, author and artist, both of whom had been with Deutsch from the beginning. Others also stayed for long periods because, if their faces fitted, it was an invigorating experience. He was primarily concerned with creative publishing, had the true publisher's flair for finding authors worthy of being seen in print and also the equally true publisher's sense of survival in buying authors who would keep him solvent. He was not markedly acquisitive of other lists although in 1961 he bought the fading imprint of Grafton, which brought him into touch with the world of librarianship, and, from the receiver of the company he directed for a while, Allan Wingate, he obtained the rights again in the works of his boyhood friend, George Mikes, a fellow Hungarian, whose *How to be an Alien* has become a classic of English humour. The Grafton list was sold to Gower Publishing in 1981.

Ernest Hecht, also a refugee from middle Europe, and founder of the Souvenir Press, once told of a visiting American publisher's remark – 'It's lovely to come to London and meet English publishers'. 'Sure,' gagged Hecht. 'Like Mr Weidenfeld, Mr Neurath, Mr Deutsch . . .'

Such visitors would have been hard-pressed to meet Mr Hecht himself who, despite building up a publishing business and diversifying into theatrical management and literary agency, was often abroad attending to his passion for watching football, cricket or athletics. He became a publisher because, on leaving Hull University, he failed to get the job he wanted as secretary to the Universities Athletic Association. His first book was a 2s. paperback about the England cricketer Len Hutton. Next he borrowed £250 from his parents and worked from home establishing the Souvenir Press, with a staff consisting of himself and a secretary. Later he moved to offices in Bloomsbury Street where he displayed a poster for a bullfight in which he was falsely billed as a toreador, and proceeded to publish quiet bestsellers about sportsmen and pop singers, and also the *Trachtenberg Speed System of Mathematics* (100,000 copies in a year). When, because he had published some fiction, Arthur Hailey came his way, he realised that his small organisation could not cope with his potential sales so he published jointly with Michael Joseph. He kept an interest in Hailey titles and expanded his own organisation to deal with other potential bestsellers, of which not a few came his way. He also developed a quality side to his list with Condor paperbacks, some of the works of Jean-Luis Borges and new translations of Knut Hamsun. A sub-division of Condor was the Human Horizons series designed to help the physically and mentally handicapped. Hecht was justifiably proud of having established it in the U.S.A. and many western European countries without government or institutional subsidy.

Ernest Hecht disproved the theory that a publisher starting in the fifties must have large capital resources. He kept his overheads to a minimum, farmed out his distribution, and remained independent, probably enjoying his publishing life more than any of his contemporaries.

One with whom he was associated through sharing reps was Jeremy Robson, who, after working at Harrap's and elsewhere, founded his own company in 1973, at the age of thirty-four. He specialised in humour and music and kept his staff small. Unlike Hecht, in 1981 he took the decision to undertake his own warehousing and distribution. He was then publishing about fifty-five books annually and had a staff of eight. It is too early to state that he successfully reversed a trend.

Others of varying sizes who survived these years as new imprints were Peter Owen, who contrived to keep a small literary list going on a shoestring (he started on £900 in 1951) and who tended towards the experimental in fiction, as did John Calder, publisher of the French avant-garde and, more profitably, of Henry Miller's *Tropics*; Desmond Elliott, whose Arlington Books was started when he had tired of being employed as a publicity manager by larger companies, and who found a market for cookery books and popular fiction; Peter Wolfe, who after making a considerable impact with various series of books of humorous appeal, became a medical publisher; Elliot Right Way Books, run by an industrious Scot who insisted on clearing each day's orders before he knocked off, and who claimed to love filling single copy orders for his instructional manuals on all subjects; Guinness Superlatives Ltd, a subsidiary of the brewing company which issued, in 1955, its *Book of Records*, a reference work designed to settle arguments in the 75,000 pubs of the British Isles, yet found increasingly in ten times that number of dwellings as each annual edition sold out its huge print run; and David & Charles, a company based in Newton Abbott, Devonshire, where it once had offices on the actual railway station. This reflected the preoccupation with trains of the founding partners – David St. John Thomas and Charles Hadfield. As they grew they embraced the whole field of general publishing although they never took to novels, which didn't stop Thomas from writing a book about writing fiction. Finally, a list which is now five years old at the time of writing – Virago, started by Carmen Callil, who had worked for various London publishers, an Australian who has made a vivid mark upon contemporary publishing by exploiting the woman's movement. She has done it by applying the sound publishing principle of reprinting books for which a market could be seen – works by writers well-known in their time but slightly forgotten now, and also by authors given a new lease of life through the media. An example is Vera Brittain's *Testament of Youth*, a book which V.G. printed once too often about thirty years ago and which was lying unwanted in every bookshop in the land.

In 1982 Carmen Callil joined Chatto & Windus on the retirement of Norah Smallwood, as joint managing director with Hugo Brunner (see also page 108), and publishing director. Virago became part of the Chatto, Bodley Head & Cape Group, although retaining, as did the other components, editorial independence, with Carmen Callil remaining chairman.

The
Paperback Revolution

The rapid growth in educational and technical books was one aspect of the meteoric rise in paperback production. The word 'revolutionary' has been applied unstintingly in this connection but it was really 'evolutionary' in that it took so long to come about, even if one dates it only from the start of Penguin in 1935. Allen Lane had a sufficiently clear field for twenty years to let him thrive on the competition when paperbacks took hold of the public imagination and he expanded at a rate which made his early progress appear snail-paced and trivial. He was undisputably in the lead in 1970, the year of his death, but ten years later, although Penguin was still the largest single imprint, the combined force of its rivals was much greater.

To return to the fifties when it all began to gain pace, alongside the popular paperbacks – mostly fiction, romance, crime and war stories – were soon ranged non-fiction series which, because of their highbrow content, came to be known as 'egg-heads'. At first these were imported from the States – Harper Torchbooks, Ann Arbor's, and so on – but the university presses in England took to the idea and issued their own academic works in paper covers. Publishers such as Faber, Macmillan, Methuen and Routledge followed suit. It soon became evident that there were no limits to what might be paperbacked, even large format art books and dictionaries.

The appearance of bookshops changed rapidly to accommodate the phenomenon, and publishers vied with each other to provide free fittings for their own ranges. Penguin took the lead, installing Penguin Bookshops either in separate premises, as at Heffer's in Cambridge, and Collet's, Charing Cross Road, or as sections of existing bookshops. By 1970 they were also undertaking to put in fittings for other paperback publishers and getting their competitors to meet some of the booksellers' costs. It was a novel situation for the bookseller who was unused to being wooed, or to receiving so much stock on a returnable basis. As a result the sale-or-return system spread to hardbacks because publishers found it increasingly difficult to place the ever-growing number of new titles which by some law, possibly Parkinson's, expanded as the demand for most individual general books decreased.

Series such as Everyman and Arden started to appear in paperback, often because they had more appeal that way and reached a public which was instinctively suspicious of the bound book, or regarded it as a luxury. The fact that it might cost only slightly less had no bearing; in some instances the paperback was more expensive than the original cased edition and by the seventies it was quite common for it to be considerably so. (Clark's *Civilisation*, for instance, began as a hardback at £4.4s.0d in 1970; in 1980, the paperback cost £7.00; the hardback £12.00.)

An important ingredient in the paperback revolution was the lack of taboos about how the books should be handled. Previously children had been taught not to illtreat books which were examples of craftsmanship whose bindings should not be broken, whose pages should not be dog-eared or annotated, and which should only be touched with clean hands. It was not so with paperbacks. They could be stuffed into pockets, left lying open and upside down, or bent back at the page last read. Coffee cups and beer mugs could be placed upon them, and they were eminently suitable for reading on beaches and in the bath, although as their price soared this became less true of the more expensive cellophane-wrapped items.

All trends being reversible, even by the setter, Penguin once again took the lead in 1967 when Allen Lane The Penguin Press was formed to publish original hardbacks from the offices in Vigo Street where John Lane had once presided over The Bodley Head. It was created to ensure that Penguins should have first call on worthwhile non-fiction in the event of traditional publishers keeping their bestselling titles for their own softback series. Until the late fifties Penguin had the automatic choice of most fiction and non-fiction, but the success of Pan, Panther, Fontana (owned by Collins), Corgi, New English Library and others made bidding inevitable. There was usually sufficient fiction to go round and Penguin, in the main, went for titles more up-market than appealed to Pan and Corgi, but the situation was fluid. Gradually the advances paid for paperback rights came to matter more and more to the original, or even intending, publishers of the hardback. Penguin's nose was thrust sideways several times. Its policy fluctuated between assumed indifference and fighting back.

'Penguin' came to mean 'paperback' which was as much a compliment to Harmondsworth as it was an irritant to those struggling to establish their own image. Of the three Lane brothers only John, killed in action in 1942, did not survive to witness the amazing expansion of the quarter of a century after the war, a time during which Allen Lane nearly always held the reins himself. The pre-war birds were joined by new breeds; some of the newcomers did not make the grade, a few of the old ones were honourably retired, but for most of the flock the flight was exhilarating.

The first Penguin classic, *The Odyssey* of Homer, appeared in January 1946, translated into modern English by Dr. E.V. Rieu, who had undertaken the task as an antidote to boredom whilst firewatching during the blitz. Dr. Rieu became editor of the series and translated other classics, among them *The Four Gospels*, work on which contributed to his conversion to Christianity. His principal colleague until 1960 was Alan Grover, who was also responsible for Pelicans.

Other ventures included Penguin Prints which, alas, never got under way; Penguin Modern Painters, edited by Kenneth Clark; Music Scores; and the Buildings of England. Modern Painters eventually foundered but had considerable success for a while at 3s.6d each for thirty-two plates, half of them in colour. The music scores were started when Allen Lane became bored at an editorial meeting. Jack Morpurgo, recognising the danger signs, thought it expedient for someone to have an idea; next day he was instructed to get the series going. The fact that Morpurgo was an historian was irrelevant to Lane who, if he liked the idea, wished to see it followed through at once. It was his genius not to question or cost a project which had the true Penguin flavour of daring and originality, but to expect those whom he employed to make it economically viable. If, after trial, it could not pay its way then it had to be discontinued. Or subsidised, as was the Buildings of England library. That incomparable series was born in Allen Lane's rose garden one afternoon when he asked his guest, Professor Nikolaus Pevsner, what he would most like Penguin to publish. Pevsner replied unhesitatingly, rapidly outlining plans for architectural guides to all the counties of England, noting their chief buildings from pre-history onwards, and also for a library of world art. Lane undertook to publish both, and they are still on the Penguin list in 1981, with volumes on Buildings of Scotland and Wales already appearing. The Pelican History of Art and Architecture started as hardbacks but went into paper from 1970; the Buildings of England began in paper at 6s. in 1951 but new titles and reprints were all in stiff bindings by 1980 when some exceeded £10 in price. Even so they represented years of painstaking work by Pevsner and those who assisted him with the later volumes. No reference books were more pithily and wittily written, and for long they were a labour of love only. For nearly twenty years no royalty was paid on them.

It was appropriate that Penguin No. 1,000, in 1954, was *One of our Submarines*; Edward Young, its author, drew the first Penguin colophons and was one of the original staff in the crypt of Holy Trinity Church. Allen Lane delighted in such acts of sentiment which helped to keep the firm human. The 1,000th Pelican did not arrive until 1968 by which time there were 2,662 books in print on the entire list, and the new warehouse at Harmondsworth housed 24 million books and could hold 40 million. By 1960 twelve titles had each sold one million copies, including Rieu's *Odyssey*, Kitto's *The Greeks*, and *Animal Farm*.

In 1956 Penguin's was a private limited company with Allen and Richard Lane owning all the shares. In 1961 it went public. The 750,000 ordinary shares were over-subscribed on the first day when their value rose by 40%. Allen Lane increased his personal holding to 51% and, three years later, made a gift of £100,000 to create a staff pension fund in memory of his brother John. He sought to safeguard the future of Penguin's by forming a trust but continued to prevaricate in naming a successor. An early candidate was Tony Godwin who lasted seven years. Under his direction, the egg-head Peregrines were introduced, also the confusingly named Modern Classics. He brought his own particular vigour to the job which made a clash of personalities inevitable because he and Lane were both accustomed to having their own way. Both could be prickly and mercurial, neither tolerated fools. A row broke out when it was apparent that large though Penguin's had grown it could not contain both men, which was a pity because if ever there was a natural successor to Allen Lane it was Godwin. When he left several of his team wrote to *The Bookseller* stating that he had 'extended the range of the list with vision and imagination, and we who were his editorial colleagues felt at every point his intense concern for quality and purpose'.

Amongst the signatories were Dieter Pevsner (son of Nikolaus), Oliver Caldecott, Giles Gordon and Charles Clark, all of whom had resigned or signalled their departure by mid-1972. One who signed but stayed was Kaye Webb, who took over the editorship of Puffins when Eleanor Graham retired. Under her dynamic and loving leadership the reputations of such excellent contemporary writers for children as Joan Aiken, Leon Garfield and Alan Garner were enhanced, and their work brought to the attention of millions. In five years from 1963 to 1968 Puffin sales trebled ($3\frac{1}{4}$ million sold in 1968) and by 1970 they had the greatest growth of all the birds. To stimulate her young readership Kaye Webb started the Puffin Club which had a membership of 50,000 by 1972. Puffin Post, sent to them four times a year, was a wittily illustrated, lightly written magazine, brimful of competitions, letters and news of club outings and plays. In some households its quarterly arrival was as eagerly awaited by the parents as by the children. Directly in the Allen Lane tradition Kaye Webb introduced original Puffins, which sometimes went to other publishers as hardbacks, and also the Young Puffin List. When the Longman–Penguin merger occurred, she took charge of the Kestrel hardback list as well. This grew out of Longman Young Books, which had itself absorbed Constable Young Books. She retired in 1979 although remaining president of the Puffin Club. Apart from her work at Harmondsworth she was active in various organisations dedicated to bringing children and books together; despite ill-health she worked almost ceaselessly to this end for twenty years.

What happened editorially continued to be exciting at Penguin in the decade after Allen Lane's death, apart from an over-proliferation of social science titles which became loosely grouped together as Penguin Education, and which down-graded Pelicans in importance. Administratively the atmosphere was tense and the turnover of top executives high.

Lane's successor was Christopher Dolley, a Unilever-trained executive, who had made a success of Penguin's in America. In 1973 he was succeeded by Peter Calvocoressi, an author, who had been with Chatto & Windus. His reign was equally short and in 1976 he departed six months before the expiration of his contract because 'his judgements as a professional publisher ... had for two years been increasingly at variance with, and increasingly ignored by, the chairman and the board ...' Anthony Mott then became editorial director until late 1978 when he too went, shortly after the appointment of the English-born American Peter Mayer as chief executive. Mayer, who had lived in the States since he was three, had had a highly successful career in paperback publishing across the Atlantic, and arrived in Harmondsworth with the reputation of being a whizz-kid. He moved the offices to Fulham and quickly became the centre of industrial unrest when he announced redundancies. In 1979 Penguin, including Allen Lane, declared a pretax loss of £381,000, but there was some improvement in 1980, and much more in 1981.

Despite the many changes of personnel at top level there were a number of survivors. Harry Paroissien, from whom Dolley took over in America, had a period of being second-in-command to Lane and was one of his trustees; Hans Schmoller, who had contributed so much to the design of Penguins, retired honourably in 1976 after twenty-six years service, while Ronald Blass, with an almost rags-to-riches story, was still in 1981 vice-chairman.

Blass was an odd-job man in the early forties who packed, drove a van and made himself generally useful, until he was called up. After demobilisation he returned to Harmondsworth to ascertain his prospects, and was told by the company secretary that he could re-start at £4 15s. a week. He declined but on his way out met Allen and Richard Lane cycling in. He was greeted enthusiastically and the King Penguin expressed regret that he was not rejoining the firm. Next morning Blass received an offer of £5 a week and so admired the effrontery of it that he accepted. Soon he was being used on special missions, travelling abroad to organise warehousing at overseas bases and even, on one occasion, being packed off to Florida for a holiday. In 1962 he succeeded Bruce Hepburn as sales director and stage-managed the introduction of a computer and a vast extension to the warehouse. He also furthered the establishment of Penguin shops-within-bookshops, of which there were more than one hundred by 1969. He was made one of

Lane's trustees and by 1976 was joint managing director. He was there at the top throughout the difficult seventies during which Pearson-Longman bought up all the shares, thus making Penguin a wholly-owned subsidiary, and a controlling interest was purchased in the American Viking Press.

Allen Lane did not in any way foresee what would happen to his brainchild. Perhaps, so huge had it grown, he could not have prevented it from becoming part of another empire even if he had lived ten years longer. When your offspring becomes a household word on all continents it is out of personal control. Whilst he lived Lane derived enormous pleasure and great wealth from Penguin, and liked to foster the various myths which grew up around him from the origin of the Pelican name to his alleged semi-literacy. He was not much of a public figure, took little part in trade affairs and, when he spoke, kept it brief. Nonetheless, official honours came his way – a knighthood in 1962, a Companionship of Honour in 1969 in which year he also received the Gold Albert Medal of the Royal Society 'for his contribution to publishing and education'. Unofficially he was honoured wherever Penguin Books were read.

I have dwelt at length on Penguin because it is part of our cultural history and its record embodies so many aspects of the trends of publishing in this period.

The records of other paperback companies pale by comparison but are by no means negligible. Pan Books started in 1944 as an independent subsidiary of the Book Society with Aubrey Forshaw as managing director, a position he retained until Ralph Vernon-Hunt succeeded him in 1970. Forshaw said of Pan 'We are in middle-of-the-road entertainment', and this remained true for most of the time, although they published a number of higher-brow titles in their Pan Piper non-fiction series. By 1980 with Simon Master now M.D. their turnover, of which almost one-third came from exports, was nearly half that of Penguin's; they were owned jointly by Collins, Heinemann's and Macmillan's, each of whom held 660,000 shares.

Ralph Vernon-Hunt, having been for a short while a bookseller's assistant at Hudson's in Birmingham after being demobbed, became Pan's sales director in 1950. He was well-known for his practice of telling booksellers that their shops were forbidding to would-be readers. This he did without offence because his forthright attitude coupled with his humour won him respect. He was certainly one of those who helped, through the paperback revolution, to make bookshops less intimidating. Having achieved this, he offered genuine inducements to booksellers in the way of bonuses on increased turnover which, when successful, led to the issuing of large credit notes. (Collins and Thames & Hudson had a similar scheme but they sent cheques.)

Pan's success was remarkable for reasons quite different from Penguin's. Whereas the latter concentrated on building a huge backlist which was its pride, Pan's method was to keep the number of titles in print to a minimum but sell more of each. (In 1955 they had 150 titles in print and sold 8 million books; Penguin had 1,000 and sold 10 million.) In 1980 Pan's turnover was almost £16m with a profit of £565,000.

Among their greatest sellers were the novels of Ian Fleming which approached 30 million by 1972, and *The Diary of Anne Frank*, the millionth copy of which was sold in 1971. In 1975, Vernon-Hunt took Pan into bookselling, opening a shop below their offices in Fulham Road, London. It aimed to stock 10,000 titles and proved so successful that more followed. (Penguin also went into bookselling, opening a shop in the Covent Garden complex in 1979.)

The early Panther books would not have won a prize from anyone for quality of production but in 1962 under the joint managing editorship of William Miller and John Boothe they became better-looking and acquired a literary status with Nabokov, Mary McCarthy, Jean Genet, Doris Lessing and Norman Mailer. (There was also *The Kama Sutra*.) In the late sixties the Paladin series of Pelican-type titles was planned by Tony Richardson, an ex-Harmondsworth man who tragically did not live to see their publication. By then Panther was part of the Granada group, which also owned Mayflower, an imprint which had achieved some notoriety under its previous American owners. The London M.D., Gareth Powell (a truck driver who became a reporter on Smith's *Trade News* before entering publishing) brought out an unexpurgated edition of the *Memoirs of Fanny Hill*, whose adventures had been a good line on the secondhand porn market throughout the century. Mayflower were prosecuted and Powell moved on to the New English Library. Boothe and Miller left Paladin to start their own company, Quartet Books, but the former returned to Granada in 1980 as deputy editorial director of a much-enlarged paperback list provided with titles published by the hardback division. In 1976 Quartet became part of the Namara Group owned by a Palestinian Arab financier long resident in Britain, Naim Atallah. Namara also ran a literary magazine and a London-based wholesaler, Pipeline Books.

By now literary agents had successfully contested the fifty-fifty royalty split between hardback and paperback publishers, so it was advantageous to the original publisher to paperback his own books. Usually, auctions were held, as when Hutchinson paid over £1m for a Frederick Forsyth title, though they did not sell it to their own paperback imprint, Arrow. Instead it went to Corgi, who from being like Panther a very down-market imprint with its books shoddily produced, rose to third or fourth place in the paperback table by 1980. As well as Forsyth, they had immense success with Joseph Heller's *Catch 22* (for which they outbid Penguin), the romantic novelist Catherine Cookson, and an author of westerns, J.T. Edson, whose books they published as paperback originals. Pat Newman who was responsible in the early days, with editor Alan Earney, for improving the look of Corgi books, became chairman and chief executive in 1979, but was succeeded by Paul Scherer in 1982.

Many of Collins' bestsellers went to Fontana but the process was not automatic, the paperback company being run autonomously, with its own sales force. It had many strands including a strong religious list edited until 1981 by Lady Collins; the Modern Masters series (egg-heads); a very healthy thriller section, leaning, obviously, on the hardback Crime Club for new titles; and a formidable selection of fiction at various levels. There was also a children's imprint, Armada.

The New English Library, now part of Hodder & Stoughton, was an off-shoot of the New American Library, started by Victor Weybright, but in 1980 owned by an American newspaper group. N.E.L. absorbed Four Square Books, a list started in the fifties by a tobacco company which had already taken over Ace Books; through N.E.L., the Signet and Mentor paperbacks, many of them quite unnecessarily duplicating classic works of English literature available in other series, were brought to Britain. Later N.E.L. branched out into hardbacks and published Harold Robbins' best-selling novels.

Other hardback publishers paperbacked their own successful titles, Batsford and Murray, for instance, and Faber who stopped leasing many of their titles to Penguin. At Macdonald's, Futura competed vigorously with the Pans and Fontanas for prestigious titles.

Many English classics appeared not only as Penguins, but in softback Everyman Library editions. These were not as attractive as they might have been, clinging to the rather stuffy appearance of their forebears. Oxford's World Classics also went into paper in 1980.

There was also the Thomson-owned Sphere Books, another imprint which survived after the big boom period during which anything, or almost anything, published in paperback sold, was over. Some firms in the seventies estimated that they had returns of 40% of what they sold which was obviously uneconomic for both sides of the trade, and by the early eighties it was being suggested that sale-or-return selling would have to be ended. But it is doubtful, given the competition for retailing space, if this will happen.

Trade Matters

Under an Act of 1966, a Restrictive Practices Court was set up one year later because of a growing feeling amongst MPs and the public that price fixing between manufacturers and traders was making certain articles, such as electric light bulbs, more expensive than they need be. The Act made it illegal for manufacturers collectively to restrain a retailer from selling at less than the recommended price, although they were permitted to take action individually against the person or company breaching their conditions of sale, at least until such time as their trade agreement was disallowed. For this reason the 1900 Net Book Agreement had to be replaced by a new one in 1957, and it was that which was in due course examined by the court. Most trade agreements were disallowed by the Registrar as being against the public interest. The book trade spent large sums of money briefing lawyers in readiness for its own case which was heard in 1962. There were few dissenting voices amongst publishers; only Paul Hamlyn and James MacGibbon, to my knowledge, spoke out against netting. Most booksellers, uneasy about the possibility of High Street supermarkets undercutting them on Oxford dictionaries and other bread-and-butter lines, gave solid support to the defence. They believed it was very much in their interests to do so rather than becoming engaged in a price war.

It fell to Gerry Davies and Ronald Barker as secretaries of the B.A. and P.A. respectively to guide their associations through the intricacies of the case, advised by Michael Rubinstein, of Rubinstein, Nash & Co. Many distinguished booksellers, publishers, librarians and others were called to give evidence at a hearing lasting twenty-four days, and costing £40,000.

Four months later came the verdict. Mr Justice Buckley, in words which echoed around the trade, declared that 'no two literary works are the same or alike in the way in which, or the extent to which, two oranges or two eggs may be said to be', and went on to express his belief that if the agreement were not upheld the number of stockholding shops in the country would be reduced, and the extent of stock held by those who survived would present less variety; that fewer titles would be published and that the retail prices of books would go up. Trade terms, he said, were neither uniform nor immutable, net profits earned by booksellers were modest compared with other branches of commerce and 'in the competitive state of the book trade publishers have so far been able to resist pressure by booksellers for higher rates of discount'.

The trade, almost to a person, cried with Shylock, 'O wise and upright judge' and then settled down to failing to protect the pound of flesh it had been awarded. Some books came to resemble each other quite unnervingly and it was not always possible to distinguish between them without comparing their ISBNs. The number of stockholding bookshops did not decline but thanks to their learning the advantages of stock control, which revealed horrific evidence of how long some titles took to sell, the extent of stock in particular categories showed less variety than before 1962, except in subjects which became suddenly popular, such as cinema and antiques. Mr Justice Buckley was correct in what he said about trade terms and their lack of uniformity but quite wrong in suggesting that the existence of the N.B.A. would keep down discounts to booksellers. They were already improving at the time of his pronouncement and went on doing so out of economic necessity, which had little to do with the 'competitive state' he mentioned. Margins increased because publishers still believed booksellers to be important as outlets for their merchandise, and because wholesalers again became necessary for effective distribution of many titles. Which meant that prices rose by more than was simply accountable for by the cost of raw material, labour, accommodation etc.

In addition to this development, unforeseen in the judgement in favour of the N.B.A., the trade – or rather the Publishers Association and W.H. Smith – then tied itself in knots to approve regulations for the introduction of new American-style book clubs.

We have seen how the original book clubs did not impinge on the traditional bookshop in taking sales from it so co-existence was unpainful. But when the clubs' membership was upset by the impact of television, the diminishing number of expatriates and the paperback revolution, book clubs declined, so understandably those running them looked for new stimulants to trade.

In America book club editions had been published simultaneously with trade publications for years. It was only a question of time before Britain followed suit, with publishers protesting that it was essential to do so if they were to go on issuing fiction and general books at all. If anyone asked, naively, why this was not an infringement of the N.B.A. he was told glibly that a book club was a club, implying membership by election, and that the cheaper price was available only to members, who received volumes with a book club imprint, not that of the original publisher. This humbug fooled no one, and publishers defending their behaviour piously pointed out that the Standard Conditions of Sale as set out in the N.B.A. had an exemption clause permitting them to sell on whatever terms they wished.

The largest operators in the new market were Book Club Associates, which was jointly owned by W.H. Smith and Doubleday, of New York. They regularly placed advertisements in the same quality newspapers which the book trade believed to be supported by book buyers. *The Sunday Times*, for instance, would carry pages of book reviews aimed at the intelligentsia, at the same time as printing a full-page spread in its colour supplement coyly wooing literate readers to become members of B.C.A., with inducements of almost free books — something not permitted to booksellers under the terms of the N.B.A. On occasion, the *Concise Oxford Dictionary*, then £6.75 in the shops, became one of a package of three books for £1 through the club.

Booksellers were mostly passive in their reactions simply because it became apparent that one half of the quality readership did not seem to be on blinking terms with the other. Shops not only did not suffer when a book club made a national special offer in a Sunday paper or the *Radio Times*, but even picked up sales at full price. This was proved by the experience of individual booksellers, publishers and B.C.A. But by 1980 there were protests that the clubs had gone too far and these were coming not only from booksellers but from literary agents who claimed that they and their clients were losing from cut-price sales. The fact that they were led by Michael Sissons, of A.D. Peters, whom all publishers respected, was a hopeful sign, but it did not prevent one club from opening High Street shops in which it sold current books at cut prices. Ostensibly sales were made only to members but even supposing this condition was strictly applied, which it was not, the operation made nonsense of the Net Book Agreement.

What was clear to everyone concerned was that there was a vast market for books amongst those who never entered bookshops either because, as Ralph Vernon-Hunt claimed, they were frightened of doing so, or because there was not one in the shopping areas they used. That must be the subject of the next chapter. To end this one, I must examine two others concerned with the law.

Since the late nineteenth century, British publishers had made agreements with their United States counterparts, when buying and selling rights, to divide the various world markets between them. The old British Empire and Commonwealth was normally regarded as an exclusive market for the British publisher, although Canadian rights were sometimes attached to the American market. During the second war British publishers had obvious difficulties in supplying their traditional overseas markets, some of which were temporarily lost through becoming enemy territory. American publishers, with a product untouched by economy regulations, competed in the old Empire market, particularly in Australasia where the trade took the reasonable view that if it could not obtain the British edition it should buy the more attractively bound and jacketed American version. This threat to markets without which its members could not exist led the P.A. to send urgent missions to the States, resulting in the British Market Agreement, which entitled our publishers to sell rights in what had been the British Empire (except Canada if the book was one of American origin), including the highly prized Australian market. Australia, sensing that it was still being thought of as colonial, which was how actual editions of novels sold to Australia were still stamped, negotiated to buy American rights direct. The Agreement received a more effective body blow when the U.S. Department of Justice indicted American publishers on a charge of conspiring to carve up world markets against the interests of free competition. The P.A. fought the ruling with the aid of American lawyers and a compromise was reached. The Market Agreement was dropped but individual companies were permitted to agree the division of exclusive rights on a book by book basis provided this reflected market strengths and broke no patterns. As a result British publishers had to fight harder to retain their export markets and, to this end, many who had formerly been content with employing agents formed subsidiary companies in the States and in Australia, to originate titles and to buy and sell rights independently of their U.K. overlords.

British publishers had other problems in Asia, where piracy, endemic since the nineteenth century, continued unabated in the printing shops of Taiwan and Singapore whose owners were not above reproducing editions of British books bearing the U.K. printers' names. There was little that could be done to prevent this in these countries, but with China and the Soviet bloc there was at least some official contact. There was no question of a Collins or a Longman setting up in Moscow or Peking but many delegations were sent to those capitals by the P.A. and other organisations which were, nevertheless, surprised when, in 1973, the Soviet Union signed the Universal Copyright Convention to which the U.S.A. had only acceded in 1955.

International copyright remained a major preoccupation of those few who understood it – notably Ronald Barker, secretary of the P.A. – and the many who thought they should. Immediately after World War Two the attitude of Russia was a major problem. As that vast country had not then become party to any U.C.C. provisions it was not breaking the law when its state publishing house issued translations from British books without permission and, usually, without paying any royalties. Russia was theoretically in the same position as was the U.S.A. until 1955 but, for the States, signature of the U.C.C. was only a regularisation of the status quo. American and British publishers were so close that it would have been inconvenient for either side not to have kept gentlemen's agreements. The Russians behaved differently and capriciously. Sometimes royalties were paid on foreign works, sometimes not. Missions from the P.A., always including Ron Barker, went to argue the case for international copyright in Moscow and presumably influenced the Russians into signing it. At least Russia had an understanding of copyright and had a domestic law about it. China had not, although after the death of Mao Tse Tung trainee publishers were sent to the West to study trade practices, at the same time as delegations of top British publishers were led courteously along the Great Wall as a reward for attempting to sell the glories of international copyright to their hosts.

The emergent nations of Africa and elsewhere presented further problems. They needed textbooks desperately but could not afford to pay for them. Their leaders, however, in some cases educated in British universities, understood that textbooks would not be written in the first place if the authors were not remunerated, a point which publishers had to underline. Some countries which wished to abide by the U.C.C. still could not afford to do so, and in their cases compromises were sometimes found, thanks often to the expertise, goodwill and patience of Ron Barker whose sudden death in 1976 removed from the world of books not only a lovable man but one who played a key part in international negotiations.

Trade Associations, Institutions and Fairs

Both the P.A. and the B.A. extended their activities to cope with their members' problems in a world which was changing more rapidly than ever before. At the P.A. Frank Sanders, an outstanding secretary for twenty-five years, resigned in 1958 to become managing director of Book Centre. He was succeeded by R.E. Barker, deputy secretary for a while before spending two years as a literary agent with Curtis Brown. Ron Barker, who was also a detective story writer, had been export secretary in the years immediately after the war when he alerted publishers to the growing importance of the Frankfurt Book Fair. He stayed in office for eighteen busy years, during which he travelled widely, as mentioned in the previous chapter, to meetings of the International Congress of Publishers and UNESCO, to conferences and on numerous missions. When he died, aged fifty-five, he had recently been joined in Bedford Square by Clive Bradley, who became joint secretary with him, and also Chief Executive. Bradley, a trained lawyer, was appointed as a consequence of the Brown Committee's examination of the P.A.'s structure and activities. (Sir John Brown, then of O.U.P., was a former president of the Association.) Barker's health was already poor, the enormous gusto with which he had lived and worked for so long having over-strained him, and one of the Committee's recommendations was that a newcomer at top administrative level should relieve him of the day-to-day running of the Association. He had served ten presidents himself and been faithfully served by two assistant secretaries, R.C. Gowers and Peter Phelan. In his reign the Book Development Council was sponsored in 1965 to foster the spread of British books overseas. Fourteen founder publishing houses provided the original finance but there were also grants from government in recognition of the fact that books spread an understanding of British achievements and values, and assisted the export drive. The P.A. took over the Council in 1970 and, eight years later, with the object of increasing

173

demand for books at home, set up the Book Marketing Council, which added a new dimension to the Association and one enthusiastically promoted by the new secretary. Bradley took over at a time when many problems of long standing had not been solved and when new ones connected with the U.K.'s acceptance into the Common Market of Europe arose regularly.

Barker's opposite number at the Booksellers Association for many of his years of office was Gerry Davies who succeeded Bruce Hepburn in 1955. Apart from a break from 1966-70, when he managed a British subsidiary of the American-owned Bowker imprint and, afterwards, worked for *The Bookseller,* Davies served thirteen presidents. He saw the establishment of BASH (Booksellers Association Service House Ltd.) which answered the criticism of some members that the Association was of little practical use. BASH supplied stock control cards and various items of stationery, and also promoted a Book of the Season campaign which ran into trouble in its infancy but which may yet, like similar schemes in New Zealand and elsewhere, succeed in its aim of drawing a new public into bookshops. Davies worked closely with Barker on the defence of the Net Book Agreement and on other matters of joint concern to their members, but one item of organisation with which he and his colleagues were solely concerned was the annual Conference which publishers attended by invitation only, although their numbers grew steadily.

The Conference was an occasion when booksellers large and small could turn their backs on the chores of actual business and commiserate together about the awfulness of it all. The venue was often a watering place far from London, and the exercise lasted at least six days for most of the delegates. It was undoubtedly a social success providing opportunity not only for booksellers and publishers to meet, but also for their wives and families. Many lasting friendships were founded on these occasions and for most this was the chief value of an increasingly expensive operation which involved hours of speeches and discussions, late nights, too much to drink and, at the end of it all, a brain reeling with all that had been said and repeated over and over again.

At its best the conference hall was a useful place in which to sound out opinion but some felt that the same old grievances were aired from year to year, chief amongst which was the cry of booksellers for higher discounts. Figures presented sought to prove to publishers that booksellers were living on the breadline, a state of affairs not exactly confirmed by their appearance and behaviour at Conference. Not a few sported luxurious cars, and on one occasion the Blackwells even brought their yacht, but they were an exceptional case, never pretending to be other than affluent, and always on the side of their less fortunate colleagues.

An annual item on the Conference agenda was the Book Tokens report, presented for more than twenty years by its chairman, Henry Schollick, who also watched over the emergence of Book Trade Improvement Ltd, a company formed to lend money to booksellers wishing to open new shops or develop existing ones. Book Tokens, whose administration was streamlined by Humphrey Tenby after the war, accumulated capital through the unexpected non-cashing of stamps, by many Tokens being redeemed long after the issuing bookseller had paid for them, and by wise investment. Thus booksellers who were unable to attract outside investment, as publishers often could, were helped, and funds were used to promote Tokens through television and other advertising.

There was wide disagreement on most issues with which booksellers were faced at Conference and elsewhere but most allowed that the wages paid on the retail side of the trade were too low, although few were willing to take practical steps to increase them. In 1970 a Charter Group survey of 94 cases found that only 2% of managers were likely to earn more than £2,500 p.a., and only $7\frac{1}{2}$% more than £2,000. About 15% earned £800 or less and only one exceeded £3,000. For assistants it was worse, new entrants outside the London area being unlikely to earn more than £11 per week before they were twenty and, unless they rose to middle or top management, only a few pounds more at twenty-five. The official scale laid down by the relevant wages council in March 1970, *as a proposal,* provided £10.15 a week minimum for a female assistant aged twenty-two or over in the London area, and £12.75 for a male. The rates were even lower in the provinces, so there was no real improvement in the 1950 situation when Thomas Joy had quoted the minimum wage of £4 5s. for a woman assistant of twenty-four in the London suburbs as disgraceful. In 1980, the comparable *official* scale was, for the London area, £48 per week for assistants aged twenty or over of either sex, and £52.40 for managers; in the provinces, £47.50 for assistants, £51 for managers, which was equally disgraceful.

It was scarcely surprising that young men and women of ability tended to leave bookselling, often to become publishers' representatives, earning three or four times as much. Few obtained jobs within publishing houses although many hankered to become editors, as did a large proportion of arts graduates from all universities. In fact, editorial work below the grade of commissioning editor was not the romantic task that many imagined and usually amounted to little more than subbing with perhaps some opportunity of reading, in their own time and for very small fees, typescripts submitted for consideration. Nor were most in-house jobs in publishing much better paid than in bookselling although by 1970 the position for the former was improving because, not surprisingly, trade union leaders had become active. There had been unions involved in the larger publishing houses for much of the century. One effect of the growth of publishing from a cottage industry into the world of the conglomerates was to make union organisation more widespread, and, in some cases, absolutely essential for the welfare of the less senior employees. As in all trades, when there was an industrial dispute, sometimes it was unfair on the management, sometimes on the workers. The gap between the two occasionally closed; more often it widened. In London, especially, it was exacerbated by members of one union, SOGAT, who were particularly powerful through their association with the newspaper industry which they had been over-manning, whilst being overpaid, for decades. This was one reason for some publishers moving into the provinces. (SOGAT was for warehouse staff; white collar workers joined the N.U.J. and A.S.T.M.S. in increasing numbers as a greater level of redundancy threatened.) Booksellers, by 1980, had not been much affected by union activity. The shop workers' union (U.S.D.A.W.) was one of the least powerful in the nation, but mergers within the retail trade gave it greater bargaining power and resulted in strikes and disputes at some shops. At others, which were not union houses, enlightened management kept staff aware of the state of business and awarded bonuses and wage increases when they were earned.

For all the bickering about terms of trading, and hardships resulting from a low wage structure, the book trade was essentially a friendly one at all levels – at least until the 1979 recession – and this was often the deciding factor for those who remained in it. Conference apart, there were many opportunities for publishers and booksellers to meet. At official level there were the various committees and sub-committees spawned by the two associations; at unofficial, the Society of Young Publishers, which among other activities hired a bus in 1964 and took it to the bookless areas of Luton with discouraging results; the Publishers' Publicity Circle and the Paternosters, which held lunchtime meetings, addressed by trade and national figures; the Galley Club and the Double Crown Club – mostly concerned with printing and production; the Children's Book Circle, founded in 1962 for editors only, but later extended to include anyone involved in writing, publishing and selling to the young; and the Society of Bookmen (which brought itself up to date by electing women members for the first time in 1972) which met in the evening. The ladies also came to grace the annual dinner of the B.P.R.A. at the Connaught Rooms because by the end of the seventies many publishers were employing female reps.

There were other organisations which led to publishers and booksellers meeting on neutral ground. The National Book League had on both its Council and Executive Committee, representatives from the P.A. and the B.A., and from other organisations, some only on the fringe of the book trade. It was invariably in poor financial health, was supported generously by too few publishers and only a handful of booksellers, and came to rely on the support of the Arts Council for its survival. The good work it did behind the scenes, especially in bringing books to the young, was ignored by many in the trade, some of whom were openly hostile to it. It often worked as a catalyst and was consulted by governmental and book trade organisations in all parts of the world. Its library of books about books, based on the personal collection of its first secretary, Maurice Marston, was much enhanced when following the death of Mark Longman (who was chairman of the N.B.L. from 1967-71) a memorial appeal was heavily subscribed. The library subsequently bore Longman's name.

Under Robert Lusty's chairmanship, the League became a registered charity in 1951. It was the year of the Festival of Britain and, appropriately, a book exhibition was mounted at the Victoria and Albert Museum for four months. John Hadfield was then director but handed over in 1954 to J.E. Morpurgo who had to spend too much of his fifteen years of office worrying about raising money. He nevertheless travelled extensively, spreading the gospel of British books about the world. His successor, in 1970, was the Banstead bookseller, Martyn Goff, who instantly began to plan another public event, the Bedford Square Book Bang, an imaginative open-air and under-canvas exhibition to which many were attracted but which was marred by an atrocious spell of summer weather. Under Goff, leading authors came to play important parts in the League's affairs – Angus Wilson, Michael Holroyd and Margaret Drabble each took the chair for two years and sat on the executive for many more – and the move from Albemarle Street, where a complicated lease situation was satisfactorily resolved, to what had been Wandsworth Town Hall in south west London was effected in 1980. The Town Hall, re-named Book House, was jointly owned with the Unwin Trust. It also housed the training department of the P.A. and had facilities open to the trade and allied organisations. To the pleasure of those who moved the N.B.L. headquarters away from central London to an unfashionable suburb, the first Children's Book Exhibition, an event of great significance in the League's year, drew good crowds.

The Arts Council of Great Britain, from which the N.B.L. benefited, was a controversial organisation much resented by some journalists and authors. It had a literature panel, chaired by a succession of distinguished authors, opened a bookshop in Long Acre, in central London, and for a few years offered literary awards one of which was rejected by the historian, Hugh Thomas, who regarded state intervention in the arts as pernicious.

Another government-funded department concerned with the welfare of the written word was the older-established British Council. John Hampden, author and ex-publisher, remained head of the books department until 1963 when his unit was divided and Richard Goffin was put in charge of a book exhibitions department which was a major feature of most book fairs. Goffin served on the executive of the N.B.L. and liaised closely with publishers. In 1968 the British Council held 143 exhibitions and issued five and a half million books from its libraries to 300,000 members, from a stock of two million; by 1982, when Goffin retired, the British Council was organising more than 250 exhibitions a year all over the world. It published *British Book News*, giving regular information about new publications, and administered the English Language Book Society (ELBS), the government scheme for providing subsidised, low-priced books for foreign markets. Under this scheme about two million books are sold overseas every year. The British Council was often under pressure from governments looking for ways of saving money as well as being attacked by Fleet Street, but it survived to carry out much good work, and in its book division it had a dedicated public servant in Richard Goffin.

Goffin was a familiar figure at book fairs round the world, of which the principal was undoubtedly at Frankfurt. In 1948 205 publishers were represented there; in 1981 the number had grown to more than 5,000 from 86 countries, displaying their wares in several vast halls. Stands of varying size – the British Council's usually the largest of all – lined each and every aisle, with oases at certain points where exorbitantly expensive refreshment in plastic containers could be obtained. Wherever one looked there were more books, more publishers, and although it was possible to talk to those who manned the stalls, the last thing possible at that mammoth feast of the written word was actually to open a book and read it.

It was not a simple task to run the Fair but Dr. Sigfred Taubert, a distinguished bibliophile who directed it until 1974, not only maintained a high standard of efficiency, but was well-liked by those who attended year after year, amongst them some booksellers who had managed to convince themselves that it was in the interests of their foreign books department to be present. The Fair was basically about selling rights. Printers and journalists were also to be found there, but very few authors. It was not really a literary occasion.

Book fairs became so numerous that publishers had to become selective about which to support. Apart from Frankfurt, the first to become a 'must' for all publishers of children's books was Bologna. Nice, for all its attractions of climate and location, never became popular; Cairo and Jerusalem did better, in some years, but Montreal, Moscow and Tokyo did not become firm dates in either the annual or three-year diaries of most publishers. In contrast the annual American Booksellers Association meeting was a trade fair which increasing numbers of British publishers found it essential to attend. More convenient for them, if more parochial, was the London Book Fair which grew out of SPEX, a modest one-day affair arranged in a Bloomsbury hotel by two enterprising young independent publishers, Clive Bingley and Lionel Leventhal. Bingley, with some experience at André Deutsch, had a dull but profitable list of books for librarians. Leventhal, an ex-bookseller who had worked for Herbert Jenkins and Hamlyn, specialised in militaria, from his Arms and Armour Press. The fair they started in 1971 as The Specialist Publishers Exhibition for Librarians (there were 23 stands), soon outgrew its venue and its organisation. Bingley and Leventhal were both much concerned with managing their individual lists so they hired John Brushfield, then marketing manager of Book Tokens, to run the London Book Fair, as it became known. By then some of the largest publishers were exhibiting (400 stands in 1979) and the object of the Fair had become blurred. It was originally held in the autumn to attract foreign publishers making for Frankfurt, but, in 1982, it was decided to change the venue from a Park Lane Hotel to the Barbican, and the season to the spring, and to rely on its own image and appeal.

Leventhal and Bingley, in their different ways, had showed that to specialise was a golden rule for the small publishers, and that a forum like the London Book Fair was needed by them. Leventhal himself did not wait for customers to come to him, his salesmen travelled far and wide to exhibit and sell at fairs and exhibitions, catering for the military minded, even attending mock battles. It would have been as foolish of him not to have gone out actively to his public, as for Landsman's, booksellers, to have sat at home in Bromyard in Herefordshire waiting for their customers to come trekking to them for the volumes on farming and horticulture which their mobile bookshop took to agricultural shows all over the country. Specialist publishers and specialist booksellers needed to operate differently from their colleagues concerned with general literature, not that the latter were impervious to the attractions of a wider market.

Bingley, with a list less capable of exploitation to the layman, sold out to Klaus-Saur, a German firm which in turn sold to the Library Association, which then invited Bingley to manage it!

Of those small publishers who exhibited at the London Book Fair it is not feasible to mention all, or even most. Two deserve the attention of book trade historians if only for the fact that they survived in a small and independent way for more than a quarter of a century. Martin Eve started the Merlin Press in the fifties shortly after Jon Wynne-Tyson had issued his first titles from the Centaur Press. The similarity between the two is confined to the fact that each dealt in books and was ruggedly individualistic. Eve came to concentrate on Marxist literature, from the annual Socialist Register to translations of the Hungarian literary critic Georg Lukacs, and settled in offices on the Isle of Dogs in London's far east end; Wynne-Tyson dabbled in fiction and expensive reprints of neglected classics and allowed himself the indulgence of publishing his own work of liberal political-philosophy, from a farm complex in Sussex. Wynne-Tyson enlarged upon his operation entertainingly in letters and articles to *The Bookseller*; Eve's name filtered into the trade press usually only as a committee member of the union endeavouring to bring about better conditions for workers in publishing.

Small poetry presses were also amongst the exhibitors at the London

Book Fair when they could afford it but many existed on rather less than a shoestring and had to rely on leaving their wares, often messily cyclostyled, with such booksellers who were willing to accommodate them, on a sale-or-return basis. Many of the poets so published had to pay for the privilege and were sometimes also required to hawk their own work around. Most literary bookshops had a corner which became the final resting-place of many tiny muses thrown upon the harsh commercial world. Rising above these piteous graveyards of humble vanity were the books produced by such small firms as the Fortune, Scorpion, Marvell, Fulcrum and Carcanet presses which operated at various times during this period.

Many of those who published for particular small markets were members of the Independent Publishers Group, who, in toto, may not have brought much extra profit to High Street booksellers but who made their contribution, with some of what they had to offer, to the literary market place.

The activities of all publishers and booksellers, of all sizes, were faithfully recorded week by week in *The Bookseller*, the trade journal which survived, in others which surfaced towards the end of the seventies, and in *British Books* into which the *Publishers' Circular* was transformed in 1959 but which disappeared in the following decade, as did Smith's *Trade News*. *Publishing News* brought a breath of air and vulgar tabloid journalism to bear and soon became essential reading for anyone wishing to keep an ear cocked for trade gossip.

The Bookseller continued to be edited by Edmond Segrave until his death in 1971, and justified its sub-title *The Organ of the Book Trade*. Segrave, a short man of Anglo-Irish stock who had been intended for the priesthood, was a perfectionist who would spend hours worrying a sentence into shape. If the sense struck him as obscure or the phrasing ugly in a letter received for publication, he would often phone the writer and tell him at length how he proposed to alter it; in more arrogant mood he would change it without consultation. He seldom wrote letters himself or replied to those he received. He never acknowledged articles sent in for publication but paid for those published. If rejected, they joined the mass of typescript and printed matter which accumulated in his room on the second floor of 13 Bedford Square, an office with a strong resemblance to a secondhand bookshop. John Hadfield who once edited *The Bookseller* when Segrave was away, recorded in his obituary of him that a small area of the desktop was kept clear for work on the current number. Segrave had many close friends and a very small and select number of enemies whom he cherished almost as much. He didn't suffer fools at all, let alone gladly. He attended few trade functions; but when he did he could be witty, indiscreet and fascinating because he probably knew more about the contemporary book trade than anyone else. He built up *The Bookseller*'s circulation by opening its columns to controversy and encouraging readers to send in news items rather than gossip.

He started features, usually with a pseudonymous byline, at least one of which he wrote himself. There was much speculation as to the identity of the various columnists; most, though not all, were revealed in time. During his last years he became a trifle stale but his foresight gave his successor, Philothea Thompson, who had served him since 1945, some new contributors and colleagues, one of whom, Michael Geare, had been with Dent. Geare remained to serve two more editors, David Whitaker and his successor in 1980, Louis Baum, a professional journalist from South Africa, who soon began to alter the layout and contents.

David Whitaker, son of Haddon, had joined the family business in the fifties and became much involved in the launching of ISBNs and, later, the production of *British Books in Print* on microfiche. He was joined in 1973 by his sister Sally who organised the move from stately but inconvenient Bedford Square to premises in Dyott Street where the whole Whitaker operation, apart from printing, could be contained in one building. The famous *Almanack* continued to appear annually and to enjoy a larger sale than many of the titles which appeared in bestseller lists, one of which became a feature of *The Bookseller*.

All the subjects which have been discussed here, and many others, were regularly commented upon in the columns of *The Bookseller*. A perennial was the problem of obscenity, the law concerning which continued to be an irritant to authors and the trade. In the early fifties there were a number of prosecutions, notably of Fredric Warburg for publishing *The Philanderer* by Stanley Kauffman. He was found not guilty, Mr Justice Stable, in summing up, uttering these significant words:

'Are we to take our literary standards as being the level of something that is suitable for the decently brought-up young female aged fourteen? Or do we go even further back than that and are we to be reduced to the sort of books that one reads as a child in the nursery? The answer to that is: of course not. A mass of literature, great literature, from many angles, is wholly unsuitable for reading by the adolescent, but that does not mean that the publisher is guilty of a criminal offence for making those works available to the general public.'

Wise words, and to printers, publishers, booksellers and authors, all of whom were liable to prosecution, it seemed that the law had at last embraced common sense. Alas, other judges were not bound by Mr Justice Stable's strictures. Mrs Webb of Hutchinson, the company itself and the printer of *September in Quinze* were all fined heavily when found guilty of publishing an obscene work. A.S. Frere of Heinemann was more fortunate over Walter Baxter's *The Image and the Search,* although he had to endure three trials before being acquitted.

The most celebrated case of all occurred when Allen Lane announced his intention, in 1960, of publishing the unexpurgated text of D.H. Lawrence's

Lady Chatterley's Lover in Penguin at 3s.6d. Proofs were sent to booksellers, which was not Penguin's usual practice and, in August, the Director of Public Prosecutions decided to prosecute. The defence called thirty-five witnesses, including distinguished authors and critics who expressed their opinion that Lawrence was a great writer and that no passage in the book would tend to deprave or corrupt anyone. The case was national news, the subject of discussion in pubs and trains between people who had scarcely heard of Lawrence but who held strong views on censorship. The jury acquitted the lady and the 200,000 copies waiting in Penguin's warehouse were supplied to the trade who instantly demanded more. Lorries stopped outside bookshops, with their engines throbbing, as rough-handed drivers strode inside to buy *Lady C.* without even having to say what they wanted.

The verdict brought a glow of optimism to the trade because the nonsense of the law at last seemed settled. Allen Lane was hailed as a saviour and every novelist who wished to be with it sprinkled the word 'fuck' about his typescript. But it was not all over. British justice does not work that way. More prosecutions took place, though less frequently, but the effect was always the same – to make a book of which there had previously been little knowledge desirable. Those who wished to ban books never heeded this, nor was there evidence of a diminishing taste for what the public, despite all the acquittals, persisted in thinking of as desirable pornography. It was usually overlooked that the taste for porn was often a normal, even healthy one. By 1980 few of the famous 'dirty' books of former times had been denied to the public. One, Terry Sothern's *Candy*, had still, however, appeared only in an abridged edition, the reason being that Sothern did not treat his subject in the solemn manner which enabled literary pundits to swear under oath that it was culture. He played it for laughs.

One main argument of those opposed to literary censorship was the impossibility of defining 'obscenity' and 'pornography'; the other was that freedom of speech implied the freedom to publish whatever one liked. Even the most liberal became worried about the latter view, however, when manuals written deliberately to instruct terrorists in the making of bombs, and similar works, appeared. The argument goes on, with the Society for the Defence of Literature, sponsored by eminent lawyers and publishers, on one side, and self-imposed keepers of the public conscience, plus teachers and other lawyers, opposed to them.

The Bookseller provided a platform for all of them. Less provocatively, it reported on such matters as literary awards, for which it had to find increasing space as commerce was persuaded to take over the role of the patron of the arts.

Tom Maschler, of Cape, having noted Booker Brothers' interest in his author Ian Fleming, suggested to them the promotion of a prize to be the

British equivalent of the Prix Goncourt and the Femina. Booker agreed, the National Book League were called in to administer and the first Booker Prize for a work of fiction by a British author published in Britain within a named period, was awarded in 1968. For the first two years the winning author got little beyond the tax-free prize money of £5,000. Then there was a breakthrough, possibly because of the rude way in which two winners ungraciously received their award, one of them naming Booker's as exploiters of Caribbean labour and giving half (*half* – note) of his prize to a political liberation organisation. In the tenth year, by which time publishers and booksellers were recording vastly increased sales for winning books, the prize was doubled to £10,000. In the following year, the leaks about the winner, which had had ample channels through which to flow, were stopped by arranging for the judges not to announce their decision until shortly before the celebratory dinner. This led to problems for the winning author's publisher but to much wider publicity and sales.

There were many other prizes, none as prestigious as Booker-McConnell's (as it came to be known), but worth hundreds or thousands to the authors who won them. Whitbread's, the brewers, awarded some of them; others were financed by funds left specifically by authors as eminent as Somerset Maugham or as little known as John Llewelyn Rhys, who was killed fighting during the Battle of Britain. Whatever the material gain, most winning authors felt a deserved boost to their egos when they were named. As Iris Murdoch admitted at a Claridges' reception when awarded the Booker 'If there is a prize going, I like to win it.' (Some very famous authors, however, refused to have their books submitted.)

Non-book trade sponsors were found to aid the National Book League, but responsibility for the book trade's particular charities remained, properly, at home. The Book Trade Benevolent Society, started in the nineteenth century at the instigation of John Dickinson's, manufacturing stationers, and the National Book Trade Provident Society found support from all sides of the trade which led to new building at the Retreat, in King's Langley, Hertfordshire. Here the original building erected to house retired stationers and booksellers came to be surrounded by purpose-built bungalows for those without pension provision or other means, who had worked within the trade.

An extra boost was given to this cause in the seventies when it was recognised that many of those retired preferred to remain in their own homes, even though some needed assistance. For their benefit Bookrest was formed, and supported by leading publishers and booksellers, with Harold Macmillan as its Patron. It captured the imagination of the trade and every year from 1976 a sponsored walk around central London was organised to raise money. It became an annual trade event supported by everyone from chairmen of publishing companies to packers and booksellers' assistants.

Authors walked, so did printers and literary agents. For three hours on a June evening crowds of those involved in the book trade, some in elaborately fancy-dressed contingents, paraded the West End of London ending in massive array at the Connaught Rooms, Holborn, where the fastest walker, and the youngest, oldest, best dressed, etc., were awarded prizes. In 1976 the Walk raised over £6,000; in 1979, £10,000; in 1980, just under £8,000.

The Walk was evidence of the trade's continuing to be a friendly organisation in which so many of the workers knew so many others at all levels.

University Bookselling

New universities meant new bookshops and the birth of two large groups – University Bookshops, Oxford, and Bowes & Bowes. U.B.O., jointly owned by O.U.P. and Blackwells, was a natural extension of the two great Oxford businesses. Nepotism can break as easily as make a family firm. Basil Blackwell was fortunate in the two sons who followed him into his business and contributed energetically to its expansion, but dealt a sad blow in 1980 when the elder, Richard, died of cancer.

From being the wealthy and established leading booksellers to one of the two main universities, and also publishers of note, Blackwell's also became important exporters and the home base for U.B.O. The bookshop in Broad Street, which had started in an area of twelve square feet, absorbed the premises on either side of it and was extended underground into the spacious Norrington Room. It also took over other Oxford shops and opened offices and warehouses elsewhere in the city for its mail order business. By the end of the seventies it employed over 700 people, had a turnover of £26m with customers in all parts of the world whilst remaining, in its native city, an inviting, peaceful shop in which town and gown could browse uninterruptedly. There were notices informing customers that they would not be approached by salesmen unless they signalled for attention. Despite this courtesy the company was managed in a thoroughly businesslike manner. With their large buying power, they were the first to demand better trading terms for other booksellers as well as themselves (although, curiously, as publishers they were not automatically generous to their fellow booksellers) and individual executives of the company were always prominent in trade affairs.

Richard Blackwell, like his father Basil a president of the B.A., developed the export business, formed Blackwell's North America Inc., acquired two printing houses, and helped to found U.B.O. His younger brother Julian (known as Toby), also a president of the B.A., became well-known for his league table of publishers' delivery performances and for his persecution of the postal authorities on behalf of all mail users. Within Blackwell's he was responsible for the transformation of the vast area lying beneath Trinity College into the Norrington Room.

Here a great cavern of books, entered down a ramp from the original bookshop, was intriguingly designed to allow vistas of an acreage of books below, above and beside one. The room's mausoleum-like tendencies were nicely tempered by such homely architectural touches as retaining an iron spiral staircase, and letting in daylight through a window high up on one side. It was a striking achievement of modern design providing a foil to the nineteenth-century aspect of the Broad Street shop front.

'The Gaffer', as Basil Blackwell was called, was knighted in 1956. He lived for more than half a century in a house near Abingdon which he designed and helped to build. It has its place in trade history not only as the home of the outstanding bookseller of his time, and one who was also a publisher, but for having a garden in which Allen Lane claimed he invented Penguins under an apple tree.

Blackwell's, with the Alden Press, bought the school bookshop at Eton College in 1946 and Alden itself ten years later. There were other small acquisitions and developments but the largest came with the creation of U.B.O. The object was to extend the services of university bookselling to other cities and towns. An equal, majority or total holding was purchased in existing businesses. Willshaw's of Manchester joined in 1964, John Prime, from Collet's in London, becoming M.D. A year later Parry's of Liverpool came in under Alan Wilson, followed over the next four years by Eric Bailey of Lear's (Cardiff), William Smith (Reading), Thomas Godfrey (York), W. Hartley Seed (Sheffield), Thorne's Students Bookshop (Newcastle-upon-Tyne) and Bisset's (Aberdeen). It was a formidable line-up from which Thorne's withdrew in 1975. Bailey, of Lear's whose shop was re-named University Bookshop (Cardiff) Ltd, became managing director of U.B.O. after the retirement of Henry Schollick.

George's of Bristol, long under Blackwell's ownership, headed a small academic group which embraced Blakey's of Exeter and bought the S.P.C.K. shop on the university campus there. Blakey's name, like Lear's, later disappeared when his former shop became George's.

Chief among the non-family members of the board of Blackwell's was H.L. Schollick (known as 'Uncle Henry'), whose name recurs in these pages in other connections, and Per Saugman. Schollick was close to the Gaffer and involved in both publishing and bookselling; Saugman, a Dane who was also an executive of Munksgaard in his native country, became head of Blackwell Scientific Publications Ltd and in 1963 acquired for the group the century-old medical and scientific Dutch house, Kooyker of Leiden. Other

Blackwell employees who joined the chiefs from the Indians were the brothers Sam and Harry Knights, who started as apprentices and became directors. Sam, who died suddenly in 1972, was described by Sir Basil as 'a precious colleague', one who was 'essentially a front shop assistant who not only assimilated the spirit of Blackwell's but did much to mould it as his career developed'. He had a marvellous memory for titles, authors and publishers and for the history of particular books. No bookseller could wish for a finer epitaph. His brother Harry became a bookseller in Abingdon.

In 1979 The Gaffer celebrated his ninetieth birthday and his firm its centenary.

The other university bookselling group was based on Cambridge and was owned by W.H. Smith, whose own progress during these years will be noted later. When George Brimley Bowes retired in 1946 his business passed to Denis Payne, who developed the publishing side with a series of critiques of European writers, and then sold the bookshop to W.H.S. in 1953, afterwards establishing himself on the Continent as representative for various publishers. Smith's appointed Esmond Warner, who had made a notable success of their branch in Brussels, as manager and under him the Bowes & Bowes group was formed. At Trinity Street he gutted the oldest bookshop in the land and rebuilt it internally from basement to roof. In 1963 he opened a science bookshop along the street and, later, a modern languages branch. By 1970, with Heffer's three shops in the same winding, narrow thoroughfare, Trinity Street had as great a density of bookshops as Charing Cross Road.

In 1961 Bowes & Bowes started empire building when Sherratt & Hughes of Manchester was transferred from W.H.S. who had bought it in 1946. Joe Cheetham, Jnr, a bookseller for over fifty years, apart from a short spell as a pupil farmer to which task his father had put him because 'there was no money in books', remained until 1967 when he reached Smith's compulsory retirement age of sixty-five.

In 1963 came the first campus shops at Southampton and Norwich, then another among the bleak grey tower blocks of the University of Essex in Wivenhoe Park, outside Colchester. It was roughly U-shaped which provided the management with a permanent shop-lifting problem.

In 1965 the W.H.S. branch in fashionable Milsom Street, Bath was transferred to Bowes, and Bryce's, of Museum Street, London, was bought. Three years later Alan Ward sold his Sheffield shops and, with them, his services for a limited period. It was the policy of B. & B. to take over the former owners as well as their shops, but Smith's retirement rule was rigid, and Ivan Chambers, to the great regret of his colleagues in the trade, and of his customers, departed in 1971 from the business he had made so very much his own after the death of William Jackson Bryce. For Alan Ward, regarded with equal affection by his friends, the wrench was not so great because he had never enjoyed actual bookselling, as Chambers had. Esmond Warner also stepped down in 1971, and was succeeded as chairman by Simon Hornby and as manager by M.A.C. (Tony) Reavell, who stayed until 1974. Truslove & Hanson's in Sloane Street (the Clifford Street and Oxford Street branches had closed in 1958 and 1963) was added to the group but Bryce's was sold to E.J. Brill. The twelfth shop was opened in the University Building at Hull University a year later.

Hugh E. Butcher was appointed managing director in succession to Reavell and it was announced in 1976 that a small loss had been turned into a profit of £136,000. W.H.S. persevered with Bowes & Bowes which was greatly to their credit though the operation was clearly a vastly different one from running their own ever-more diversified main company.

Heffer's moved out of their rambling Petty Cury premises in 1970 and into a new shop in Trinity Street which rivalled Blackwell's Norrington Room in ingenuity of design, use of space and splendour of fittings. Ernest Heffer died in 1948 and was succeeded by his son Reuben, who brought in his own sons, Nicholas and William but also went beyond the family in search of senior colleagues. John Welch, who had wide publishing experience, became M.D. in 1968 and organised the move to Trinity Street where the children's bookshop, another triumph of design, was the first to open. It has since moved into larger premises nearby. In 1977, by which time there were more Heffers active (although Reuben's son William had defected to antiques), separate divisions were confirmed for bookselling, stationery and printing.

Bowes & Bowes and Heffer's dominated Cambridge bookselling but not exclusively. Gustave David's son, Hubert, kept his stall in the market and his two shops in St Edward's Passage; the sons of the first Porter, of Galloway & Porter, also took over from their father; and there was the Student's Bookshop which moved from Trumpington Street to Silver Street in 1965, establishing branches at the University of Keele, and in Henley. It later took over in Lancaster from Maxwell but closed down in Cambridge. Deighton, Bell's became entirely antiquarian in 1963, four years after the share capital had been bought by William Dawson's, the London wholesalers and exporters.

Some universities chose to run their own bookshops, the first being at Leicester where the authorities claimed that local booksellers had declined the offer to install a campus shop. The faculties at Sussex and Warwick also decided to do it themselves, despite rumblings of disapproval from both trade associations. In Birmingham, however, the resident booksellers, Hudsons, were successful in gaining the concession.

In Leeds, it was the Austicks who catered not only for the student population but for industry and the general public also in several shops in the city. A university bookshop was opened in Woodhouse Lane in 1950 and moved to Blenheim Terrace in 1965. A medical bookshop was opened in 1952, the main shop in Cookridge Street was extended two years later, followed by a specialist paperback shop in Eldon Street, a book room in the Huddersfield College of Technology, another in a college at Horsforth and a big new general shop in The Headrow. Mrs Hilda Austick, who died in 1960, had been justified in ignoring the advice given to her when she was widowed before the war, to leave bookselling and wind up the business. Aided by her two sons Paul and David she made Austick's the principal booksellers of Leeds.

Sheffield's main booksellers both sold out to Oxbridge, but had to face competition from the City Council which had been allowed by some publishers, with the P.A.'s approval dating back to 1917, to buy its textbooks direct at higher discounts than the booksellers could afford. This caused great bitterness because, in the previous year, at the request of the Chief Educational Officer, several booksellers including Ward's, Hartley Seed, and the Methodist Bookshop, had opened a showroom for local teachers. In 1970 they closed it because it was not being used. Most publishers, however, declined to supply the Council direct. Had it been a question of allowing the city fathers to buy only textbooks from educational publishers, the Sheffield booksellers would possibly have not objected but they were fearful of losing the valuable school library business in net books as London booksellers had to the G.L.C. It was this factor which determined the attitude of many booksellers, in all parts of the kingdom, to supplying schools.

The competition in Manchester was more straightforward. Haigh & Hochland opened near the campus in 1959 and claimed to be the first specialised university bookshop to start in the provinces. Ernest Hochland operated a mailing service on index cards, and by 1969 two-thirds of his turnover came from mail order. (Blackwell's started a similar operation at the same time without knowing what Hochland was doing.) He had three shops by the end of the sixties, one specialising in technological books and another in paperbacks, with a total staff of forty-one, including three working directors. In 1972 he moved into Manchester University's new Precinct Centre where the office was integrated with the retail part of the premises. The minute shop in Portland Street, built up by the Misses Jardine and Davison over many years, may not have looked like serious competition but in fact had many institutional as well as private customers. Grace Jardine, who took the shop in 1924, was an ex-suffragette who had worked with Harriet Weaver on *The Egoist*. Kathleen Davison was a member of the first B.A. Charter Group Committee. She sold the shop to Paul Underhill, a publisher's rep who moved to larger premises in St. Peter's Square, and opened branches in Knutsford and Macclesfield. Many Manchester shops closed during the immediate post-war period; Willshaw's changed hands, its new owner, Frank Gabbutt, moving his new acquisition to John Dalton Street in 1956. According to his successor John Prime, Gabbutt, who survived the lean years in Blackburn, had an open mind, anticipating the demands of late-twentieth century bookselling, zestfully promoting the expansion of his Manchester shop at an age when most would have been thinking of retirement.

At the other end of the ship canal most of the Liverpool closures had occurred between the wars. Of the survivors, Philip, Son & Nephew opted out of school contracting in 1969 and concentrated on the retail branches already opened in West Kirby, Formby, Southport and Wirral. Parry's which had only just entered the new book market was bought in 1948 by Alan Wilson who under U.B.O. opened a new shop, at that time the largest built specifically to serve the needs of a provincial university. Charles Wilson and Henry Young also survived.

At Nottingham, Sisson & Parker opened a university bookshop in Portland Buildings. There, and at their main shop in Wheeler Gate, they claimed in 1963 to have a range of books unequalled outside London and Oxbridge (although the Bible was still their bestseller). Walter Gisborne, a nephew of Walter Sisson, who died in 1947, managed the company, which opened various branches in Nottingham and elsewhere, until the Pentos purchase which was reported as costing £957,000.

Of the U.B.O. shops already mentioned, Kenneth W. Adlam bought William Smith of Reading in 1960 and ran it independently for seven years during which time he opened a branch on the campus; Godfrey's of York endured inadequate accommodation in the university buildings for ten years before new premises were provided; and Lear's of Cardiff made do with similarly makeshift rooms in a basement until the re-named University Bookshop was opened.

The two leading cities of Scotland did not require outside aid in coping with their student population. John Smith's had been meeting the demands of Glasgow University for many decades. They achieved steady if unspectacular expansion under John Knox, head of the firm until 1969, when he handed over to his ward, Robert Clow. Clow had for some years been occupied with the shops in Gibson Street, near the university, and had used his architectural training and knowledge to turn a relatively small shop into one which appeared much larger. Under his management more development took place, not only in St Vincent Street where the space for bookselling came to occupy six floors, but in branches further afield. For these the name John B. Wylie was revived for a chain of self-service shops where customers could write out their own orders, including ISBNs.

Wylie's was a subsidiary of Smith's directed for many years in a highly personal way by Ross Higgins. In Sauchiehall Street he created a haven of peace in an area of Glasgow which, for years, lay in the bulldozers' path. On the ground floor, customers entered something resembling the hall and library of a country house, where stood a large round table on which books were carefully but informally arranged. There was even an open fireplace although it was not much used. At the back, on a dais, was a stationery department, and up the pleasant wooden staircase was the children's department and Higgins' office, not unlike an actor's dressing-room with its signed photos of authors adorning the walls. At busy seasons he opened during the evenings for the benefit of those who could not shop at normal times. He was partly dependent on mail order and many customers relied on the Higgins choice of the month for their reading. If he did not consider there was a suitable book then no selection was made. It sounds a gentlemanly form of bookselling but immense thought and energy went into it and valuable lessons can still be learned from it. When the bulldozers came too close the shop was closed and Ross Higgins moved back to St Vincent Street for some years.

Of the other Glasgow booksellers, W. & R. Holmes became a company in 1947 and later merged with George Outram, publishers of the *Glasgow Herald* and part of the Lonrho Group. After a spell in the newspaper building they moved into Wylie & Lochhead's store (nothing to do with John Wylie), where, despite appearances, it was a separate entity. Later they became Holmes-McDougall, taking over the Edinburgh firm, and sold their educational contracting division to E.J. Arnold. They also took over Blacklock Farries, of Dumfries, and the Standard Bookshop at Kilmarnock. Jackson, Son & Co closed down in 1968.

In Edinburgh the Thins and Bauermeisters presided over the bulk of the university trade, with both shops close to the campus on South Bridge and George IV Bridge. Thin's occupied the older premises, rambling across several buildings with the same abandon as John Smith's in Glasgow. James Thin IV joined the family partnership in 1950, started the mail order side and was the first bookseller (in 1956) to use a computer; his cousin Ainslie joined him at the end of the fifties. The Thins tended to dislike the computer and even to express regret at having gone into mail order, but they appeared to thrive in their lovely city from which Ainslie was often absent on B.A. affairs. They opened a new shop for engineering and scientific books in the university in 1972, and also controlled Melven's Bookshops in Inverness and Perth. In 1980, having used a computer bureau for fifteen years, they installed their own machine presumably having come to love the electronic beast.

Bauermeister's moved in 1966 from the Mound to George IV Bridge into a modern shop built on to the old premises of W.F. Henderson, theological bookseller. It had a spacious air compared with Thin's. During the second war Bauermeister's was sold out of the family although a daughter of the founder remained as managing director. When William, her brother, returned from the services, he purchased all the shares from the Mound Bookshop Company then owning them, and his wife and son joined him in partnership. He opened a university branch at Dundee in 1964 but sold it two years later to Frank Russell. He died in 1979.

In Dublin the chief booksellers were still those mentioned in earlier sections. A.P.C.K. had a foot in both Eire and Ulster, as did Eason's. Browne & Nolan, another distinguished bookseller-publisher, formed an associated company with Longmans in 1967 to publish for the educational market. All in the Irish book trade were constantly beset by the censorship problem, and those in the north, especially Belfast and Londonderry, lost all or part of their premises from time to time, by fire or bombing during the prolonged civil disturbances which started in 1968. The Eireann booksellers were ever on good terms with their British colleagues but the comparative poverty of the Emerald Isle, plus the absurdities of the censorship, made selling books there difficult. Indeed, Victor Gollancz is said to have remarked that he sold more books to Harrods in one week than he did to Ireland in a whole year.

Bookselling Chains

The place of W.H. Smith & Son as booksellers was unique and complicated. The company operated more shops selling books than any other firm, in many places maintaining the only retail outlet, though most were not primarily bookshops but newsagents, stationers and selling points for various other goods ranging from gramophone records to toys. The closure of their commercial library system led to Smith's allocating more space within their shops for goods other than books, yet for all large and medium-sized publishers they were customers with immense buying power. In the ten years 1970-80 the W.H.S. book turnover increased just under six times. There were fifteen branches with book sales of more than £½m per annum, and the large two-level department at the Brent Cross shopping complex in north-west London was only a fraction below the million in 1979. In 1959 Smith's had 371 branches; in 1969, 318. In the seventies they closed thirty-four shops in small towns but opened sixty in urban centres where they had not previously traded. No fewer than 123 existing shops were either re-sited or extended though 118 railway bookstalls were closed.

W.H.S. was often sneered at by other booksellers, and more especially by authors, for not being more literary, but it never pretended to be other than what it was, a huge public company, dealing in many commodities. In many trades and industries a more ruthless policy would have been implemented. To the book trade it behaved impeccably, upholding the Net Book Agreement which it was in a very strong position to ignore, not attempting to have one vote per branch at B.A. Conference which could have given it a trade-union-like block vote, and supporting charities generously.

W.H.S. wholesaling policy changed direction several times. After the demise of Simpkin Marshall it was the largest available to the trade, which it served first from Strand House, off Kingsway, then from Bridge House in Lambeth, finally from Swindon in Wiltshire where it became computerised.

Service to other booksellers ended soon after although a limited range of books, hardback and paperback, was still supplied from its other wholesale warehouses spread around the country. In 1978 a new management structure gave autonomy to the company's Wholesale Group which came to have two large bases, at Woking in the south, and Warrington in the north, with a van service to bookseller and newsagent customers.

From 1943 the head of the book buying department at Strand House was Kenyon Foat who succeeded David Roy, and handed over to Reggie Last, an experienced shop manager. Last was under pressure constantly from general publishers to buy in large quantities but he contrived to do his best for the company and remain on friendly terms with the trade. His deputy, Tom Hodges, took over from him in 1965, emphasising a policy at that time of promotion from within. The life of a chief buyer for such an organisation demanded an iron nerve. Both Reggie Last and Tom Hodges kept their integrity and their friends, as did their successor Michael Pountney, an Oxford graduate who had been with W.H.S. and Bowes & Bowes since 1962. With his appointment there were changes in the buying structure. He became merchandising manager for books, heading a team including John Hyams, a Bournemouth bookseller who had not risen from the Smith ranks.

The Hon. David Smith became governing director of W.H.S. when his elder brother died in 1948. His first task was to make Smith's a public company in order to pay death duties. This meant that for the first time outsiders had shares in the company, although David Smith and Michael Hornby, his vice-chairman, endeavoured to keep something of a family atmosphere. In so large a body this was difficult, but Smith made a point of meeting as many of his widespread staff as possible and in being available to hear their problems. The retirement rule applied to him as to everyone else and his chairmanship ended in 1972 although he remained on the board of the holding company. A new position of chief executive was created in the seventies. Simon Hornby, son of Michael, succeeded to this post in 1976, and with it the management of a company with world-wide ramifications, and much diversification. In 1979 he reported to the shareholders that after years of increased profits there had been a 7% fall which was due to costs rising faster than sales. In the following year it fell again to £13.68m from £17.27m. The turnover, however, had risen from £474.13m to £570.85m, and it was noted that wholesaling in both Britain and America had lost over £3m between them.

W.H.S. involvement in book clubs, noted elsewhere, began in 1966 with a cookery book club which gained 60,000 members in two years. Later that year the Reprint Society (World Books) was bought for £280,000. It then had a membership of around 50,000, having dropped from the quarter million figure of the late forties. Under B.C.A. (jointly owned by W.H.S. and Doubleday of America) it rose to six figures again within eighteen months.

The Menzies chain expanded vigorously from 1945, in which year it had only five retail shops, to 1965, when there were 150, including all those previously known as Wyman's and Stoneham's. The latter were sold by Simpkin Marshall during World War II to Hatchard's who disposed of them (23 in all) in 1952. Some of the Stoneham shops were so tiny as to be uneconomic; others were sizeable and could hold a representative stock – for example, the branches in Old Broad Street and Cheapside, where Chris Pemberton displayed large photographs of authors to indicate that although he was part of a chain dealing in all manner of goods, his was primarily a bookshop. All of these were renamed Wyman's, only Stoneham's Public Library Service remaining a separate entity until it was sold to Zwemmer's. The name Wyman also disappeared when Menzies took over in 1959, although it was perpetuated in the printing firm of Cox & Wyman (later owned for a time by Thomas Tilling, the proprietors of Heinemann) and also in Wyman-Marshall, a company incorporated in 1963 as a wholesaler. The 'Marshall' of the title referred, not to Simpkin's, but to Horace of that ilk, a nineteenth century firm purchased in 1962.

As Menzies altered all the fascia-boards yet again, so that only their name remained, the shop fronts and interiors came to resemble those of W.H.S., rather as different makes of car grew alike in appearance. Menzies, still based upon Edinburgh, where their Princes Street premises underwent elaborate modernisation in 1979, bought a number of private businesses – Douglas & Foulis, also in the Scottish capital; the Helensburgh Bookshop, David Robertson's of Perth, Dunn & Wilson's of Falkirk, and others. The family remained in control of the company throughout the period, John Maxwell Menzies succeeding his grandmother in 1951, at the age of twenty-five. Diversification took a different direction from Smith's into communications systems, photographic equipment and commercial radio, and their profits rose, although, like W.H.S., their wholesaling side entered a bad period, mainly because of industrial disruption, in the late seventies. Turnover for 1979-80 increased from £197.67m to £233.36m, and pretax profit from £5.94m to £6.66m.

By 1980, the S.P.C.K. had forty-five shops in Britain (five fewer than in 1969) but none overseas, although many of the latter remained in business under local ownership. At Salisbury, their attractive old premises on three floors in the cathedral precincts held the best stock of new books in the city; at Lincoln the panting visitor climbing Steep Hill to the cathedral could pause to browse at their shop there; in Winchester, a former book room was closed when the Gallery Bookshop was taken over in 1977; in Durham they became the university booksellers and also had a shop in the cathedral undercroft catering both for tourists and the needs of the diocese; Bristol held one of their main religious shops, two more of which were in actual churches in Guildford and Edinburgh. In London the new premises opened in 1968 were sold for redevelopment two years later, so the business was moved to the headquarters of the Society in that same Holy Trinity Church, in Marylebone, where the Penguin adventure began. The number of shops operated in centres of education dropped steadily towards 1980 because of college closures and mergers.

John Elsley joined his parents in Bookland & Co, based on Chester, in 1945, after serving a year's apprenticeship with Charles Wilson of Liverpool. By 1977, when his father died, (Mrs Elsley predeceased her husband in 1960) he was a leading provincial bookseller who had established good bookshops in towns which previously lacked them. In 1969 he controlled a staff of over one hundred in two shops in Chester (where there was also a wholesale house), three in Bangor (which became a separate company) and one each in Stafford, Newcastle-under-Lyme, Wolverhampton and Wallasey. In 1973 he opened in Shrewsbury and a third shop was started in Chester in 1978 in attractive premises dating from the mid-seventeenth century and boasting a thirteenth-century crypt (perhaps to be used for remainders?).

It was John Elsley's policy to delegate widely to his branch managers, allowing them to run their shops as they wished, but to centralise accounting and research so far as this was compatible with local efficiency. In 1978 Ainslie Thin, of Edinburgh, became a director of Bookland.

As an outlet for books Boots Pure Drug Stores declined during this period, although for a time in the late fifties, under Philip ('Books can be sold like soap') Jarvis, the departments were administered with great zest. Boots, however, had never been primarily concerned with selling books but lending them, so that their importance to publishers declined with the circulating libraries, the last of which ceased to issue books in 1966. Many branches continued to keep a small stock of books for sale after this and there were indications by 1979 that this was to be widened.

Another small chain, much involved in lending, was Countryside Libraries Ltd which closed its last branch at Hitchin in the same year as Boots. Run by Audrey and Basil Donne-Smith for over thirty years, it had boasted twenty-five branches at its peak. The Donne-Smiths retired to Crewkerne Abbey in Dorset where he dabbled in bookselling from home until his death in 1978. He was one of the most prominent trade politicians of his time and wrote and spoke much about the economic plight of booksellers, despite which he and his wife were well liked.

A new chain expanded rapidly in the south of England from 1973 when Websters Bookshops opened in Guildford and Dorking. Other shops followed in Croydon, Winchester, Bournemouth and Brighton. The parent company, Webster's Publications, took over Bookwise, the wholesaling company started by Christopher Barclay in 1969. Barclay, previously owner of South County Libraries which he started in 1948, helped paperback publishers to expand their market by finding new outlets for them. By 1970 he had a sales force of approximately forty servicing 5,000 accounts south of Newcastle-upon-Tyne. By 1978 Bookwise, which he no longer owned, had opened a hardback and children's distribution centre at Leamington Spa and their vans were a familiar sight all over the country. Webster's had a turnover of almost £12m in 1976. (The Hammick chain, equally expansive, has been dealt with on page 122.)

W.G. ('Bill') Smith, a trained librarian and once editor of *Books & Bookmen*, turned to selling remainders when he ceased being a journalist, and subsequently opened his Booksmith shops in London, Kingston and Brighton. His turnover in 1977 was quoted as being £750,000 of which two-thirds was in remainders. (At what Smith called his pedigree outlet, the New City Bookshop in Byward Street which he bought from Elwyn Fisher in 1975, he sold new publications as well.) A determined opponent of the Net Book Agreement, he wrote from this address to *The Bookseller* in the same year to say that like John Menzies, who were offering a £1,000 holiday to the winner of a lucky paperback, he was installing a 'Lucky Dip'. Prizes would range 'from a fiver to a photograph of Thomas Joy holding an urn containing the ashes of the Net Book Agreement'.

Thomas Joy, sometime merchandising manager of the Army & Navy Stores, where he had previously run the book department, and ex-president of the B.A., was by then managing director of Hatchard's group of shops which included the Ancient House Bookshop at Ipswich, and specialised in opening book departments in retailing strongholds such as Harvey Nichols and the Civil Service Stores, in London's Strand.

Lastly, and a major irritant to the trade, was Susan Reynolds, run by Michael Reynolds, and dealing exclusively in remainders. Much of his stock came from the United States and not infrequently included books which were still selling at full price in the U.K. It was Reynolds' practice to take shops temporarily available because of planning dispute or other cause, pay a low rent and fill them with thousands of volumes priced from 30p upwards. He opened on Sundays and late in the evening and undoubtedly had real bargains to offer for which the public, who had no interest in the affairs of the book trade, was grateful. In 1981 a number of publishers obtained an injunction against him on copyright grounds.

The Charter Group

Books were often news, frequently because some person eminent in politics, sport or showbiz had written an autobiography; sometimes because of their supposedly scandalous or salacious nature; occasionally because the author was already so famous as an author that any new publication by him or her warranted comment. This was fine for publishers and booksellers, and made the latter the envy of their fellow main street traders whose wares were not so often subjected to intense media scrutiny. There was a disadvantage, however, because members of the public who wanted a book because they had read about it, or heard it mentioned on the radio, expected to be able to obtain it immediately, or within a short while. This had once been possible because of cheap labour, low postal rates and a smaller output of new titles. Soon after the war the position had changed, as it had with many other commodities. As modernisation took effect service deteriorated. The working day was shorter, terms of engagement came to favour the employed more than the management, and the increased volume of business was more than the new technology could cope with swiftly. There had to be a scapegoat. Long before the computer was named as the villain, the bookseller came to be blamed. Who else was the would-be purchaser of a book to castigate when his needs were not satisfied instantly?

Such are the qualifications for efficient bookselling that all too often the member of the public appeared to be correct in nailing his complaint on the retailer's door. A bookseller, ideally, needs to have wide general knowledge, an intimate acquaintance with classical and current literature, an encyclopaedic awareness of publishers and titles in constant need of updating, and to be patient, helpful and resourceful in dealing with the public. Saintliness, in fact, is called for. So, the often poorly paid bookshop assistant came to symbolise the inefficiency of the publisher, who then called for better training, to which booksellers agreed on condition that they received better terms of trading, in order to afford it. (There was a basic error in this point of view to which reference will be made later.) After numerous heated sessions at the annual B.A. Conference, many letters to *The Bookseller,* and speeches at meetings of this and that society influential in the trade, the Charter Bookselling Group of the B.A. was formed, and a committee which included publishers appointed. This laid down standards about minimum stocks, floor space, window frontage, training, stock control and other matters, and required those participating to complete an annual questionnaire which became the basis of an economic survey of bookselling. Nearly every contemporary bookseller mentioned in these pages, and a great many more, automatically became Charter booksellers. The conditions, except over training, were not onerous, perhaps because a senior member of the B.A. hierarchy of the time had so small a shop that they couldn't be, without embarrassing him. And, where training was concerned, so many members failed to meet the commitments that, certainly up to 1981, they were seldom penalised.

The Charter Group was formed in 1964. Almost immediately it became preoccupied with screwing better terms out of publishers. It had wide areas of success so that this, for many booksellers, became its *raison d'être.* There were other benefits which might or might not have come about through the ordinary activities of the trade associations – standard order forms, stock cards, returns labels, various rationalisations which aided efficiency. And it was no great labour to complete the yearly economic survey, interpretation of which was another matter. Annual publication was invariably accompanied by an outraged commentary on the poor returns of bookselling. Figures for net profit and return on capital were discussed angrily, without any reference to the thought which might have gone into deliberately making a loss. Some highly successful businesses made as little net profit as possible, preferring to pay higher dividends to shareholders, bonuses to directors and staff, and to increase the pension fund rather than pay away profits in corporation tax. Nor did the survey differentiate sufficiently between booksellers.

In *Publishing and Bookselling,* revised for Jonathan Cape in 1974, a national survey of booksellers, town by town was attempted. It had to be invidious. What follows will be even more so. Businesses will be mentioned only when they relate to some specific theme, or if their names have occurred in earlier sections of the book, so that some continuity of history may be maintained.

Take a population map of the British Isles and mark on it those places which had well-stocked and well-run bookshops in 1970, or 1980, and no very clear pattern emerges. Some of the largest cities, and all of those with universities attached, were reasonably well served but many others were not. Some comparatively small places supported one bookshop, or even two. In many of the sprawling suburbs of big cities the absence of a bookshop was explained because book-buying was done by workers at lunchtime in the centre.

In Newcastle-upon-Tyne, Mawson, Swan & Morgan, now grown to the size of a store with a book department, celebrated its centenary in 1978, by which time it had been owned by the Midland Educational Company for five years. T. Robson Dring, an experienced bookseller who left the Charter Group because of the training demands, ran a shop here and another in Carlisle for many years. At first he tried to buy for both at Newcastle but found the tastes of each city so different, though only sixty miles apart, that he delegated the responsibility to the Carlisle manager. In 1973 he gave up his shop in Newcastle and concentrated on the other. In 1980 he noted, 'it is often said that small bookshops are falling by the wayside, but recently four different kinds have opened in Carlisle, and two in towns close by'. Hill's of Sunderland spread their wings to Newcastle where they bought two existing businesses in the seventies. Also in Sunderland was Binns, a department store allied to twelve other outlets selling books. G.N. Boddy, who took over his father's business in Middlesbrough in 1952, sold it in 1976 to Thorne's of Newcastle-upon-Tyne, and the House of Andrews, at Durham, changed hands in 1963, later losing its status as bookseller to the university.

Industrial Lancashire provided paradoxes, with some of the best bookshops in the country, yet having, in 1970, towns such as Bolton with only branches of the big chains and the Send the Light Trust. In Preston (with a smaller population) Harold Sweeten, whose father had died ten years earlier, bought Robinson's Bookshop in 1955. There, in drab Fishergate, near the centre of a city of no great beauty, he and his two sons Christopher and David created a bright, modern shop with fitted carpet. Sweeten's was a veritable oasis of learning and well-supported by the local population, although the proprietors resolutely insisted that new general publications would not sell in Preston where the stock, all recorded on computer, consisted of backlist items and big technical and educational sections. The Sweetens prided themselves on their professionalism and businesslike approach so it was good for Blackpool when, having closed their shop there in 1965, they decided to reopen in other premises five years later. They also took their light to Bolton in 1980 when they bought the Chapter and Verse Bookshop which had opened there a few years before. The Sweetens carried out a customer survey in 1978 with the help of students which showed that 47% of their customers were able to find the book they wanted, and another 30% something on the subject in which they were interested.

Lancashire was a centre of library suppliers – Askew's, Holt-Jackson, and Jackson's Library Service. F.T. Bell became manager of Holt-Jackson in 1946, the year in which the founder sold out to Marlborough, a London wholesaler. He was much respected and liked by publishers because his was a creative approach to library supply. He bought speculatively and sold positively, sending his travellers off to libraries all over Britain, and establishing personal relations with his institutional customers. The staff at Holt-Jackson increased from eight in 1945, housed in three rooms, to 175 in 1968, occupying premises of 20,000 square feet, and accounting for an annual turnover of £1m. Like other suppliers Holt-Jackson processed books (at the rate of 3,500 per day), fitting them with plastic jackets and performing many of the tasks which older librarians had been trained to carry out themselves. The charge for processing provided an area for competition amongst library suppliers, many of whom performed the service at cost which led to bitterness amongst booksellers who could not afford to do so but would have liked more of a stake in such business.

The non-university towns of Yorkshire were not rich in bookshops and two became the object of special campaigns. Children in schools in Bradford were subjected to a flood of books, donated by publishers, at the instigation of the National Book League, whose director Martyn Goff had noted a similar scheme in New Zealand. The results, being long-term, cannot yet be fully assessed. That was in 1976; four years later the Book Marketing Council planned a mission to Barnsley which was chosen as typical of a town of large population without a bookshop. An initial survey unearthed great enthusiasm for book-buying and led to the opening of a shop in time for Christmas 1980. The actual event in 1981 received nationwide publicity.

Norman E. Lucas opened in Altrincham, Cheshire, on 'a poor site' in 1946 and he stayed for sixteen years building up business with libraries and schools on credit, selling little for cash. To correct the imbalance he had the courage to move to a better shopping street and was rewarded. G.W.M. Blewett, in Dudley, Worcestershire, started in 1949 and moved premises several times but not to his satisfaction; in 1967 he wrote to *The Bookseller* to complain that the public would not buy books even at sale prices. He blamed publishers for not supporting small booksellers and declared that they could not afford to lose such outlets!

At Over's in Rugby books were moved onto the first floor to allow expansion of the stationery department and customers were not, apparently, upset. Over's started a Technical Book Service in the sixties. Albert Gait's of Grimsby, after one hundred years in the Old Market Place, moved to a new shopping precinct in 1970. Of the non-industrial towns which might have been thought likely to support pedigree bookshops, there were at least two exceptions – Buxton, Derbyshire, and Stratford-upon-Avon. Buxton, a small spa, had large hotels and an air of prosperity but, in 1969, not even one moderately well-stocked bookshop. Stratford, a busy market town as well as a major tourist centre, had branches of W.H.S. and the Midland Educational apparently selling as many souvenirs as books.

In contrast, East Anglia, known as 'the graveyard' by book reps who had trailed round it unrewardingly, had more shops than seemed reasonable given the size of the population. Probably, some of the owners ran them as a hobby. One who certainly did not was John Prime who, having inherited a legacy, left the U.B.O. group and his comfortable position in Manchester, and chose the market town and port of King's Lynn in which to establish a shop which Sir Allen Lane officially opened for him in 1968. The population of King's Lynn was only 28,000 at that time but there was a large catchment area and Prime was proved right in his choice, although he worked hard at it, holding literary lunches and taking an active role in the annual King's Lynn Festival. He moved premises, was partnered in the business by his wife, Maureen, and came to be regarded as something of a barometer by *The Bookseller*. Whenever things seemed to be going well, or ill, John Prime was asked to comment on how it was in King's Lynn and if, as usually occurred, cautious optimism was expressed, the trade felt relieved. (His appearance was not unlike a Buddha.)

In the south-west there was little outside Exeter and Bristol to excite the publisher's rep. An exception was the Harbour Bookshop at Dartmouth, started by Christopher Milne and his wife in 1951. The small Devon port had a population of only 7,000 but the Milnes served an extensive hinterland, exhibiting and selling to schools in the classrooms of the county. They drove their mobile showroom within a radius of sixty miles and were truly dedicated booksellers. In 1980 they put the Harbour Bookshop up for sale so that Milne, son of A.A., and the original of Christopher Robin, could devote himself to writing and be free, after nearly thirty years, of being recognised by his customers.

At King's of Lymington, which dated back to 1735, the printing side was sold in 1976, which left Miss Mary King, a descendant of the founder, in charge of the bookshop in the Hampshire town. At Penzance, farther west in Cornwall, Bridger's closed down in 1970 leaving the Truro Bookshop as the main stockholding shop in Cornwall.

Dorset, although sparsely populated, had good bookshops in Sherborne, Shaftesbury, Blandford Forum, Dorchester and even the little port of Lyme Regis, where Serendip Fine Books, the Chapmans' emporium on the steep main street, was temporarily given a new frontage for the filming of resident author John Fowles' *The French Lieutenant's Woman*.

In Hampshire there were two formidable women booksellers: Irene Babbidge at Havant, Molly Way at Emsworth. Miss Babbidge, after selling the Ibis at Banstead, set up as a librarian and bookseller in 1941, moving twelve years later to larger premises. From 1965 she sold only books in an urban district serving a population of 100,000. When she retired Rayner Unwin, then president of the P.A., said she was in the great tradition of personal booksellers. She wrote a book about her craft published by André Deutsch.

In the neighbouring county of Sussex Miss Santoro, of Crowborough, moved her shop to larger premises, having closed down her library service in 1966 and sold her branch at Uckfield ten years earlier.

In the Home Counties it was often preferable for a bookseller to operate farther away from London than in one of its sprawling suburbs, because there was less likelihood of the local population going up to town for shopping sprees and the working population, which commuted on five days, might well become customers on Saturdays. Frank Weatherhead at Aylesbury prospered in an attractive town which spread too far into the countryside for the pleasure of conservationists though that was probably good for business. At Slough, which could be called 'industrial Windsor', there was a first class bookshop which was as unexpected as Sweeten's in Preston. Leslie and Louie Wheeler started in 1945, in partnership with Herbert Carter, hence Carter & Wheeler. Carter withdrew two years later – the Wheelers stayed in command until 1981 when they accepted an unsolicited offer from the Bowes & Bowes Group.

Surrey, whose countryside almost disappeared under the urban encroachment of greater London, was catered for patchily. Tom Dally ran a personal, small shop at Woking; the Houbens had a pleasant site in a paved way off the main shopping street at Richmond; Reigate had its Ancient House Bookshop (no relation to Ipswich's) and in the ultra-suburban and quite undistinguished centre of Banstead which was only about quarter-heartedly mock-Tudor, Martyn Goff presided over Miss Babbidge's former Ibis from 1950 for most of the next twenty years. His tycoon-father had told him to open in Esher which had a much richer class of resident; he chose Banstead which became famous in the book trade almost immediately because of his habit of writing to *The Bookseller* from the Ibis and highlighting the various problems, as he saw them, of the small bookseller. He also wrote novels and books about L.P.s. He was a super salesman whose talents were rather wasted in a Surrey dormitory town, as they were in St. Leonard's-on-Sea where he had his first bookshop in 1948 and scandalised the respectable inhabitants by clearly labelling a section in his shop – SEX. He sold the Ibis in 1979.

The Sussex coast, apart from Brighton, was not great bookselling territory, being much populated by the retired, and the sick, although Tony and Cynthia Reavell made a personal success of the Martello Bookshop in Rye's ancient high street, opening on Sundays as well as weekdays, and attracting many buyers to signing parties. Brighton, which soon acquired a university on its northern outskirts, had in particular Bredon & Heginbotham, a shop which was not a great favourite with many representatives of publishers because Kenneth Bredon was an astute buyer who took few risks. He and Margot Heginbotham (who left quite soon to marry) bought the shop from Frank Ward, of Baker Street and Chelsea, soon after the war.

T.H. Rayward continued at Goulden & Curry, Tunbridge Wells, until 1956, when the onset of blindness led to his retirement from the splendid book department he had created. In 1981, his exemplary assistant Miss Elizabeth Woodhams was still there, working with the manager, Julian Fall, who had joined in 1948 as a £3 a week apprentice.

Kent was as patchy as Surrey, with the Medway towns, perhaps because of their proximity to London, having fewer shops than Canterbury, for instance, where Jill and Alec Rae took over the Pilgrim's Bookshop in St. Margaret Street in 1955. Alec Rae had retired early from the colonial civil service, which was a non-growth industry by then, and added his name to the long list of those who came to bookselling by way of another career. When they retired in 1979 their business was bought by Dillon's and later transferred to another address. In Canterbury also was Alan Kemp, a professional librarian who turned to bookselling, and had outlets in Ramsgate, Margate and Broadstairs as well. They were called Albion Bookshops.

London bookselling did not go from strength to strength in this period although there were areas in the suburbs which improved.

The losses included Bumpus, the Times Book Company, Better Books, Alfred Wilson (in the City and Victoria Street), many of the Stoneham shops, two of Truslove & Hanson's, Bryce's, Batsford's, and a great many others which may not have contributed greatly to the home turnover of the book trade but which possibly added something more to the ambience of a shopping street than is gained from the presence of boutiques selling the same garments, or of dry-cleaners and Wimpy Bars.

The gains included the enlarged Dillon's, the Economists', Grant & Cutler, Berger & Tims, more of Collet's, John Sandoe, Karnac's, new shops in Highgate, Kentish Town and Muswell Hill to the north; in Bromley, Greenwich and Sydenham to the south; and in branches of Gill's and the Booksmith.

That Hatchard's, Foyle's, Zwemmer's, Heywood Hill's, Mowbray's remained, plus ever-active departments within Harrods, the Army & Navy Stores and Selfridge's was a mercy for both publishers and those who bought books.

Hatchard's was saved as an important outlet for new books when one publisher bought it; Bumpus was reprieved for only a while when a consortium took it over. Hatchard's, which has been in the doldrums more than once in its long history, enjoyed a new phase of prosperity after Collins bought it. It also became a refuge for some of those who had worked for Bumpus, notably Peter Giddy who was appointed manager, and later managing director.

In the thirties J.G. Wilson raised the money to buy Bumpus, but after the war failed to realise the value of the Oxford Street lease. When it came up for renewal he was faced with having to pay an uneconomic rent. Once the war was over Bumpus had some lean years and J.G. had to seek support from publishers, who took out debentures and invited Tony Godwin to become M.D. The company was losing £1,800 per month, there was a staff of nearly fifty, many of them over seventy, and no pension scheme. Numerous accounts, including those of some very celebrated people indeed, had not been paid for years and the shelves were over-stocked. Godwin had to be ruthless. He moved to new premises in Baker Street, reduced the staff to about twelve and refused long-term credit, thus ridding himself of unwanted customers. Every bookseller in London felt the repercussions and some learned to be equally firm in refusing to take on Bumpus's fleeing customers on their terms. The foreign department was sold to Dillon's, and the Book Society purchased for £12,000. The latter with its ten thousand members helped restore the fortunes of the shop. Then, in 1960, Allen Lane, one of the consortium, offered Godwin the chief editorship of Penguin's. The latter's bookselling career was nearly over; so was Bumpus's, which was sold, despite bids by W.H.S. and Claude Gill, to Bendor Drummond who had not previously been in the trade. He moved the shop to Mount Street, to premises which had for long been Day's Library, and sold out to Robert Maxwell in 1966. Bumpus was merged with the library supply business of Haldane's which Maxwell had just bought from Foyle's.

Charing Cross Road remained the principal book street in London although much of it was under threat of demolition from the fifties onwards. Foyle's premises were extended in 1966 when the Goldbeaters' House building was opened at a cost of £250,000. The firm at that time received 3,000 letters a day from all over the world and had thirty-two departments. The literary luncheons continued to attract the public and the press, which also gave space to a strike of shop assistants in the 1960s. This lasted about two weeks during which time the shop remained open, but picketed. Some publishers supported the strikers and refused to deliver books, perhaps in order not to damage their own industrial relations, possibly because they had sympathy with the lowly-paid assistants. The wage structure was capricious and the wonder is that union intervention had not occurred previously. The strike did not markedly improve conditions for bookshop assistants generally and, after it was settled, Foyle's tended to employ temporary foreign labour.

William Foyle died in 1963, having spent some of his fortune on purchasing Beeleigh Abbey in Essex. His son Richard was already dead so effective control of the shop was in the hands of his daughter Christina and her husband, Ronald Batty, who had come to Foyle's as an antiquarian bookseller. Foyle's Educational was run as a separate company under William's brother Gilbert, who founded an educational trust in 1944 to provide grants to university students. Eric and John, his sons, succeeded him and, under them, left Charing Cross Road, to take offices in Upper Berkeley Street, Mayfair.

Almost opposite Foyle's, on a corner site, were the small premises occupied by Miller & Gill. The name was changed to Better Books when Tony Godwin bought it just after the war and embarked upon his self-imposed task of waking up the trade he had chosen. His was not the first modern bookshop but it was the one which had most influence on other booksellers. The old-fashioned style bookshop, ill-lit, over-crowded with dark-brown high shelving, some of it inaccessible without a ladder, and with windows dressed in a way which would have seemed pleasingly familiar to a Dodsley or a Tonson, had an atmosphere to which many a bibliophile responded warmly, so there were some regrets at its passing. Not that it is altogether extinct even now.

A new approach was inevitable and essential, the younger generation had to be a little brash and insensitive in its approach.

At Better Books Godwin had a fascia board designed, after Mondrian, by John Sewell and got himself talked about by advertising amusingly on London Transport and in the *New Statesman*, using such artists as Ronald Searle and André Francois. He took apparent risks, ordering one-tenth (1,000 copies) of the whole first edition of Chrisopher Fry's play *Venus Observed* and filling his window with it. His huge competitor opposite had subscribed only twenty-four, most of which went on staff sales on publication day. Better Books became *the* fashionable shop for poetry, contemporary fiction and philosophy in surroundings which were bright and unfusty. When Alfred Wilson's collapsed in 1956 Godwin took over the City branch in Ship Tavern Passage, gutted it and turned it into a beguilingly attractive shop in which individual books stood out. This was in stark contrast to the effect made under the former management, when it was necessary to pass through two doors before gaining access to a veritable forest of books in which the trees could not be detected, although previous years' leaves could. Later, at Bumpus's new premises, Godwin gave too much prominence to statuary and seating at the expense of books and the shop was always too dark. Next he acquired a unit beside Better Books and dreamed up a horror of a bookshop. The walls were used not for books but for notices and posters, and the stock was held on snaky aluminium stands which could be removed when poetry evenings were held. And everything was painted silver. It was, however, a reflection of contemporary taste and of his desire to make his shop a social centre; it also had a coffee bar.

When he became a publisher Godwin lost interest in his shops, sold the City premises for the value of the lease, and disposed of Better Books as a going concern to Hatchard's, who in turn sold it to another publisher, John Calder. He planned to return it to its avant-garde image, which suited his books, but received notice to quit from the G.L.C. after only two weeks. He took premises further up Charing Cross Road but the company went into liquidation in 1974, for £40,000, with Calder himself the largest single creditor. The premises were taken over by the Booksmith.

In the lower part of the road Zwemmer's continued to be primarily an art book shop, run by the sons of the founder who died in 1979. One of their shops was rented to O.U.P. as a central selling point for their publications. Their near neighbours Collet's expanded from the Bomb Shop into modernised and enlarged accommodation and added first a Penguin bookshop and later another large store just above Foyle's called Collet's International Bookshop. The founder, Eva Reckitt, died two days after the opening, aged eighty-six. Collet's by then had many other shops in London and elsewhere with its headquarters in Wellingborough, Northants, on a new industrial trading estate. Joan Birch, managing director from 1976, spent much time in travelling this dispersed empire. She died, whilst planning her retirement, in 1981.

Bryce's and Dillon's have already been referred to in the section on university bookselling; another academic shop, the Economists', has not. This was started in 1947, close to the London School of Economics, as a joint venture of *The Economist* journal and the L.S.E. The first manager was Mrs Gerti Kvergic, another remarkable woman bookseller who worked on Basil Blackwell's dictum that a bookshop must be able to function behind closed doors, so she built a strong mail order department. Under her successor, Gerald Bartlett, the staff tried to close the doors but failed, although for many bitter months they picketed the shop entrance whilst a wrangle about the right to have a staff association and other matters was fought out. When it was finally settled Bartlett, who as the youngest-ever president of the B.A. had made fierce anti-union speeches, left, and published an account of the affair. It was ironic that Gerald Bartlett's rather dazzling career in books should have been interrupted in this way because he was a persistent fighter for better wages and a firm supporter of training schemes.

Denny's, from having shops in the Strand and Ludgate Hill, came to concentrate on library supply in Carthusian Street in 1967, but another City bookseller, Barker & Howard, extended its activities from the small shop in Fenchurch Street, which it retained, to a new site in the Barbican development. At Jones & Evans, in small premises in Queen Victoria Street, George Downie exercised his prejudice against Book Tokens and paperbacks but contrived to remain a good, personal bookseller of the old school. Alfred Wilson's, alas, followed Simpkin Marshall's into the receivers' hands. Publishers struggled to save it because it had a turnover, through its three shops and export department, of £100,000 p.a. in books, which was large for 1956. The solution came when Hubert Wilson bought back from the receiver the export books and magazine subscriptions department. The Victoria Street shop was closed down, Godwin bought Ship Tavern Passage and Hampstead was sold with the tax loss of the whole company to a very famous London bookseller who contrived to remain anonymous.

Mowbray's switched from purely theological to general bookselling and became an unquoted public company. They opened and closed branches in various provincial cities but in London settled into redesigned premises in Margaret Street, Oxford Circus. At Heywood Hill's in Curzon Street, Handasyde Buchanan, who had worked in other nearby shops before the war, presided over an emporium which had an air of carefully organised muddle without a speck of dust. He also wrote and edited books, retiring in 1974.

The Times Bookshop declined gradually during these years. First its library was closed down, the remaining subscribers being transferred to Harrods; then in 1968 it was sold to W.H.S. who closed it and transferred the goodwill to Truslove & Hanson in Sloane Street.

Harrods' Subscription Library was the only one which survived and its book department remained one of the best accounts for nearly all publishers, whose reps queued willingly and regularly to do business with the buyer, Geoffrey Van Dantzig who was rare in that he didn't follow the pattern of his times in moving from one post to another. He joined Harrods in 1949 and was still there in 1981. At the Army & Navy Stores and Selfridge's, books were allocated more space than the average bookshop occupied but were subject to the rules of departmental store buying where the finance director, when he notices purchases have reached a certain level, bans all buying. This is hard on the department which is being careful and especially difficult for bookbuyers faced with demand for an unexpected bestseller.

Wholesale exporting declined from 1946 but did not disappear altogether. William Jackson (Books) Ltd moved from Took's Court to Southampton Row where it also had a retail shop, but one in which the customers were not allowed to handle the books or to use the door off the street. Instead they had to enter by a side passage and ask for what they wanted. The books were kept behind glass. The shop is now a stationery mart. Jackson's, like Clark's and Dawson's, ceased also to be exporters. One which kept going was Gordon & Gotch, which took that side of Dawson's and W.H. Smith's businesses and also bought Alfred Royle & Willan.

There were many specialist bookshops. Captain O.M. Watts, in Albemarle Street, dealt in maritime literature; the Fabian Society had its own retail outlet in Westminster not far from the Conservative Party Bookshop in Victoria Street, and the Labour Party had a book room in Transport House, but these disappeared along with larger shops in the area. J.A. Allen owned the Horseman's Bookshop in Buckingham Palace Road;

H.K. Lewis's remained the chief medical booksellers, in Gower Street, and in Great Russell Street were Luzac and Probsthain still dealing in orientalia, and the more recently arrived Cinema Bookshop. (As the cinema declined as a popular art form, its literature grew.) A book department was also formed within the Photographers' Gallery in Great Newport Street which opened, with Arts Council backing, in 1971. Photography was another much exploited subject for books and the Gallery catered for both technical and general markets. Quite whom the Arts Council's own bookshop in nearby Long Acre was supposed to attract was less obvious. It moved there in the late seventies from smaller premises in Mayfair and it was questionable whether it was necessary for public money to support a general bookshop in an area which had more old-established book businesses than any other in Britain, and close to which both Penguin and Hammick had opened new, unsubsidised branches at the same time. And neither Penguin nor Hammick was required to pay assistants at Civil Service rates. The Arts Council had a literature director, Charles Osborne (a noted author himself) and a panel which correctly backed the National Book League and supported other worthy causes but its entry into retail bookselling both in Long Acre and elsewhere caused some concern.

The young were specifically catered for at the Children's Book Centre, first in Church Street, Kensington, later in the High. It grew out of Mary Glasgow and Baker. When Mary Glasgow decided to concentrate on publishing, Eric Baker kept the shop and became an authority on bookselling for children, issuing a quarterly newsletter to which other booksellers subscribed to give away to their customers. In 1978 the financier Jim Slater bought 75% of the shares and one year later he and Baker parted company amicably. This time Slater retained the shop and Baker concentrated on his Book Services company which continued the newsletter and supplied school bookshops.

The government ran other specialist shops under the aegis of H.M.S.O. One of these, in Oxford Street, closed down in 1968 for the curious reason that it was doing too much business. It could not accommodate the vast Stationery Office output nor would funds stretch to take additional premises.

In 1977 Peter Braithwaite and Bing Taylor developed a specialist approach to the sale of general books by issuing from a P.O. Box number in Battersea, S.W. London, *The Good Book Guide*. Their mail order business served the whole world but 30% of sales were in the U.K., and they reached a turnover of £500,000 at the end of their third year (1979). Leading authors selected books for them, no inducements were offered to customers, except guidance and service, and Taylor claimed that, far from harming High Street booksellers he was helping to attract trade to their shops. What he was really proving was that there are many ways of selling books, and every single one of them may be right.

S.W.7, S.W.3 and N.W.3 were all good areas for bookselling. Frank Ward opened a shop in King's Road, Chelsea when he returned from the war and there it remained until colleague and successor Edward Sheppard died in 1971. Around the corner in Blacklands Terrace John Sandoe started an attractive small shop on three floors in 1957. It became a mecca for booklovers in the area. In Gloucester Road, Knightsbridge, Harry Karnac opened in 1950, specialising in psycho-analysis and psychiatry. He was the one who survived. Several others in the neighbourhood closed as the character of Kensington changed. In 1950, Karnac said, it was still in the hands of the Galsworthian middle classes who thought paperbacks were vulgar, so that revolution reached S.W.7 a little later than elsewhere, but not in time to prevent some shops going out of business.

When the tax loss of Alfred Wilson was sold it was necessary for the new owners to keep open a branch of the business. This became Hampstead's High Hill Bookshop in 1957. The turnover in books was £8,000 in 1956 but had risen to more than £½m by 1980 with over 80% in direct retailing over the counter. This figure would be more impressive if W.H.S., Brent Cross had not reached that turnover in one year's trading and doubled it three years later. And by then there were other personal bookshops in North and N.W. London which had not been the case in 1957, apart from a Collet's branch, now the Belsize Bookshop, owned by Donald Woodford. Antony Wilson opened in Highgate in 1967, Michael Flanagan in Muswell Hill, Southgate and elsewhere, about the same time and in 1974 two ex-Dillon's assistants, Margaret Lally and Robert McLeod, had the courage to take premises in Kentish Town Road, a shopping street from which Marks & Spencers and others were about to withdraw because trade was not good enough. The new Owl Bookshop soon outgrew its premises and moved into a larger, attractive L-shaped space which became the reason why many people shopped in Kentish Town. By 1980 Finchley, Barnet, and other suburbs which had been deprived of them for so long had bookshops.

South of the river Wimbledon had two good shops, Nigel Hamilton ran another by Greenwich Pier for a while, but there were vast areas which were not well catered for and the same time was true of west London, although W.H.S. had a huge branch at Ealing. Of all unlikely places Dalston, in London E.8., acquired a bookshop in 1971. Unlikely, because the borough of Hackney in which it was situated was classified as 'an area of special social need'. To this outback of semi-slum urban sprawl came an American-born social worker, Glenn Thompson, whose special gift was to interest charitable trusts in backing the venture he named Centerprise. In run-down premises Thompson created a community centre including a commercially viable bookshop which moved into larger accommodation on a main street a few years later. Soon after seeing it launched Thompson hived off to oversee the Writers' and Readers' Publishing Co-operative, an imprint no more in the mainstream than Centerprise, but which became one of the few effective bridges between the official trade, as represented by the P.A./B.A., and that part of the untapped market for books which spokesmen for the trade were always lamenting as being out of reach. Outside the London postal district but still within the great conurbation, the Caxton Bookshop, at Romford, was started by Arthur Andrews and successfully transferred to larger premises. It is still there though Andrews was killed in a car accident in 1978. Harrow and Enfield were two large areas with middle-class populations which did not fare well in these years, the former losing an old-established shop and the latter having nothing apart from a semi-open-air stall-cum-shop (now gone) near the station and Don Gresswell's showroom for children's books and school equipment tucked away in a side street. Gresswell ceased to deal in books in 1980.

This brief survey, though highly selective, does have general import in that it indicates that in the literate Britain of 1980 there were still a great many urban areas without anything approaching a properly stocked and efficiently run bookshop.

Epilogue

In 1980 the British book trade reaped a harvest of misfortune. For eighteen months an overvalued pound had crippled exports and interest rates had soared to record heights. Inflation pushed up manufacturing costs to uneconomic levels yet publishers allowed others under their own control to rise even faster. In the ten preceding years the number of publishers had risen by over 40% while the total output of books, swelled by imported titles, had grown by more than 90%. Under this load the distribution system between publisher and book buyer broke down monotonously often. When, in addition, economic pressures forced cut-backs in public spending on books for schools and libraries, the trade was in trouble.

Since the invention of printing authors and publishers had multiplied in number to cater for an ever-increasing public. The arrival of mass literacy combined with a world population explosion suggested a potentially unlimited market for the book trade, but long before 1980 it had become obvious that even in those parts of the world where everyone was officially literate, a substantial proportion of people managed their lives without the direct help of books. Where a use was found for them, it was often not one inspired by the love of reading; satisfaction came from manuals on catering, car maintenance, wireless-telegraphy and computers. Progress towards the Miltonian ideal of the book seen as the blessed life blood of a master spirit was neither swift nor widespread. Magazines, ephemeral by nature, first distracted the newly literate in hordes, soon followed by alluring scientific inventions, visual and aural, less demanding than a page of type.

Thus it became of prime importance for book publishers to hold their existing market, although they bravely pretended that they were actually concerned with extending it. Mercifully for them, and their bookseller customers, affluent sections of the population had already come to regard books as acceptable status-symbol gifts. Volumes designed for the coffee tables of the rich looked expensive, which was what mattered, but were usually modestly priced between £10-£20. Publishers and booksellers valued this trade not only for the profit it generated but because it helped to subsidise literary works − books of travel, biographies, verse, experimental novels (although some coffee table books were also of literary value). In Caxton's time there were all those Sarum Ordinales which helped to keep him in business whilst he was at work on his next translation; the late twentieth-century bookseller tolerated with equanimity the latest hyped-up novel, the swift turnover of which made up for slow-moving works of historical research or slim, sensitive evocations of childhood, which might remain on his shelves for a year or so, and then leave them only to find a new home on a church bazaar stall. Not that bookseller or publisher could afford too many of those at a time when the life of most trade books was less than three months. Mistakes had to be speedily dealt with by remaindering or, in the case of the bookseller, de-stocking, a hideous term invented during the current recession.

The American practice of denying the existence of a book more than three months old, unless it was still a bestseller, had not hit Britain except at a few outlets modelled on the New World-style store, but Charter booksellers found it increasingly unprofitable to adhere to that condition of group membership which laid down that any book required by a member of the public should be obtained for him or her. There was a let-out clause about 'reasonable request ... where economically possible' and many grasped it, advising the customer to apply direct to the far from familiar-sounding publisher.

The 1980 book trade had to be concerned with profitability because no government was likely to underwrite its losses like those of some industries employing vast numbers of workers. It had to rely on private backing, or borrow from the bank; either way it was expensive and had its effect on the price of books, as did the alarmingly inflated price of petrol, paper and postage.

It would not be unreasonable to suppose that all those problems might have resulted in fewer titles being published. In fact, in the first year of recession, 1979, there were over three thousand more, and in the second, over six thousand making an all-time record of 48,158. When, against all the odds, an outsider attracted media attention and thus orders from the public, there were often delays in meeting the demand because there were no copies of the book in the shops. Interest was not always sustained and sales were permanently lost. There was even more exasperation when the number of copies in print was inadequate and a reprint had to be ordered. Readers, being articulate types, criticised the trade in the correspondence columns of newspapers, crying 'do publishers really want to sell their books?' Their frustration was understandable, yet publishers *really* did want to, so did booksellers, but both were hampered by there being too many titles available (theoretically) and by the capriciousness of the media whose attention was sought for every publication but which found it impossible to review or mention more than a small proportion. Books were news regularly, whether or not advertised by publishers; and when editors or feature writers decided they were big news, the effect on sales could be impressive, provided the publisher had backed his fancy by printing a large edition, and had control over his distribution machine.

Some believed that the answer to the distribution problem would be found in teleordering. Electronic terminals would be installed in bookshops and publishers' warehouses, the erratic and costly letter post would thus be by-passed, the publisher would be able to service orders by return and customers would be satisfied as quickly as the post, which was still involved at this stage, would permit. Committees were formed to investigate the proposals, arguments were heard for this or that system but, finally in 1979, teleordering went live, with four booksellers participating in a trial run with a larger number of publishers. A year later there was crisis because Software Sciences Teleordering were making moan at having already lost £168,000 and asking for greatly increased support from the book trade which was exhorted by the presidents of its two associations to react more positively and back the new technology. Deadlines were set by S.S.T. and then extended; finally the company agreed in November 1980 to a two-year reprieve for the system, which as younger booksellers succeed more traditionally inclined ones, will no doubt become part of the daily hazards confronting the public which wishes to buy one of the too many titles produced by too many publishers.

The recession was the first which most people in the book trade had experienced, although there had been a nasty hiccup in 1974-75 when inflation began to take off. In all but a few publishing houses staff were laid off, or not replaced when they retired or resigned. A number of companies went out of business, were amalgamated to reduce overheads, and yet others were absorbed into larger organisations. Some of those who found themselves unemployed started their own imprints (thus adding to the annual total of new titles), others went into literary agency, or into the consultancy world, a grey area apparently capable of assimilating infinite numbers of axed executives.

Bookselling was similarly affected, although there were fewer dramatic news stories than in publishing. The failures were quieter on the whole, often involving small shops run by husband-and-wife teams.

At the same time the world of books was poised for changes which at the most pessimistic assessment of them would relegate it, within a decade, to the size of a one-roomed cottage industry. If the microchip proved to be everyman's answer to the book and much else, providing information which twenty-five generations had become accustomed to obtaining from printed matter, then the book trade would find itself part of the world of antiques, which might prove to be a lucrative transformation for those canny enough to adapt swiftly.

During the previous thirty years the trade had comforted itself by noting that such innovations as the newspaper, the cinema, radio and television, had all spelt doom to the book; yet the trade had always had more than its share of adroit entrepreneurs, so it survived by learning to profit from the threats. There was similar optimism about the chip, even though those who understood its implications insisted that it would bring about changes more sweeping than anything which had happened during an already tumultuous century. Were those who believed the book would survive whistling in the dark, or would they be proved correct?

Some publishers did not wait for the answer. Both Butterworth and the Thomson Group set up electronic publishing systems in the legal field, while Longman made major investments across the whole field of communication. There had long been data banks in which information was stored, corrected, up-dated and then regurgitated in the form required for conventional printing and binding in book form. Now there were processes to replace the traditional methods of printing and binding and give the reader direct access to information through a so-called terminal. Whether or not general literature would be appealing given this treatment was not apparent, but there were obvious advantages for compilers and perhaps users of works of reference or any other branch of literature, such as guide books, requiring regular revision. Perhaps reference books were doomed to be replaced by cassette containers, just as Whitaker's unwieldly two-volume *British Books in Print* had already been banished from some bookshops in favour of its microfiche counterpart.

This was a long-term problem. Of immediate concern to authors and publishers was the theft of their property, on an ever-increasing scale, through piracy and photocopying.

Carbon paper was the means of making instant copies for most of the century. Inserted between sheets of ordinary paper, it was capable of making eight or more copies, increasingly illegible. The photocopying machine altered all this. For much less than the cost of a box of carbon paper numerous readable copies of documents could be produced in minutes. It became painfully clear to publishers that this invention threatened their sales. Multiple copies of pages and sections from books were taken (often by schools and public libraries) without payment to the owners of the copyright. There was argument about what constituted fair usage for purposes of quotation, and over what steps could be taken to stop it being abused. The Whitford Report favoured a licensing system backed by legislation and the British Committee of Copyright Owners produced a series of draft licences to aid discussion. The Music Publishers' Association, whose members had long benefited from the fees collected by the Performing Rights Society, *acted* instead, and successfully, against both a local authority and a public school. The M.P.A. estimated that there were about eight million unlawful abuses of copyright music and written material every year in British schools. So much for the good organisation of the M.P.A.

Piracy on a staggering scale was almost endemic in some parts of the world, where governments tended to look on it as no concern of theirs and leave the aggrieved parties to seek a belated (and costly) remedy in their local courts. A solution looked even further away than in the case of photocopying.

In 1980 a success was recorded when the Society of Authors, backed by the P.A., the N.B.L. and other bodies finally cornered the politicians and established officially the right of authors to be paid for the loaning of books through public libraries. The Public Lending Right Act reached the statute book, a sum of £2m was made available, but the likelihood of any author receiving more than a piffling token amount receded fast.

Chip and copying apart, the trade remained obsessed by old problems, one of which was how to get more books into state schools. Statistics showing how much per head was spent on each child at school made dismal reading. When The Schools Council was first set up by government (it received £3m of public money in 1980) some educational publishers reacted ambivalently, wondering if this might not be a tentative step towards establishing a state publishing house for textbooks; later they co-operated with it. At all levels publishers stated their case to official bodies for higher government spending on books for education. In this, an area where they could be said to have a vested interest, they were supported by teachers, by the findings of public investigations and by the National Book League – there was absolute agreement that the child having access to books at home and at school was more likely to benefit from education than the child who was deprived of them. Political considerations, however, caused councils and Parliament to stop further specific funding of books, although teachers often complained that money could have been diverted from the purchase of less important equipment without adding to the overall bill. Publishers were, naturally, not too much concerned about adding to the cost of education by increasing the book funds, but the trade usually found itself on the losing side. Politicians expressed sympathy, as they did with P.L.R., but seldom acted effectively because the parliamentary system did not make it easy to take a line independent of that laid down by a party caucus. The N.B.L., with its emphasis on the need for adequate book provision, explored the possibility of starting a movement for parents to supply their state-educated children with textbooks, but it received little support from either the Book Marketing Council or the Educational Publishers' Council. Free education for all was supposed to imply free books, just as public libraries were expected to lend books free, although everyone – especially in the book trade – conveniently forget that 'free' meant paid for out of taxes, local or national.

Expenditure on books by local authorities for their libraries was reduced at the beginning of the recession and it appeared likely at the time of writing that it would be even more severely curtailed in the immediate future. If so, a consequence could be the revival of a lobby which gained little support in the sixties when it demanded that public libraries should buy direct from publishers at full trade discount. In 1979-80 public library spending on books was £58m, (some 18% of the total cost of public libraries), and given so great a sum it is at least possible that by the end of the century, if not well before, the political masters of the librarians will insist on more favourable terms of supply, whether or not through booksellers and library suppliers. The same applied to purchase of books for state schools and colleges – as indeed it had for most of this century in the case of the G.L.C. and some other authorities – which made a good reason for booksellers to concentrate on selling more books in their own shops, or by mail.

The difficulties of remaining on High Street sites increased for booksellers through horrendously high rents and rates. Publishers could move onto trading estates in country areas – booksellers could not. They had to be where the actual shopping public was. Against the tide of book clubs, simultaneous and otherwise, and the latest brainchildren of science, they had to sell in the main market places. If publishers wished them to remain there as their traditional outlets it was obvious that they would have to demand wider margins – larger discounts – which could only lead to yet higher prices for books.

The picture at the end of 1980 was one of apprehension, if not of gloom, to most people in the book world. But as time wore on it became increasingly possible to find publishers and booksellers who would guardedly admit that they were doing fairly well. Most of the problems remained, though some at least were being tackled vigorously, and at last the number of new titles pouring on to the market began to decline. Some companies announced trading figures which made far from depressing reading and a feeling grew that, given responsible, efficient management and entrepreneurial enterprise whether on the bookshop floor, or in the commissioning editor's or sales director's office, there might still be a place in the world for books. A somewhat different place as time went on but, looked at historically, perhaps one born of no greater upheaval than that which Gutenberg, by his invention, imposed on the illuminators of manuscript.

Appendices

1. Total number of titles published

Year	New books	Total, including new editions
1900	5670	7149
1905	6817	8252
1910	8468	10804
1915	8499	10665
1918	6750	7716 (lowest war year total)
1920	8738	11004
1925	9977	13202
1930	11856	15494
1935	11410	16678
1937	11327	17137 (pre-war record year)
1940	7523	11053
1943	5504	6705 (lowest war year total)
1945	5826	6747
1950	11638	17072
1955	14192	19962
1960	17794	23783
1965	21045	26358
1970	23512	33489
1975	27247	35608
1976	26207	34434
1977	27684	36322
1978	29530	38766
1979	32854	41940
1980	37382	48158
1981	33651	43083

Source: J. Whitaker & Sons Ltd. (Figures pre-1928 taken from *The English Catalogue of Books*, thereafter from *The Bookseller*.)

2. Subject areas of titles published

These tables, reprinted by permission of J. Whitaker & Sons, Ltd, show the books
recorded in *The Bookseller*

CLASSIFICATION	1937 (Pre-war record year)				1943 (Lowest war year total)				1955			
	Total	Re-prints and new edns.	Trans.	Edns. de luxe	Total	Re-prints and new edns.	Trans.	Edns. de luxe	Total	Re-prints and new edns.	Trans.	Edns. de luxe
Aeronautics	50	9	—	—	148	19	1	1	107	37	1	—
Annuals and Serials	123	101	—	—	47	33	—	2	52	50	—	—
Anthropology	46	5	2	—	23	1	—	—	38	2	1	—
Archaeology	60	6	3	—	17	—	—	1	58	9	4	—
Art and Architecture	230	46	6	9	67	12	1	1	591	89	33	22
Astronomy	43	3	1	—	21	2	—	—	78	21	1	—
Banking and Finance	42	13	—	—	40	14	—	—	220	82	—	—
Bibliography	98	44	3	3	55	4	—	—	304	47	9	9
Biography	789	188	43	4	281	40	5	1	496	89	34	3
Botany and Agriculture	178	39	1	1	58	6	1	2	285	78	5	4
Calendars	67	31	1	—	7	1	—	—	15	14	—	—
Chemistry and Physics	133	27	4	—	52	16	1	—	335	71	8	—
Children's Books	1597	552	6	1	671	110	4	—	1756	482	14	—
Classics and Translations	87	57	40	3	26	15	8	4	64	27	22	—
Dictionaries	62	15	—	—	22	5	—	—	116	22	—	—
Directories	166	92	—	—	16	9	—	—	411	258	2	—
Domestic Economy	79	12	—	—	45	11	—	—	221	42	—	—
Educational	1337	223	20	—	312	41	1	—	1844	383	10	—
Engineering	155	53	3	—	101	26	—	—	413	165	3	—
Essays	462	96	16	1	124	26	1	2	118	25	12	3
Facetiae	61	9	—	—	54	11	1	—	66	10	5	—
Fiction	5097	2944	81	6	1408	347	30	1	3702	1453	255	6
Geology	56	10	—	—	18	2	—	—	157	67	12	—
History	458	87	22	1	192	20	4	2	235	40	15	1
Illustrated Gift Books	234	31	2	21	39	1	—	4	32	9	—	—
Law and Parliamentary	248	97	2	—	103	29	1	—	437	164	3	—
Maps and Atlases	30	4	1	—	15	1	—	—	81	22	—	—
Mathematics	38	4	1	—	46	14	—	—	87	22	3	—
Medical and Surgical	543	155	9	1	212	72	2	—	785	239	13	—
Music	83	13	3	—	43	12	2	—	121	25	7	—
Natural History	186	34	1	1	48	7	—	—	295	57	6	2
Nautical	99	18	—	1	14	3	—	—	133	57	4	—
Naval and Military	62	6	—	—	229	21	5	—	305	86	18	—
Occultism	58	13	2	—	28	5	1	—	48	17	2	—
Oriental	169	25	11	2	34	5	4	—	15	4	7	—
Philately	13	6	—	—	11	2	—	—	23	12	—	—
Philosophy and Science	164	36	18	—	62	5	3	—	187	41	31	1
Poetry and Drama	569	211	20	9	329	56	15	4	658	104	29	14
Politics	633	66	23	2	596	44	23	—	651	122	15	—
Psychology	59	1	—	—	25	5	1	—	119	26	13	—
Religion	927	135	60	3	425	41	6	1	1058	202	81	3
Sociology	264	26	2	—	165	10	1	—	405	96	10	1
Sports and Pastimes	260	34	5	2	57	9	—	—	433	129	10	6
Technical Handbooks	322	80	2	—	104	44	1	—	881	320	4	2
Topography	139	18	—	—	59	6	—	—	399	59	12	4
Trade	81	22	—	—	47	9	—	—	626	246	3	—
Travel and Adventure	411	107	19	—	102	18	5	1	199	31	31	—
Veterinary and Stockkeeping	38	11	1	—	73	6	—	1	204	84	—	—
Wireless	19	5	—	—	34	5	—	—	98	33	2	—
Totals	17137	5810	434	17	6705	1201	129	28	19962	5770	750	81

CLASSIFICATION	1965				1981			
	Total	Reprints and new editions	Trans.	Ltd editions	Total	Reprints and new editions	Trans.	Ltd editions
Aeronautics	149	31	1	—	237	35	—	—
Agriculture & Forestry	313	42	6	—	451	79	4	1
Architecture	209	26	8	—	347	69	9	1
Art	649	100	69	6	1383	238	92	7
Astronomy	88	11	5	1	120	35	1	—
Bibliography and Library Economy	238	51	1	3	788	138	2	—
Biography	707	125	44	2	1243	302	48	4
Chemistry and Physics	828	139	46	—	682	115	19	—
Children's Books	2484	343	105	—	2934	496	97	1
Commerce	507	83	3	—	1213	312	4	1
Customs, Costume, Folklore	61	7	4	—	158	37	6	—
Domestic Science	264	41	9	—	695	181	13	2
Education	562	63	2	—	1040	194	6	—
Engineering	756	166	42	—	1488	239	29	1
Entertainment	161	25	10	1	630	117	12	—
Fiction	3877	1633	307	—	4747	1837	118	5
General	41	8	2	—	557	96	5	—
Geography and Archaeology	229	36	8	—	476	102	9	—
Geology and Meteorology	165	30	6	—	340	41	5	—
History	1073	233	65	1	1432	347	50	2
Humour	104	23	1	—	171	24	1	—
Industry	561	130	23	—	492	96	1	—
Language	292	45	3	—	657	136	10	—
Law and Public Administration	526	109	3	1	1399	304	9	—
Literature	745	121	63	1	1151	190	54	5
Mathematics	466	87	47	—	726	138	8	—
Medical Science	1227	262	31	—	2838	497	27	—
Military Science	94	12	7	1	113	28	1	—
Music	178	32	11	1	365	97	12	1
Natural Sciences	690	146	23	—	1234	190	14	1
Occultism	70	14	2	—	251	59	19	—
Philosophy	230	39	18	—	431	111	49	—
Photography	86	18	4	—	237	27	—	1
Plays	220	47	19	—	256	102	51	2
Poetry	361	34	20	13	620	70	61	38
Political Science and Economy	1559	221	40	—	3764	868	79	—
Psychology	268	38	6	—	725	121	14	—
Religion and Theology	1227	179	88	—	1363	274	138	3
School Textbooks	1869	175	31	—	1991	261	16	—
Science, General	113	11	3	—	55	12	1	—
Sociology	525	70	8	—	1031	149	19	—
Sports and Outdoor Games	353	59	5	1	511	87	15	—
Stockbreeding	170	29	3	—	264	69	2	—
Trade	313	47	—	1	536	141	3	1
Travel and Guidebooks	545	129	27	—	677	279	8	1
Wireless and Television	205	43	8	—	264	47	3	—
Totals	26358	5313	1237	33	43083	9387	1144	78

3. U.K. Book Sales, Home and Export

Year	Total £	Home £	Export £	Percentage Export
1939	10,321,658	7,167,059	3,154,599	30.0
1949	34,297,252	24,498,414	9,798,838	28.6
1959	66,945,183	41,551,223	25,393,960	37.9
1969	145,693,000	77,170,000	68,523,000	47.0
1971	179,099,000	101,243,000	77,856,000	43.5
1973	230,106,000	134,251,000	95,855,000	41.7
1975	342,408,000	203,787,000	138,620,000	40.4
1977	467,036,000	263,132,000	203,904,000	43.7
1979	582,433,000	387,131,000	195,302,000	33.5
1980	644,213,000	431,355,000	212,858,000	33.0

Source: The Publishers Association, derived from *Business Monitor* PQ 489

Note 1: These figures are for 'contributing establishments' only. The Business Statistics Office calculates that from 1974 on these represent about 68 per cent of total turnover.

Note 2: Before 1979, allowance is made in the export figures for certain sales by export booksellers. Discontinuance results in a decrease of the export percentage of about 5 points.

4. Charter Group overall results

	1969	1970	1971	1972	1973	1974	1975	1976	1977	1978	1979	1980
Number of questionnaires analysed from booksellers	229	179	192	352	353	376	355	335	342	343	346	347(†)
Total new book sales £'000	19235	18159	24593	43227	45800	55996	65542	81747	93016	103503	109700	122800
Sales — other goods £'000	12562	11707	13638	18644	18849	24424	29560	32432	39485	46199	52400	45750
Total sales £'000	31798	29867	38231	61871	64649	80421	95102	114181	132501	149702	162100	168550
% Sales — new books — Retail*	46.1	47.1	49.4	50.5	51.2	51.2	53.0	54.47	56.4	53.49	54.8	60.1
Library*	8.1	8.3	8.3	9.4	9.6	8.9	9.3	9.3	8.0	9.4	8.9	8.2
Book Agents*	—	0.2	0.3	0.6	0.4	0.4	0.5	0.9	0.4	0.3	0.3	0.4
Schools*	6.3	5.2	6.3	9.4	9.6	9.1	6.1	6.7	5.4	5.5	3.7	4.2
	60.5	60.8	64.3	69.9	70.8	69.6	68.9	71.6	70.2	69.1	67.7	72.9
% Sales* — other goods	39.5	39.2	35.7	30.1	29.2	30.4	31.1	28.4	29.8	30.9	32.3	27.1
	100.0	100.0	100.0	100.0	100.0	100.0	100.0	100.0	100.0	100.0	100.0	100.00
*Gross profit %**	25.9	25.0	25.4	26.3	26.6	26.7	27.8	27.9	28.1	28.9	29.1	29.2
Total expenses %	22.3	21.7	22.0	21.6	21.7	22.3	23.5	24.6	25.0	25.8	26.3	27.3
(a) Wages and salaries %*	13.7	13.3	12.7	12.7	12.9	13.3	14.1	14.7	15.2	15.1	15.7	16.8
(b) Rent and rates %*	2.7	2.5	2.7	2.9	2.7	2.7	2.9	3.5	3.5	3.6	3.7	3.9
(c) Other working expenses %*	5.9	5.9	6.6	6.0	6.1	6.3	6.5	6.4	6.3	7.1	6.9	6.6
*Net (trading), profit %**	*3.6*	*3.3*	*3.4*	*4.7*	*4.9*	*4.4*	*4.3*	*3.3*	*3.1*	*3.1*	*2.8*	*1.9*
Net (trading) profit as % of capital employed	12.6	10.8	11.1	—	—	—	—	—	—	—	—	—
Number of times book stock turned over per annum	4.0	4.3	4.3	4.7	4.9	4.2	4.0	4.2	4.1	3.9	3.6	3.8
Sales per person employed (£)	6177	7180	7936	9025	10153	11588	13747	14427	19319	22900	24900	28900
Sales per sq.ft. of floor space (£)	28.1	38.7	42.3	41.9	45.7	52.8	58.0	71.1	82.1	87.0	93.3	116.0
% by which retail book stock written down to cost or valuation	—	—	—	—	—	—	—	39.5	39.7	39.5	40.4	39.3

* Figures expressed as % of total sales.

Note: † 347 questionnaires returned, representing 407 shops.

Figures taken from a survey prepared for the Booksellers Association by the Manchester Business School and David Sutton of System Six.

5. Officers of the Publishers Association

Date	President	Vice-President	Treasurer
1896-98	C. J. Longman	John Murray	Frederick Macmillan
1898-1900	John Murray	C. J. Longman	Frederick Macmillan
1900-2	Frederick Macmillan	John Murray	C. J. Longman
1902-4	C. J. Longman	Frederick Macmillan	John Murray
1904-6	Reginald J. Smith	William Heinemann	C. J. Longman
1906-9	Edward Bell	C. J. Longman	William Heinemann
1909-11	William Heinemann	Edward Bell	Arthur Waugh
1911-13	Frederick Macmillan	William Heinemann	James H. Blackwood
1913-15	James H. Blackwood	Frederick Macmillan	John Murray
1915-17	Reginald J. Smith	James H. Blackwood	W. M. Meredith
1917-19	W. M. Meredith	Humphrey Milford	G. S. Williams
1919-21	Humphrey Milford	W. M. Meredith	C. F. Clay
1921-3	G. S. Williams	Humphrey Milford	C. F. Clay
1923-4	C. F. Clay	{ G. S. Williams / Humphrey Milford }	H. Scheurmier
1924-5	C. F. Clay	G. S. Williams	H. Scheurmier
1925-7	H. Scheurmier	G. S. Williams	G. C. Rivington
1927-8	{ W. M. Meredith / Edward Arnold }	H. Scheurmier	G. C. Rivington
1929-31	W. Longman	G. C. Rivington	Bertram Christian
1931-3	Bertram Christian	W. Longman	Stanley Unwin
1933-5	Stanley Unwin	Bertram Christian	W. G. Taylor
1935-7	W. G. Taylor	Stanley Unwin	G. Wren Howard
1937-9	G. Wren Howard	W. G. Taylor	Geoffrey C. Faber
1939-41	Geoffrey C. Faber	C. Wren Howard	Walter G. Harrap
1941-3	Walter G. Harrap	Geoffrey C. Faber	R. J. L. Kingsford
1943-5	R. J. L. Kingsford	Walter G. Harrap	B. W. Fagan
1945-7	B. W. Fagan	R. J. L. Kingsford	R. H. C. Holland
1947-9	R. H. C. Holland	B. W. Fagan	J. D. Newth
1949-51	J. D. Newth	R. H. C. Holland	Kenneth B. Potter
1951-3	Kenneth B. Potter	J. D. Newth	Ralph Hodder-Williams
1953-5	Ralph Hodder-Williams	Kenneth B. Potter	J. Alan White
1955-7	J. Alan White	Ralph Hodder-Williams	Ian Parsons
1957-9	Ian Parsons	J. Alan White	R. W. David
1959-61	R. W. David	Ian Parsons	John Boon

Date	President	Vice-President	Treasurer
1961-3	John Boon	R. W. David	John Brown
1963-5	John Brown	John Boon	John Attenborough
1965-7	John Attenborough	John Brown	Peter du Sautoy
1967-9	Peter du Sautoy	John Attenborough	Mark Longman
1969-71	Mark Longman	Peter du Sautoy	Rayner Unwin
1971-3	Rayner Unwin	Mark Longman	Colin Eccleshare
1973-5	Colin Eccleshare	Rayner Unwin	Peter Allsop
1975-7	Peter Allsop	Colin Eccleshare	Graham C. Greene
1977-8	Graham C. Greene	Peter Allsop	Frank Whitehead
1978-9	Graham C. Greene	Ian Chapman	Frank Whitehead
1979-80	Ian Chapman	Graham C. Greene	Peter Allsop
1980-1	Ian Chapman	Tim Rix	Peter Allsop
1981-2	Tim Rix	Ian Chapman	Philip Attenborough
1982-3	Tim Rix	Philip Attenborough	Robin Hyman

Secretaries

1896-1933	William Poulten
1934-58	Frank Sanders
1958-76	Ronald E. Barker
1976-	Clive Bradley (Secretary and Chief Executive)

226

6. Officers of the Booksellers Association of Great Britain and Ireland

Date	Chairman	Hon. Secretary	Hon. Treasurer
1895-9	H. W. Keay, J.P.	E. Pearce	
1900-2		E. Pearce	F. Calder Turner
	President		
1903-11	H. W. Keay, J.P.	E. Pearce	F. Calder Turner
1912-20	H. W. Keay, J.P.	E. Pearce	F. Hanson
		Secretary	
1921	H. W. Keay, J.P.	W. J. Magenis	F. Hanson
1922	H. W. Keay, J.P.	W. J. Magenis	H. Shaylor
1923	F. A. Denny	W. J. Magenis	H. Shaylor
1924	F. A. Denny	W. J. Magenis	H. Shaylor
1925	G. A. Bowes	W. J. Magenis	H. Shaylor
1926	G. A. Bowes	W. J. Magenis	H. Shaylor
1927	C. Young	W. J. Magenis	W. J. Prior
1928	C. Young	W. J. Magenis	W. J. Prior
1929	H. E. Alden	W. J. Magenis	H. L. Jackson
1930	H. E. Alden	Miss H. M. Light	H. L. Jackson
1931	T. N. Philip	Miss H. M. Light	H. L. Jackson
1932	F. Bacon	Miss H. M. Light	H. L. Jackson
1933	F. Bacon	Miss H. M. Light	H. L. Jackson
1934	Basil Blackwell, M.A., J.P.	Miss H. M. Light	H. L. Jackson
1935	Basil Blackwell, M.A., J.P.	Miss H. M. Light	H. L. Jackson
1936	David Roy	Miss H. M. Light	H. L. Jackson
1937	David Roy	Miss H. M. Light	H. L. Jackson
1938	C. H. Barber	Miss H. M. Light	H. L. Jackson
1939	{ A. S. Jackson / J. H. Ruddock }	Miss H. M. Light	H. L. Jackson
1940	J. H. Ruddock	Miss H. M. Light	H. L. Jackson
1941	J. H. Ruddock	Miss H. M. Light	H. L. Jackson
1942	H. L. Jackson	Miss H. M. Light	F. G. Bryant
1943	H. L. Jackson	Miss H. M. Light	F. G. Bryant
1944	A. F. Mason	Miss H. M. Light	F. G. Bryant
1945	F. J. Aldwinckle	Miss H. M. Light	F. G. Bryant
1946	F. J. Aldwinckle	Gordon M. Smith	F. G. Bryant
1947	H. M. Wilson	Gordon M. Smith	F. G. Bryant
1948	H. M. Wilson	P. B. Hepburn	F. G. Bryant

Date	President	Secretary	Hon. Treasurer
1949	K. V. Saville	P. B. Hepburn	F. G. Bryant
1950	K. V. Saville	P. B. Hepburn	F. G. Bryant
1951	F. G. Bryant	P. B. Hepburn	T. A. Joy
1952	F. G. Bryant	P. B. Hepburn	T. A. Joy
1953	Cadness Page	P. B. Hepburn	T. A. Joy
1954	Cadness Page	P. B. Hepburn	T. A. Joy
1955	Basil Donne-Smith	G. R. Davies	H. H. Sweeten
1956	Basil Donne-Smith	G. R. Davies	H. H. Sweeten
1957	T. A. Joy	G. R. Davies	H. H. Sweeten
1958	A. B. Ward	G. R. Davies	H. H. Sweeten
1959	A. B. Ward	G. R. Davies	H. H. Sweeten
1960	J. Wells	G. R. Davies	H. H. Sweeten
1961	H. S. Hitchen	G. R. Davies	H. H. Sweeten
1962	H. S. Hitchen	G. R. Davies	H. H. Sweeten
1963	C. R. Edgeley	G. R. Davies	R. Blackwell
		Director	
1964	H. H. Sweeten	G. R. Davies	R. Blackwell
1965	H. H. Sweeten	G. R. Davies	H. E. Bailey
1966	R. Blackwell	G. Lane	H. E. Bailey
1967	R. Blackwell	J. Newton	H. E. Bailey
1968	Ross Higgins	J. Newton	G. R. Bartlett
1969	Ross Higgins	J. Newton	G. R. Bartlett
1970	H. E. Bailey	G. R. Davies	D. Ainslie Thin
1971	H. E. Bailey	G. R. Davies	D. Ainslie Thin
1972	T. Hodges	G. R. Davies	D. Ainslie Thin
1973	T. Hodges	G. R. Davies	D. Ainslie Thin
1974	G. R. Bartlett	G. R. Davies	J. May
1975	G. R. Bartlett	G. R. Davies	J. May
1976	D. Ainslie Thin	G. R. Davies	J. Blackwell
1977	D. Ainslie Thin	G. R. Davies	J. Blackwell
1978	J. May	G. R. Davies	J. Elsley
1979	J. May	G. R. Davies	J. Elsley
1980	J. Blackwell	G. R. Davies	R. Grant Paton
1981	J. Blackwell	T. E. Godfray	R. Grant Paton
1982	J. Elsley	T. E. Godfray	J. F. Hyams

Bibliography

History and Trade Practice

Barnes, James J. *Free Trade in Books:* A Study of the London Book Trade since 1800 (O.U.P., 1964)

Bingley, C. *The Business of Book Publishing* (Pergamon, 1972)

Blond, Anthony *The Publishing Game* (Cape, 1971)

Booksellers Association of G.B. & Ireland and the Publishers Association *Report of the 1948 Book Trade Committee* (London, 1954)

Briggs, Asa (ed) *Essays in the History of Publishing* in Celebration of the 250th Anniversary of the House of Longman, 1724-1974 (Longman, 1974)

Corp, W.G. *Fifty Years:* A Brief Account of the Associated Booksellers of Great Britain and Ireland 1895-1945 (Blackwell, 1945)

Curwen, Peter J. *The U.K. Publishing Industry* (Pergamon, 1981)

Duff, E. Gordon *A Century of the English Book Trade, 1457-1557* (The Bibliographical Society, 1906)

Gross, John *The Rise and Fall of the Man of Letters* (Weidenfeld & Nicolson, 1969)

Hampden, John (ed) *The Book World Today:* A New Survey of the Making and Distribution of Books in Britain (Allen & Unwin, 1957)

Hepburn, James *The Author's Empty Purse and the Rise of the Literary Agent* (O.U.P., 1968)

Joy, Thomas *The Bookselling Business* (Pitman, 1974)

Kingsford, R.J.L. *The Publishers Association, 1896-1946* (C.U.P., 1970)

Lewis, John *The Left Book Club:* An Historical Record (Gollancz, 1970)

McKerrow, R.B. *Dictionary of Printers and Booksellers 1557-1640* (The Bibliographical Society, 1968)

Mumby, F.A. & Norrie, Ian *Publishing and Bookselling* (Cape, 1974)

Myers, Robin *The British Book Trade:* From Caxton to the Present Day. A Bibliographical Guide (Deutsch/National Book League, 1973)

Plant, Marjorie *The English Book Trade* (Allen & Unwin, 3rd ed 1974)

229

Plomer, H.R. *A Dictionary of the Printers and Booksellers who were at Work in England from 1641 to 1667;* and supplementary volume 1668 to 1725 (Bibliographical Society, 1907)

Plomer, H.R., Bushnell, G.H. and Dix, E.R. McC *A Dictionary of the Printers and Booksellers who were at Work in England, Scotland and Ireland from 1726 to 1775* (Bibliographical Society, 1968)

Sanders, F.D. (ed) *British Book Trade Organisation:* A Report on the Work of the Joint Committee (Allen & Unwin, 1939)

Scheurmier, H. *The Book World* (Nelson, 1935)

Unwin, Philip *Book Publishing as a Career* (Hamish Hamilton, 1965)

Unwin, Stanley *The Truth about Publishing* (Allen & Unwin, 1st edition, 1926; 7th extensively revised edition, 1960; 8th edition partly rewritten by Philip Unwin, 1976)

Ward, Audrey & Philip *The Small Publisher* (Oleander, 1979)

Company Histories

Arnold, Martin (foreword) *A Service to Education:* The Story of the Growth of E.J. Arnold & Son Limited of Leeds (Arnold, 1963)

Attenborough, John *A Living Memory:* Hodder & Stoughton Publishers 1868-1975 (Hodder, 1975)

Barker, Nicolas *The Oxford University Press and the Spread of Learning 1478-1978* (Oxford, at the Clarendon Press, 1978)

Blackie, Agnes A.C. *Blackie & Son 1809-1959* (Blackie, 1959)

Bolitho, Hector (ed) *A Batsford Century:* The Record of a Hundred Years of Publishing and Bookselling 1843-1943 (Batsford, 1943)

Darwin, Bernard *Fifty Years of COUNTRY LIFE* (Country Life, 1947)

(Duckworth) *Fifty Years 1898-1948* (Duckworth, for private circulation, 1948)

Fabes, Gilbert H. *The Romance of a Bookshop 1904-29* (Privately printed for Foyles, 1929)

Grant, Joy *Harold Munro and the Poetry Bookshop* (Routledge, 1967)

Griest, Guinevere L. *Mudie's Circulating Library and the Victorian Novel* (David & Charles, 1970)

Hodges, Sheila *Gollancz:* The Story of a Publishing House 1928-78 (Gollancz, 1978)

Jones, H. Kay *Butterworths:* History of a Publishing House (Butterworth, 1980)

Keir, David *The House of Collins* (Collins, 1952)

King, Arthur & Stuart, A.F. *The House of Warne:* One Hundred Years of Book Publishing (Warne, 1965)

Liveing, Edward *Adventure in Publishing:* The House of Ward, Lock, 1845-1954 (Ward Lock, 1954)

(Menzies) *The House of Menzies* (Menzies, 1958)

Menzies, John *The Menzies Group* (Menzies, 1965)

Morgan, Charles *The House of Macmillan* (Macmillan, 1943)

Mumby, F.A. & Stallybrass, F.H.S. *From Swan Sonnenschein to George Allen & Unwin Ltd* (Allen & Unwin, 1955)

Mumby, F.A. *The House of Routledge, 1834-1934* (Routledge, 1934)

Newth, J.D. *Adam & Charles Black 1807-1957* (Black, 1957)

Nowell-Smith, Simon *The House of Cassell 1848-1958* (Cassell, 1958)

Nowell-Smith, Simon (ed) *Letters to Macmillan* (Macmillan, 1967)

(Penguin) *Twenty-Five Years 1935-60* (Penguin, 1960)

Roberts, S.C. *The Evolution of Cambridge Publishing* (C.U.P., 1956)

Ryder, John *The Bodley Head, 1857-1957* (Bodley Head, 1970)

Sutcliffe, Peter *The Oxford University Press:* An Informal History (O.U.P., 1978)

(Sweet & Maxwell) *Then and Now 1799-1974* (Sweet and Maxwell, 1974)

Unwin, Philip *The Publishing Unwins* (Heinemann, 1972)

Wallis, Philip *At the Sign of the Ship, 1724-1974* (Longman, for private circulation, 1974)

Warner, Oliver *Chatto & Windus* (Chatto, 1973)

Williams, W. Emrys *The Penguin Story 1935-56* (Penguin, 1956)

Autobiography, Biography

Dent, J.M. *Memoirs* (Dent, 1928)

Dickson, Lovat *The House of Words* (Macmillan, 1963)

Howard, Michael S. *Jonathan Cape, Publisher* (Cape, 1971)

Joseph, Michael *The Adventure of Publishing* (Wingate, 1949)

Kennedy, Richard *A Boy at the Hogarth Press* (Whittington, 1972)

Lusty, Robert *Bound to be Read* (Cape, 1975)

Morpurgo, J.E. *Allen Lane, King Penguin* (Hutchinson, 1979)

Richards, Grant *Author Hunting by an Old Sportsman* (Unicorn Press, 1960)

Unwin, Stanley *The Truth about a Publisher* (Allen & Unwin, 1960)

Warburg, Fredric *All Authors are Equal* (Hutchinson, 1973)

   An Occupation for Gentlemen (Hutchinson, 1959)

Woolf, Leonard *Beginning Again* (Hogarth, 1964)

   Downhill all the Way (Hogarth, 1967)

   The Journey not the Arrival Matters (Hogarth, 1969)

(Zwemmer) *Anton Zwemmer:* Tributes from some of his friends on the occasion of his 70th birthday (Privately printed, 1962)

The above is only a small selection of the vast literature of the book trade which runs into thousands of volumes and pamphlets, some offered for sale to the public, others circulated privately. Whitaker's *Reference Catalogue of Current Literature* lists more than any other publication, the various editions of Frank Mumby's history run it close and have the advantage of explanatory notes, and Robin Myers' *The British Book Trade* (see above) records as much as, probably more than, many students will require. *The Bookseller,* published regularly since 1858, and usually at weekly intervals, is a mine of information about the personalities and politics of the trade. Within its pages may also be found detailed histories of publishing and bookselling companies.

Two useful trade reference books are *Writers' and Artists' Yearbook* (A. & C.

Black) which is published annually, and Cassell and Publishers Association *Directory of Publishing*.

In addition, there are the annual reports of the Publishers and Booksellers Associations, and numerous pamphlets on such subjects as international copyright, export, distribution etc. issued from the same sources. The house magazines of such publishers as Jonathan Cape and Oxford University Press, compiled with an awareness of the general reader, will also reward researchers into book trade history, as will the files of the *Times Literary Supplement,* the *Publishers' Circular* (later *British Books*), *Books and Bookmen, Smith's Trade News* (later plain *Trade News*), *Books* (the journal of the National Book League), *The Author* (journal of The Society of Authors), and, more recently, the group of newssheets headed by *Publishing News*.

Abbreviations

A.A.A.	Association of Authors' Agents
A.B.	Associated Booksellers
A.B.P.	Associated Book Publishers
A.L.C.S.	Authors' Lending & Copyright Society
A.P.C.K.	Association for Discountenancing Vice and Promoting the Knowledge and Practice of the Christian Religion
A.S.L.I.B.	Association of Special Libraries & Informational Bureaux
B.A.	Booksellers Association
B.A.S.H.	Booksellers Association Service House
B.C.A.	Book Club Associates
B.C.C.	British Copyright Council
B.D.C.	Book Development Council
B.M.C.	Book Marketing Council
B.P.B.I.F.	British Paper & Board Industries Federation
B.P.C.	British Printing Corporation
B.P.C.C.	British Printing & Communication Corporation
B.P.I.F.	British Printing Industries Federation
B.P.R.A.	Book Publishers' Representatives Association
C.B.S.	Columbia Broadcasting System
C.C.M.	Crowell, Collier-Macmillan
C.L.A.	Copyright Licensing Authority
C.U.P.	Cambridge University Press
E.F.L.	English as a Foreign Language
E.L.B.S.	English Language Book Society
E.P.C.	Educational Publishers Council
E.U.P.	English Universities Press
F.P.P.C.	Financial & Provincial Publishing Company
H.E.B.	Heinemann Educational Books

H.M.S.O.	Her Majesty's Stationery Office
I.P.A.	International Publishers Association
I.P.C.	International Publishing Corporation
I.P.G.	Independent Publishers Guild
I.S.B.N.	International Standard Book Numbering
L.A.	Library Association
M.P.A.	Music Publishers Association
M.T.A.	Minimum Terms Agreement
N.B.A.	Net Book Agreement
N.B.C.	National Book Council
N.B.L.	National Book League
N.E.L.	New English Library
N.P.A.	Newspaper Publishers Association
O.U.P.	Oxford University Press
P.A.	Publishers Association
P.A.C.H.	Publishers Accounts Clearing House
P.D.L.	Publishers Databases Ltd
P.E.N.	Poets, Playwrights, Editors, Essayists, Novelists
P.I.R.A.	Printing, Paper, Packaging Industries Research Association
P.L.R.	Public Lending Right
P.L.S.	Publishers Licensing Society
P.P.A.	Periodical Publishers Association
P.P.C.	Publishers Publicity Circle
P.P.I.T.B.	Printing & Publishing Industries Training Board
P.R.S.	Performing Rights Society
R.K.P.	Routledge & Kegan Paul
S.C.M.	Student Christian Movement Press
S.O.A.	Society of Authors
S.P.C.K.	Society for Promoting Christian Knowledge
S.T.M.	(International) Scientific, Technical & Medical Publishers Group
S.Y.P.	Society of Young Publishers
T. & H.	Thames & Hudson
T.A.B.S.	Transatlantic Book Services
U.B.O.	University Bookshops (Oxford)
U.C.C.	Universal Copyright Convention
U.L.P.	University of London Press
W.G.	Writers Guild
W.H.S.	W.H. Smith
W.I.P.O.	World Intellectual Property Organisation

Index

243

244